Movie Mistakes
That Made the Cut

Matteo Molinari
and
Jim Kamm

CITADEL PRESS
Kensington Publishing Corp.
www.kensingtonbooks.com

For Mom and Nonna

CITADEL PRESS BOOKS are published by

Kensington Publishing Corp.
850 Third Avenue
New York, NY 10022

All Kensington titles, imprints, and distributed lines are available at
special quantity discounts for bulk purchases for sales promotions,
premiums, fund-raising, educational, or institutional use. Special book
excerpts or customized printings can also be created to fit specific needs.
For details, write or phone the office of the Kensington special sales
manager: Kensington Publishing Corp., 850 Third Avenue, New York, NY
10022, attn: Special Sales Department, phone 1-800-221-2647.

Design by: Leonard Telesca

First printing: April 2002

10 9 8 7 6 5 4 3 2

Printed in the United States of America

Library of Congress Control Number: 2001099189

ISBN 0-8065-2319-0

CONTENTS

LET'S SAY THANKS TO . . .

Our families and friends, first and foremost. As you know (and fear), all inspiration stems from you.

Many of you have also "tipped us off" to bloopers. And so, to all of these great minds—and eyes—THANKS!:

Carlo Alberini, Sean Astin, Brad Bernstein, Lorenzo Bertacchi, Dave "Kennedy" Beyer, Elisa Bozzo, Charlotte Breeze, Fabrizio Campelli, "Amazon" Bob Carter, Mick Crowley, Domenico "Dom" Del Zotto, Allison Donnelly, Dave Edison, Holly Ellwood, Bevis Faversham, Michael French, Ariana Fronti, Silvia Gasparini, Alberto Ghè, Piero and Marina Girotti, Max Greggio, Bill LeBoeuf, Erik Lichtenfeld, Giuseppe Macchion, Francesco Mattarelli, Marco Mazzocchi, Nicoletta Molinari, Mike Montes, Manuel Nardi, Paul Navidad, Paolino T. Orsini, Jeff W. Owens, Francesco Pannacciulli, Tito Parodi, Jacopo and Valerio Peretti Cucchi, Emilio Pozzolini, Ryan Prince, Timothy "Texas Chainsaw" Ramage, Riccardo Recchia, Carlo Romanò, Jeremy Ross, Stefano Ruscitti, Alessandro Sgorbati, Larry Sher, Simona and Stefano Sordi, Laurent Soriano, The Stantons (particularly Chris, Joel and Sam), DeWitte Stewart, Elle Struzziero, Josh Tundra, Pietro Vezil, Joel Viertel, Graham Winick . . . and if we forgot anyone, it's a blooper. Our bad.

And thanks to all blooper hounds, past and present. Even on the Internet, where it's easier to hack the CIA than it is to find real bloopers.

Also, thanks to Dave's Video, Laser Blazer, Toshiba, Matsushita, Philips, Sony and others, and to the much-abused Netflix.com.

And a special thanks to everyone who makes movies, for using your amazing talents to make us laugh, cry, and dream. The world is a better place because of you. Keep plying your craft, if only so we can write more obnoxious books!

INTRODUCTION

We're the weirdos behind it all. Yes, we're the culprits. We found and collected thousands of evident mistakes in the final cuts of movies—then verified, sorted, organized, and slaved over them for years, just to bring you the very best movie blooper guide available.

Every blooper you can find in this book we have seen with our very own eyes—in other words, no rumors have gone unchecked, no "secret satanic messages" have slipped through the cracks, no international conspiracies . . . but we digress. Oh—and we've marked the exact minute where each one occurred. Pedantic perhaps? You don't know the half of it . . .

Since we started this endeavor, everybody we know has become a blooper hound, including friends, loved ones, and business associates. Several times a week, someone says to us something along the lines of: "Hey, did you see the screw up in that new movie? Yeah, right before they blow up the mothership, if you look real close . . ." You get the picture. Fact is, it's downright addictive. We hope that reading this book won't take you to the dark side as well, but we can't make any guarantees.

We also want you to know that we wrote *OOPS!* because we absolutely love movies, not because we're trying to bust the filmmakers. It's practically impossible to make a movie without some errors, and our most beloved movies are filled with them (mostly because we've seen them so many times!). So we salute the world's great filmmakers, and say, "Hey, man . . . bloopers happen!" And of course, we look forward to hearing about the inevitable bloopers in our book. Just let us know, and we'll snicker along heartily.

OOPS!: Movie Mistakes That Made the Cut is for anyone who has a movie or two in their possession and wants to have a little fun. You just pop in the movie, fast-forward or skip to the minute we specify, and find cheap, silly entertainment. We know you can't make a movie without a few mistakes; we just have that much more fun when there are some.

We hope that you'll find our offbeat little hobby as amusing as we do.

Tally Ho!

Matteo Molinari and Jim Kamm
The Picky, Picky, Picky Folks Who Wrote the Book

HOW TO USE THIS BOOK

Oops!: Movie Mistakes That Made the Cut is a listing of thousands of amusing mistakes and tidbits in the final cuts of movies. But before you dig in, we offer some simple guidelines.

Note: This book isn't meant to be read cover to cover. It's a reference book, and like any other reference book, to be consulted when needed. (All right, heck, if you really want to read the darned thing straight through, go right ahead—we won't come knocking at your door to poke you in the liver because you did. For all we care, you can also plow through the Oxford English Dictionary. *Nerd!)*

So, Say You Wanna Check a Flick for Bloopers . . .

Proceed as follows:

A. Grab the movie (e.g., *The Matrix*).
B. Flip the book open to the letter *M.*
C. Look up *The Matrix.*
D. Find *The Matrix.*
E. Read the first blooper.
F. Incredulously cry, "I can't believe it!"
G. Pop *The Matrix* in your player.
H. Fast-forward to the minute of the blooper.
I. Press play.
J. Enjoy.
K. Repeat steps A through J.
L. When you reach step E again, make sure to move on to the second blooper, and then the third, and so on. Otherwise, you'll find yourself quite stuck.

BLOOPER Q & A

This is a book like many other books, with a front cover, many pages, thousands of words, and the inevitable back cover.

But its content is pretty darn unique. Yes, because it lists hundreds and hundreds and oftentimes even more hundreds of mistakes from the final cuts of your favorite movies.

You most likely have a few questions in store—so let's try to intercept them, shall we?

What's a Blooper?

blooper \'blü-per\ n. (colloq., 1945)   1: an embarrassing public blunder, especially on-camera   2: a mistake, a gaffe, a flaw that's present in a released version of a movie—the same movie you can see in theaters, rent, or buy for your home video collection.

Thus, we have compiled *OOPS!*, which has hundreds of film bloopers, listed alphabetically by title. Each entry has your basic movie guide–type information followed by a chronological listing and descriptions of the movie's mistakes, with the exact placement of each error within the movie's running time (give or take a few seconds, depending on your player—or more, if you're watching a movie outside of Area 1).

Of course, as you'll inevitably find out, not all of the mistakes listed in the book are what we would call "pure" bloopers . . . we have questions, fun facts, trivia, and other stuff to keep you occupied while your popcorn pops. Some of these are *almost* bloopers, but we just couldn't be positive enough to commit them to blooperhood. The rest is eye and brain candy.

What *Won't* I Find in This Book?

Idiotic things such as . . .

- *The Return of the Son of Attack of the Creeping Boom Mikes Strikes Again.* Unless we are able to find a letterbox version of the movie with this mistake visible (see *Eraser* or *Friday the 13th Part 3D),* you won't find bloopers such as "you can see the boom mike at the top of the screen!" Boom mikes and cables are often visible at the tops and bottoms of frames in bad transfers from film to videotape.
- **Location, Location, Location!** Unless there's a very blatant landmark or marker blowing a movie's established location (see *Die Hard 2* or *You Only Live Twice),* you won't find bloopers such as "the scene is set in Chicago, but it was shot in Vancouver!" Frequently it's cheaper to shoot a scene in one place instead of another, but if the illusion is good, hey, it doesn't hurt our feelings. And for those who enjoy spotting this kind of thing, we have a news flash: George Lucas did not, in fact, shoot *Star Wars* in outer space.
- **Atrocious Accents.** No, we don't consider a bad character accent grounds for a blooper—just grounds for bad acting (see Kevin Costner in *Robin Hood—Prince of Thieves*, or Keanu Reeves in just about anything).
- **"It's There Somewhere . . . Trust Us."** We hereby promise not to list any bloopers in the following manner: "*At a certain point*, Harrison Ford has his left hand on his chin, then in the next shot he doesn't." We locate our mistakes precisely—by trying to give you a little context and by listing the minute in the movie where they actually occur. So you can spend less time searching for them and more time enjoying them.
- **And Sorry, TV Hounds . . .** No, we don't have any errors from TV shows, because they're just too darned hard to keep track of, and usually not widely available for rental or purchase. Sure, you may have taped every episode of the short-lived Bronson Pinchot sitcom *Meego* but trust us—you're the only one, including Bronson himself.

What Will I Find in This Book?

Only 100% U.S.B.A. certified, verified, and authentic bloopers . . . along with some other fun stuff just for kicks.

Anybody can write a blooper book or throw together a Web site, oftentimes being vaguely accurate, occasionally lying about flubs, frequently saying one thing for another. But we're so sure of the veridicality of ours that we've dared to put the very minute where you can find the most titillating, snazzy, rakish mistakes. If we were any user-friendlier, we'd come to your place and rewind your tapes for you.

Where Do I Start Timing the Movie?

On the first frame of the production company's logo . . . which is automatic on almost all DVDs.

If I Haven't Seen a Movie, Will the Book Spoil It for Me?

We've marked off potential spoilers, but read on at your own risk. The description of a blooper could give away plot points, twists, and surprises that you might find more enjoyable if you watch the movie first. Then you can use our book to have even more fun.

What if My Favorite Movie Mistake Isn't in Your Stupid Book?

Write it down a.s.a.p. and send it to us. We'll look it over, and if you're right we'll immortalize you in future editions.

Oops!
P.O. Box 24174
Los Angeles, CA 90024-0174

e-mail: dotell@oopsmovies.com

Is It True That You Have to Salt Sunny-Side-Up Eggs When You Put Them on the Plate?

No, the best of the best is to salt the butter while it's melting in the pan, before you even crack the eggs.

LEGEND

TITLE (number of bloopers)
also Additional Release (SE—special edition, DC—director's cut, etc.)
Year released, color specification, length in minutes

Director(s): The insufferable fools behind the camera.

Cast: The insufferable fools in front of the camera.

The "blurb," or a very quick take on the content of the movie written by the insufferable fools behind this book.

Blooper
The main course. It's an error, a mistake, a faux pas that you can easily spot in the final cut of a movie. Wrong positions, colors, names, suits, sounds . . . anything that you can actually snicker at, and which we're totally sure is wrong.

DVD Blooper
These can be seen only on those shiny little discs that go in the players with all the bells and whistles. Technology marches on, and the *OOPS!* team is there to scrutinize, as usual: subtitles, special features, and so on.

Non-Blooper
Rare, but as powerful as any urban legend, hence very hard to eradicate. There are tons of incorrectly identified non-bloopers in the naked city (the Internet, in particular) and here we focus on the most persistent and widespread false accusations. We've tried to research as thoroughly as possible, in order to bring you the truth, the whole truth, and nothing but the truth. Well, all right, maybe with a little embellishment.

Question
A tricky part of our quest. A question is not quite a blooper, but is something that, uh, smells fishy. Not necessarily plot holes (we tend to leave those for movie critics and such), but certain situations that don't sound quite right. You can have your own opinion, your friend can see it from a totally different point of view . . . discuss amongst yourselves.

Fun Fact
A little-known tidbit of juicy trivia, just to amaze friends and family (not so much ours as yours; our friends and families threw in the towel long ago).

Pan & Scan
Sometimes when a movie is "Formatted to fit your TV screen," bloopers that were outside of the frame in the cinema (or the widescreen version) come into view. Darned good reason for them not to "pan & scan" movies.

Sequel Blooper
A blooper that only exists because some filmmakers didn't pay close enough attention to an earlier movie in a series. Or maybe they did, but figured they could just "fudge it a little." Fine, but we cry, "OOPS!"

ICONOGRAPHY

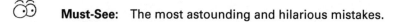

Must-See: The most astounding and hilarious mistakes.

Will They Never Learn?:   Mistakes made again, and again, and again . . . but which are still a kick in the pants.

Ignorant: Do a little research, folks!

For Maniacs Only: You have to be a major league blooper hound to appreciate it. Picky, picky, picky!

Spoiler: If you haven't seen the movie, beware!

Let the Show Begin . . .

A

ABBOTT AND COSTELLO MEET THE MUMMY (2)
1955, black & white, 90 min.

Director: Charles Lamont

Cast: Bud Abbott (Pete Patterson), Lou Costello (Freddie Franklin), Marie Windsor (Madame Rontru), Michael Ansara (Charlie), Dan Seymour (Josef), Richard Deacon (Semu), Kurt Katch (Dr. Gustav Zoomer), Richard Karlan (Hetsut), Mel Welles (Iben), George Khoury (Habid), Edwin Parker (Klaris, The Mummy).

"Hey Aaaabbooott! There's a mummy!"

Bloopers
1. Freddie tapes his threatening voice, then puts down the microphone—but in the following shot, he's holding it again. (00:26)
2. All through the picture, the two leads call each other "Bud," (00:25) "Abbott," (00:08) "Lou," (00:05) and "Costello." (01:13) But in the closing cred-

its, their character names are listed as Pete Patterson and Freddie Franklin. (01:18)

Question
How come everyone in Egypt is speaking fluent English, including the newspaper boy? (00:21)

ABOMINABLE DR. PHIBES, THE (3)
1971, color, 93 min.

Director: Robert Fuest

Cast: Vincent Price (Dr. Anton Phibes), Joseph Cotten (Dr. Vesalius), Virginia North (Vulnavia), Terry-Thomas (Dr. Longstreet), Sean Bury (Lem), Susan Travers (Nurse Allen), David Hutcheson (Dr. Hedgepath), Edward Burnham (Dr. Dunwoody), Alex Scott (Dr. Hargreaves), Peter Gilmore (Dr. Kitaj), Maurice Kaufmann (Dr. Whitcombe).

Crazy doctor wants revenge on docs who couldn't save his wife, and gets Egyptian on their asses.

Bloopers

1. Dr. Phibes plays his organ but he doesn't perform a single movement in sync with the music. (00:00)
2. Dr. Vesalius picks up a poster, holding it with his hands at the top and bottom; the detail shows that one hand is holding a side of the poster. (00:42)
3. As the plane is rolling to take off, you can see the shadow of the camera on the grass. (00:52)

Question

Dr. Phibes drills a hole in the wall above the head of a nurse, then pours cabbage Jell-O all over her. How does he end up pouring it over the lamp on her bedside table if the hole was precisely above the woman's head? (01:08)

ACE VENTURA: PET DETECTIVE (9)

1994, color, 86 min.

Director: Tom Shadyac

Cast: Jim Carrey (Ace Ventura), Courtney Cox (Melissa Robinson), Sean Young (Lois Einhorn), Tone Loc (Emilio), Dan Marino (Himself), Noble Willingham (Riddle), Troy Evans (Roger Podacter), Raynor Scheine (Woodstock), Udo Kier (Ronald Camp), Frank Adonis (Vinnie), John Capodice (Aguado), Randall "Tex" Cobb (Dog Owner).

Bizarre pet sleuth tracks down Dolphin mascot.

Bloopers

1. A dog owner crawls through the rear windshield of Ace's moving car: he's almost halfway inside the car in the inside shot; from the outside, he's still on top of the trunk. Then, he's inside again. (00:05)
2. Ace sneaks inside the shark aquarium through a door: he opens it, revealing a plant in the hallway behind him. In the inside shot, the plant is gone, yet there's a small fish tank. (00:30)
3. When Ace slams the aquarium door, the slamming sound precedes the actual shutting of the door. (00:30)
4. Once inside, Ace opens a second door that has its hinges on the right. As we cut to the inside of the room, the hinges are on the left. (00:31)
5. Ace grabs a book about The Miami Dolphins with his left hand; on a close-up, he holds it with his right hand, then again with his left. (00:34)
6. Aguado has his hands at his sides; in a medium shot, his hands are on his hips, then back to his sides again. (00:40)
7. The football players who kidnap Dan Marino from the studio switch places as they're carrying him outside. No. 99 starts on the left, No. 53 on the right, then they're vice versa once they're outside. (00:54)
8. Ace tries to hide inside a cardboard box, but he falls and smashes it. In the next shot, one of the sides of the box is restored. (01:04)

9. Lois Einhorn's true identity is revealed by Ace: she has her jacket on, then when she kneels down she doesn't, then she has it back on again. (01:20)

ACE VENTURA: WHEN NATURE CALLS (7)
1995, color, 94 min.

Director: Steve Oedekerk

Cast: Jim Carrey (Ace Ventura), Ian McNeice (Fulton Greenwall), Simon Callow (Vincent Cadby), Maynard Eziashi (Ouda), Bob Gunton (Barton Quinn), Sophia Okonedo (The Princess), Tommy Davidson (Tiny Warrior), Adewale (Hitu), Danny O. Daniels (Wachootoo Witch Doctor), Sam Motoana Phillips (Wachootoo Chief), Damon Standifer (The Wachati Chief), Kayla Allen (Airplane Stewardess).

Another case for the bizarre pet sleuth with the funky do.

Bloopers

1. Ace is on a plane, flying to Africa. A stewardess asks him if he wants some peanuts, and he grabs a bag—but for some reason he winds up spitting sunflower seed shells on Mr. Greenwall's arm. (00:12, 00:13)
2. As he's carelessly driving the car in the Nibia savanna, Ace makes a few comments, such as "Steering's a little loose!" as the car's front bumper falls to the ground. Right after that, Ace says, "Alignment's off, too!" . . . and the bumper is back in place. (00:15)
3. Still driving the car, Ace hits a branch that smashes the windshield—which is as good as new a few seconds later, as the car crosses a small stream. (00:15)
4. While dining with the Wachati tribe, Ace finds some food particularly tasty. He licks a plate made with guano, and as Greenwall tells him that guano is actually "bat droppings," Ace freezes, his head tilted to

---

FOOD PROBLEMS

Hopefully, you won't find these bloopers too hard to swallow . . .

Jim Carrey's peanuts in *Ace Ventura: When Nature Calls*	Blooper No. 1
Verne Troyer's cookie in *Austin Powers: The Spy Who . . .*	Blooper No. 12
Jeff Cohen's slice of pizza in *The Goonies*	Blooper No. 1
Grimsby's plate in *The Little Mermaid*	Blooper No. 8
John Belushi in *National Lampoon's Animal House*	Blooper No. 5
Julia Robert's sherbet in *Pretty Woman*	Blooper No. 7
Donna Dixon's pie in *Wayne's World*	Blooper No. 3

the left. When he lets the plate fall to the ground, his head is tilted to the right. (00:33)

5. Just before passing the last test, Ace is carried overhead by the Wachootoo tribe. After he says, "Do not worship me!" they toss him to the ground—which wobbles briefly (mat pad for the stunt). (00:58)

6. Ace's luck is bad in the Circle of Death, and to top that, the tiny warrior stops and yells something. After Ouda translates the line, the warrior is thrown a spear: at this point the paint over his body is much heavier and whiter than it was a few seconds earlier, when he spoke the line. (01:01)

7. In the Consulate, during Ace's speech in front of Vincent Cadby, all the chess pieces on the table vanish for no reason at all. (01:12, 01:14)

ADDICTED TO LOVE (2)
1997, color, 100 min.

Director: Griffin Dunne

Cast: Meg Ryan (Maggie), Matthew Broderick (Sam), Kelly Preston (Linda Green), Tchéky Karyo (Anton Depeux), Maureen Stapleton (Nana), Nesbitt Blaisdell (Ed Green), Remak Ramsay (Prof. Wells), Lee Wilkof (Carl), Dominick Dunne (Matheson), Susan Forristal (Cecile), Larry Pine (Street Comic).

When Ferris Met Sally.

Bloopers

1. Sam studies the stars with a telescope, then he sees it's noon and moves the telescope to watch his girlfriend. At noon, you can't see the stars, no matter what telescope you're using. (00:00)

2. During his last speech, Anton snaps the support for his arm splint—the same support that is intact one moment later, and then snapped again. (01:28, 01:29)

AMERICAN PIE (12)
also Unrated Version
1999, color, 96 min.

Director: Paul Weitz

Cast: Jason Biggs (Jim), Shannon Elizabeth (Nadia), Alyson Hannigan (Michelle), Chris Klein (Chris "Oz" Ostreicher), Thomas Ian Nicholas (Kevin), Eddie Kaye Thomas (Paul Finch), Natasha Lyonne (Jessica), Seann W. Scott (Steve Stifler), Chris Owen (Sherman), Tara Reid (Vicky), Eugene Levy (Jim's Dad), Mena Suvari (Heather).

About a guy who loves pie . . . in quite unsavory ways.

Bloopers

1. When Jim's Dad gets the remote control and the blanket that's covering Jim's tube sock, Jim is aroused only in the detail—not in the long shot. (00:01)

2. Jim is walking toward Nadia at Stifler's party. After he hits a table, it's possible to see a piece of equipment (a C-stand) peeking from behind a wall to his left. (00:08)

3. Michelle and a few other band members knock at Stifler's door, hoping to get into the party. A nerd with large glasses stands to Michelle's right (when Stifler is in the scene) and to her left (when the group is in frame). (00:09)

4. Kevin leaves a very personal "gift" in a clear cup filled with beer. When Stifler gets it from the hands of a young woman, the cup is blue (it pops up from the bottom of the screen). It's clear again after that shot. (00:13)

5. Before their parody of a kung fu movie, the four kids sit in Stifler's living room. On the couch, Finch has his legs crossed and then uncrossed and then crossed for the whole sequence. (00:18)

6. Jim's dad gives his son some porn magazines. When he grabs *Shaved*, he holds it from the top when he takes it from the paper bag, yet holds it from the bottom when he hands it to his son. (00:25)

7. When Oz waits for Heather, he's wearing a white "East Great Fall Lacrosse" T-shirt. A few minutes later, he's in the library and he's wearing a blue shirt. When he's at choir practice, singing "How Sweet It Is," he's wearing the white T-shirt again. (00:40, 00:41)

8. Jim aims the computer camera at the bed. But when his friends (and everyone else) log on to the Web site, the image they see is much wider and includes part of the room, too. (00:42, 00:43)

9. While leafing through Jim's stuff, Nadia opens a drawer: a jar of Vaseline, in the left part of the drawer, vanishes between cuts. (00:45)

10. When Finch desperately runs for a restroom, it's possible to see a microphone wire running underneath his shirt. (01:00)

11. Wandering through the house, Finch enters the door to the pool room, which has a "Please Keep Out" sign on it. He pulls the door, which swings into the hallway. The next morning, Stifler enters the very same door by pushing it open, so that it swings *into* the pool room. (01:19, 01:29)

12. Finch casually rolls one ball on the pool table, then starts a conversation with Stifler's mom. The arrangement of the balls on the table changes. (01:19, 01:20, 01:25 / 01:20, 01:25 UV)

Fun Facts

1. Jim finds an apple pie on the kitchen counter, as well as a note from his mom: "Jim—Apples—you're favorite!!!" —

she should have written "your." (00:31)

2. Sitting in the locker room, Stifler tells his friends, "She calls me up, asking for my number..." So how did she call him in the first place? (00:58)

ANACONDA (8)

1997, color, 90 min.

Director: Luis Llosa

Cast: Jennifer Lopez (Terri Flores), Ice Cube (Danny Rich), Jon Voight (Paul Sarone), Eric Stoltz (Dr. Steven Cale), Jonathan Hyde (Warren Westridge), Owen Wilson (Gary Dixon), Kari Wuhrer (Denise Kalberg), Vincent Castellanos (Mateo).

See Jaws. *Except on a river.*

Bloopers

1. Terri gets on the boat and briefly chats with Danny: he has no toothpick in his mouth, then he has one, then he doesn't, then he does... (00:06)

2. Sailing along the river, Gary says to Denise, "Is it just me, or does the jungle make you really, really horny?" During this powerful insight, Gary manages to lose the headphones he had around his neck. (00:09)

3. Gary and Denise get out of the boat at night to tape some interesting new sounds. She places a torch on a tree just behind her, but when she states, "It's unbelievable," the light seems to have disappeared. But worry not: it'll come right back. (00:20)

4. Paul and Gary are about to blow up a river dam. Gary is in the water and he's fidgeting with a few sticks of dynamite in his left hand. But when Paul pulls him out of the water, the sticks are gone. (00:31)

5. Mateo falls in, and when he emerges, swearing in Spanish, he's in the water up to his chest. In the following matching cut, when he's attacked by the snake, he's in water up to his waist. (00:39)

6. After Sarone has been captured, Terri visits Steven in his cabin: a gray sheet covers Steven either up to his chest (in the shot over Terri's shoulder), or up to his neck (from the opposite angle). (01:01)

7. After Warren is killed by the anaconda at the waterfall, Sarone is missing in action and the boat eventually sails away. Look closely... the waterfall falls *up* from the lake, in reverse. (01:11)

8. The snake opens its mouth to eat Sarone. Yet, from the bizarre angle of the inside-the-snake-cam, the beast has to open its mouth again. (01:18)

Question

One of the first victims of the anaconda is a black panther. There are no indigenous black panthers in the Amazon basin. Was this one just visiting? (00:15)

ANIMAL HOUSE (SEE "NATIONAL LAMPOON'S ANIMAL HOUSE")

ARMAGEDDON (8)
also Director's Cut
1998, color, 144 min. / 153 min. (DC)

Director: Michael Bay

Cast: Bruce Willis (Harry S. Stamper), Billy Bob Thornton (Dan Truman), Ben Affleck (A. J. Frost), Liv Tyler (Grace Stamper), Will Patton (Charles "Chick" Chapple), Steve Buscemi (Rockhound), William Fichtner (Colonel William Sharp), Owen Wilson (Oscar Choi), Michael Clarke Duncan (Jayotis "Bear" Kurleenbear), Peter Stormare (Lev Andropov), Ken Hudson Campbell (Max Lennert), Jessica Steen (Co-Pilot Jennifer Watts).

There's this big asteroid, you see . . . oh, well: see Deep Impact.

Bloopers
1. Of course, in space there is no sound, but what the heck . . . (00:00)

COLOR, COLOR, COLOR CHAMELEONS

Here are a few examples of a not-so-rare movie disease called Technicolorblindness.

William Fichtner's cables in *Armageddon*	Blooper No. 8
Mike Myers in *Austin Powers: The Spy Who Shagged Me*	Blooper No. 3
A picture in *Charlie's Angels*	Blooper No. 4
Sean Connery's car in *Dr. No*	Blooper No. 8
A balloon in *The Goonies*	Blooper No. 2
Richard Attenborough's cloth in *Jurassic Park*	Blooper No. 6
Cards in *On Her Majesty's Secret Service*	Blooper No. 3
Mel Gibson's jacket in *Payback*	Blooper No. 2
Susan Sarandon's sweater in *The Rocky Horror Picture Show*	Blooper No. 5
William Shatner's jacket in *Star Trek V*	Blooper No. 1
A soldier in *Star Wars*	Blooper No. 33
Gloria Stuart and Kate Winslet's eyes in *Titanic*	Blooper No. 1
The truck lever in *Toy Story*	Blooper No. 12
Hallee Hirsh's ring in *You've Got Mail*	Blooper No. 4

2. When Harry gets mad on his oil rig, he whacks A.J.'s door with a golf club, causing a few objects to fall on a shelf. A green fan falls again when Harry enters and slams the door closed. The same fan is back up on the shelf again when Harry makes a gesture to shut A.J. up. (00:12 / 00:12, 00:13 DC)

3. Harry places his golf club at A.J.'s throat ("I would really like an explanation"). The head of the golf club shifts from pointing to A.J.'s left in the master shot to pointing to his right in the close-up. (00:14)

4. When Harry's crew is introduced to the astronauts who will fly with them, they meet NASA co-pilot Watts. She's a gorgeous blonde who's wearing her hair down. NASA doesn't allow this: women's hair must be worn up, if not cut above the shoulders when in uniform. (00:39)

5. Chick's son sees "that salesman" on TV. His mom, who was on the phone, drops the handset. She was holding it with her right hand in the close-up, but she drops it with her left in the long shot. (01:04 / 01:06 DC)

6. When the first space shuttle (*Freedom*) takes off, a very quick shot in NASA mission control shows the boosters on a large screen. The shot is in reverse play, since the smoke and the sparks are going *toward* the reactor and not coming out of it. (01:08 / 01:10 DC)

7. *Freedom* is about to land on the asteroid: Colonel Sharp's mike—the one he has to the left of his mouth—vanishes in one shot (after Rockhound screams, "Oh, no!!") and comes back as the shuttle lands. (01:27, 01:28 / 01:30 DC)

8. The crew has to draw wires to see who's staying behind to trigger the bomb. The order of the wires changes in Colonel Sharp's hand. (02:09 / 02:11 DC)

Questions

1. In New York, a couple of bystanders read a copy of the *Daily News,* which screams on the front page, "Shuttle Explodes!" Right after that, from the ABC7 TV screens they yell "We interrupt our regularly scheduled program to bring you this special report," and newscaster Alexander Johnson says that the shuttle exploded at 3:47 A.M., Eastern Pacific Time. So, what's the deal: are newspapers extremely fast or TV stations really slow? (00:06)

2. What moron would allow a firearm on an oil rig? Matches aren't even allowed on an oil rig, much less a shotgun. (00:14)

3. While sitting in his office a few hours before the shuttle takeoff, Truman receives a page that says, "Dottie has gone public" (Dottie being the name of the asteroid). Truman comments, "So the whole world knows." Did everyone forget

what happened in New York a couple of weeks earlier? (00:57 / 00:59 DC)

AS GOOD AS IT GETS (11)
1997, color, 139 min.

Director: James L. Brooks

Cast: Jack Nicholson (Melvin Udall), Helen Hunt (Carol Connelly), Greg Kinnear (Simon Bishop), Cuba Gooding Jr. (Frank Sachs), Skeet Ulrich (Vincent), Shirley Knight (Beverly), Yeardley Smith (Jackie), Brian Doyle-Murray (Handyman), Shane Black (Frank, Cafe 24 Manager), Lawrence Kasdan (Dr. Green), Harold Ramis (Dr. Martin Bettes).

Obsessive-compulsive gets busy with single mom.

Bloopers
1. While Melvin's telling Simon never to bother him while he's working, Melvin holds his glasses in his right hand. But in the over-the-shoulder shot, when he says "You have to hold a hanky to your face" the glasses are gone. (00:07)
2. When Simon asks Vincent to hold his pose, Vincent has his right hand close to his forehead; but in the wide shot, his right hand is in another position and his left has jumped close to his head as well. (00:21)
3. When Jackie hands her pow-der mirror to Simon, the mir-ror rotates 180° in her hands between cuts. (00:31)
4. Melvin is in a thinking mood. He removes his glasses, stands up, removes his glasses again, and then stares out the window. (00:50)
5. Carol decides to go to Melvin's house and she takes the bus. As she's sitting by the window, the camera pulls away to reveal a sign on the side of the bus that says: "Subway Shuttle—Not in Service." (01:02)
6. Just before they leave for Baltimore in Frank's car, Melvin shuts the trunk and says, "Never a break . . . never." In the following close-up on Carol, the trunk is still open (upper right hand corner of the screen). (01:24)
7. On the drive to Baltimore, Carol is curious to hear Simon's story, but she wants to pull over to give him "her full attention." When she says that, the trio is riding in the convertible with the top down. As they stop, the top is up. (01:26)
8. During their conversation on the side of the road, both Simon's and Carol's headrests go up and down in various shots. (01:27, 01:28, 01:29)
9. In order to draw correctly, Simon breaks part of his arm cast. When the trio is back in New York, the cast is back like it was before being broken. (01:49, 01:58)
10. While talking on the phone

with Melvin, Carol's wrist-watch changes its position on her wrist. (02:00)

11. At the very end, the second time Melvin kisses Carol in the street, she wraps her right arm around his neck. In the wide shot, however, it's her left arm wrapped around his neck. (02:12)

Questions

1. If he has an obsessive-compulsive disorder, how come Melvin locks all of the locks (including the big black one on top) only the first time he gets home, and every other time he "forgets" about it? (00:03, 00:28, 00:37)

2. Does it happen very frequently in New York that you see a bunch of people standing still in the middle of a sidewalk staring at a bizarre guy, or do the extras in NYC simply suck? (00:10)

3. Melvin's apartment is across the hall and down two steps from Simon's apartment. How did Simon wheel his wheelchair over to Melvin's door to ask for the dog? He might have jumped down the steps, all right...but in the next scene, Simon is back in his apartment—in his wheelchair. (00:38, 00:39)

4. Melvin and Carol enter a restaurant where jacket and tie are required. The house band is playing "Everything My Heart Desires." Melvin leaves to buy the proper suit, comes back, the dinner starts and then the singer in the background says "This is a request ...happy anniversary." And the requested song is "Everything My Heart Desires." Where was the anniversary couple fifteen minutes earlier? (01:26)

AUSTIN POWERS: INTERNATIONAL MAN OF MYS-TERY (10)

1997, color, 90 min.

Director: Jay Roach

Cast: Mike Myers (Austin Powers / Dr. Evil), Elizabeth Hurley (Miss Vanessa Kensington), Michael York (Basil Exposition), Mimi Rogers (Mrs. Kensington), Robert Wagner (Number Two), Seth Green (Scott Evil), Fabiana Udenio (Alotta Fagina), Mindy Sterling (Frau Farbissina), Paul Dillon (Patty O'Brien), Cheryl Bartel (FemBot No. 1), Cindy Margolis (FemBot No. 2), Donna W. Scott (FemBot No. 3), Barbara Ann Moore (FemBot No. 4), Cynthia Lamontagne (FemBot No. 5).

Mike Myers makes us all horny baby...yeah, baby, yeah! But is it "an 'evil' horny?"

Bloopers

1. Great Britain has a Ministry of *Defence*, not a Ministry of *Defense* (that's the American spelling). (00:08)

2. Austin has been defrosted when the lab assistants remove two clips from his ears. In the next close-up, the clips are back. (00:12)

Director Jay Roach giggled while saying, "The Gaffe Squad [*Premiere* magazine's monthly flubspotter paragraph] will be tracking those earclips for a long time . . ."

3. Miss Kensington tells Austin that his private jet has been waiting for him. Austin froze himself in 1967. Jumbo jets weren't in use until 1970. (00:15, 00:22)

4. Austin goes to the restroom in a hotel. As he sits on the toilet, he fakes the action but he doesn't lower his pants (you can see he has them still on in the very bottom of the screen). But when he's attacked by Patty O'Brien, a detail shows the pants and the underwear pulled all the way down. (00:32, 00:33)

5. Austin and Vanessa are on top of a bus, while Burt Bacharach serenades them. As he begins singing, the bus is going toward the Riviera hotel, which is on the right hand side of the strip. As Austin and Vanessa stand up to dance, the Riviera has "jumped the strip," and now appears on the other side. (00:38)

6. Vanessa falls asleep against Austin. She holds a glass in her right hand. The shot cuts from the side to above the bed, and the glass moves from the hand to the floor. (00:42)

7. While still in bed, Austin receives a call via laptop. The first time we see the detail of the laptop on the nightstand, a clock behind it says it's 10:28. A few seconds later, the same clock seems to be off, as the display is no longer lit. (00:42)

8. Austin throws cigarettes into the FemBots mouths, but they all vanish in one second. (01:12)

9. Austin wants to stop the probe and Dr. Evil's evil plan, so he bursts into the room firing left and right. Every time he fires the gun, there's a flame coming out of the barrel. But when he's on top of the stairs, after two judo chops, the first bullet he fires doesn't have the accompanying flame, although it does have the sound and it does kill a henchman. (01:15)

10. In their final showdown, Austin talks with Dr. Evil, who walks by the same fireplace twice. (01:16, 01:17)

Non-Blooper
When Miss Kensington shows Austin his dental equipment, the floss box is black in the long shots, but white in the close-up (actually, it's a metal box with a reflective surface. It doesn't look very good, though). (00:49, 00:50)

Question

In Vegas, Miss Kensington tells Austin that the only reason they're "sharing a room is to keep up the context that we're a married couple on vacation." Doesn't she mean "pretext," rather than "context?" (00:27)

AUSTIN POWERS: THE SPY WHO SHAGGED ME (18)

1999, color, 95 min.

Director: Jay Roach

Cast: Mike Myers (Austin Powers / Dr. Evil / Fat Bastard), Heather Graham (Felicity Shagwell), Michael York (Basil Exposition), Robert Wagner (Number Two), Rob Lowe (Young Number Two), Seth Green (Scott Evil), Mindy Sterling (Frau Farbissina), Verne Troyer (Mini-Me), Will Ferrell (Mustafa), Elizabeth Hurley (Mrs. Vanessa Kensington-Powers), Kristen Johnston (Ivana Humpalot), Gia Carides (Robin Spitz Swallows), Tim Robbins (The President), Kevin Durand (Assassin), Woody Harrelson (Himself).

The International Man of Mystery is back . . . but so is the sinister trickster Dr. Evil. Let the games begin!

Bloopers

1. Austin emerges from the pool of water fully dressed. It's a reverse shot (check the water coming back into the sprinklers). (00:07)
2. Mini-Me's silhouette appears behind a door: the pinky trademark is lifted in front of the mouth, but as the door opens, Mini-Me's hands are far from his face, no pinky showing. (00:14)
3. Dr. Evil from time to time sports either blue eyes (e.g., during the declaration that he can make, instead of trillions, "billions"), brown eyes (e.g., while drinking Austin's mojo), or both (when talking for the first time to the president of the United States). (00:16, 00:37, 00:55)
4. While getting sexy with Ivana, Austin swallows a pawn from a chessboard, and spits it to the right of Ivana, breaking a vase. But when she invites Austin to the bed, the broken vase is behind the international man of mystery, way off from where it should be. (00:20, 00:21)
5. In the Secret Projects room, Austin backs up the VW and hits a tower of computers, a table, and a pile of white plastic drums. In the following shot, when Austin says, "Here we go, here we go," the drums are back in place. (00:25)
6. While in 1969 London, we hear "American Woman"—a song released in 1970 by Canada's The Guess Who. (00:25, 00:39)

7. During a dance with one of Dr. Evil's henchwomen, Robin Swallows, Austin looks into her eyes and sees an assassin tossing a knife at him. But the reflection in her eyes is not a reflection: the thug raises his right arm in both the reflection and the non-reflected shot. (00:28)

8. Felicity fires at the front right tire of Mustafa's car. The tire goes flat, but when the car skids, the tire looks fine. (00:31)

9. Just before Mustafa reveals the secret lair of Dr. Evil, Mini-Me blows an almost lethal dart into Mustafa's neck. From Mini-Me's position in the baby carriage, it is impossible to hit the right side of Mustafa's neck. But he makes it. (00:33)

10. During the dance to "I'll Never Fall in Love Again," just before the end of it, a couple of extras sit at a table. The male, who wears sunglasses, appears not interested in the dancing, then extremely interested and pleased, then not interested, and then enthusiastic again. (00:42)

11. Dr. Evil shows his Alan Parsons Project and aims the "laser" model at Washington, D.C. But as he says, "www.shh.com.org," the "laser" is aiming in a totally different direction—without anybody having touched it. (00:50)

12. In 1969, Number Two and Mini-Me both try to grab two cookies from a plate, but when the diminutive evil man wins the race, he grabs only one cookie from the plate, which now looks empty. (00:54)

13. During the "Just the Two of Us" rap, Dr. Evil talks about Scott, who's disgusted and walks from the left to the right. Dr. Evil turns to Mini-Me to tell him "you complete me," and Scott is behind Dr. Evil, to his left, as if he never walked away. (01:03)

14. Mini-Me draws a good-bye card to Scott. But as soon as the small sidekick grabs the sheet of paper to start drawing, it's possible to see the drawing already on it. (01:05)

15. During their terrible fight, Mini-Me lifts Austin and spins him above his head. In the long shots, Mini-Me rotates as well. But in the close-ups, he stands still and makes Austin spin only with his hands. (01:06)

16. After Frau Farbissina yells "Go!" and the rocketship takes off, Number Two, seen from above, pushes in the antenna on his remote control and places it on the table. In the next close-up he's holding it again, and he pushes in the antenna one more time. (01:07)

17. In a pause during the fight on the Moon Base, Mini-Me grabs Austin's glasses: the

glasses rotate in his hand in one cut (lenses away from him—lenses toward him). (01:16)

18. During the second sequence of synonyms for "penis" (which takes place "back in 1969"), a woman asks Woody Harrelson for his autograph. No offense, but Woody, born in 1961, was just an unknown kid back in 1969. (01:27, 01:28)

Fun Facts

1. While Vanessa (as a FemBot) fires her guns at Austin, he runs to hide and grabs the Swedish-Made Penis Enlarger. But he used it to kill Random Task at the end of the last movie . . . who brought it back? (00:04)

2. When Fat Bastard puts everyone to sleep in order to steal Austin's mojo, one of the Scottish guards, fainting, re-veals some white underwear. But Scots traditionally don't wear anything under their kilts. (00:23)

3. Austin and Felicity spend one day in London, buying clothes, harassing Royal Guards, and dancing; then there's one night in Austin's shag pad (where Austin leaves); then the next day they meet again in the London streets. Well, while in London during both days, Austin and Felicity wear the same clothes—but at night they changed. Mmmh . . . (00:39, 00:45, 00:51)

4. Dr. Evil shows what his "laser" can do, and plays a clip from the movie *Independence Day*. Well . . . that sequence is actually from the trailer of *Independence Day*. The sequence in the movie also had a helicopter blowing up on the right side. (00:57)

B

BACK TO THE FUTURE (22)
1985, color, 111 min.

Director: Robert Zemeckis

Cast: Michael J. Fox (Marty McFly), Christopher Lloyd (Dr. Emmett "Doc" L. Brown), Lea Thompson (Lorraine Baines / McFly), Crispin Glover (George McFly), Thomas F. Wilson (Biff Tannen), Claudia Wells (Jennifer Parker), Marc McClure (Dave McFly), Wendie Jo Sperber (Linda McFly), George DeCenzo (Sam Baines), Lee McCain (Stella Baines), James Tolkan (Principal Strickland), Norman Alden (Lou Caruthers).

Michael J. Fox hops in a DeLorean that transports him back to the 50s . . . and spawns a trilogy.

Bloopers
1. While playing a guitar, Marty causes the explosion of a

speaker in Doc's lab. He flies
back against a bookshelf,
which falls on top of him: papers and books drop to the
floor. The shelf is now empty
. . . but in the following close-
up, a few more sheets of
paper fall on top of Marty.
(00:04)

2. Marty enters his house when
Biff and George are talking
about George's totaled car.
Marty stops near a book-
shelf, on which there is a
vase filled almost to the lid
with jelly beans. After Biff
grabs a few jelly beans, we
see that the number of jelly
beans has dropped dramati-
cally. (00:12, 00:13)

3. Doc sends Einstein into the
future, for 1 minute. Or, to be
precise, for 1 minute and 21
seconds. (00:21)

4. During the dog's time-jump,
the strip of fire left by the
DeLorean passes by Doc's
legs three times: in the long
shot, the detail shot, and
from behind. (00:21)

5. Speaking of which, the strip
of fire goes underneath Doc's
legs. In the following shot,
Doc is far away from the fire.
(00:21)

6. Doc tells Marty that he can
go and see the birth of Christ,
and punches in Dec. 25, 0000.
Actually, there never was a
year 0000. Humanity jumped
from 1 B.C. to A.D. 1. (00:24)

7. The time circuit seems to be
on (or at least lit) when Marty
gets the DeLorean into gear
the first time. But a few sec-

onds later, when he hits the
switch, the time circuit turns
on again. (00:30)

8. During the chase with the
Libyans, the DeLorean's
odometer reads 33061, then
after one shot 32994. Later
on, when Marty's going back
to the future, the odometer
reads 33051. (00:30, 01:39)

9. In the same chase, the
DeLorean's "trip meter" reads
86.4. In the next shot it reads
19.0. (00:30)

10. The car encouraging people
to vote for Red Thomas has
two loudspeakers (one in
front, one in back) and a sign
in-between. As the car turns
a corner, the rear speaker
vanishes and the sign rotates
90°. (00:36)

11. When Marty approaches his
future dad for the first time
at Lou's in 1955, a menu in
front of the them rotates 180°
without anybody touching it.
(00:39, 00:40)

12. The *Honeymooners* episode
that Marty and his future
family see on the night of
November 5, 1955, actually
aired for the first time on
December 31, 1955 (The title
of the episode was "The Man
From Space"). (00:46)

13. When Marty does his Darth
Vader impression for George,
he has a hair dryer in his
belt. The hair dryer vanishes
and comes back in the belt in
four different shots. (01:02)

14. Chased by Biff and his gang,
Marty takes off on a skate-
board. Marty grabs on to the

back of a truck. Marty is holding on to the right side, but his stunt double has a hold of the left side. (01:06)

15. During the same chase, after Marty bumps into two pedestrians, Biff's car approaches — and the red sun visors on the car appear and disappear all through the final part of the chase. (01:06)

16. When Biff's car hits the manure truck, from one shot it hits the rear end; but when the manure falls on the kids, the car has moved at least three feet back. (01:07)

17. Marty talks to George, trying to convince him to be aggressive. The flap of Marty's left pocket is out, then in when he mumbles "Da da da, daddy-o," and then out again. (01:12)

18. Marty writes a note to Doc warning him about the future, but Doc tears it into pieces and pockets them. In 1985, Doc shows the same note taped back together, but the message on the note is different. (01:15, 01:45)

19. Marty's guitar is a Gibson ES-335, a model which came out in 1958, not in 1955. (01:16)

20. Principal Strickland takes his hands away from his ears twice: the first time in a wide shot (he's on the left side of the screen), the second time 10 seconds later, in a close-up. (01:29)

21. Back in 1955, Doc wears a pair of sneakers with velcro fasteners. True, velcro was invented in Switzerland in 1948, but shoes with those particular stripes weren't manufactured until the 1970s. (01:38)

22. Marty jumps back to the future in order to reach Doc before the Libyans. But his car fails, and as he jiggles the key in the ignition, we catch a glimpse of the "Time Where You Were" monitor. It reads "OCT" — but when Marty was in 1955, it was November. (01:42)

Non-Blooper
When Marty goes to Doc's test of the time machine, he stops at the Twin Pine Mall. Once he's back in the future, it's called the "*Lone Pine Mall*." It's because Marty ran over one of the two pines while dashing away from the angry farmer in 1955. (00:18, 00:33, 01:43)

Back to the Future Cameo

Huey Lewis, whose band did music for the movie, is the "Battle of the Bands" judge. (00:07)

BATMAN (13)
1989, color, 126 min.

Director: Tim Burton

Cast: Michael Keaton (Batman / Bruce Wayne), Jack Nicholson (The Joker / Jack Napier), Kim Basinger (Vicki Vale), Robert Wuhl (Alexander Knox), Pat Hingle (Police Commissioner

Gordon), Billy Dee Williams (Harvey Dent, Gotham District Attorney), Michael Gough (Alfred Pennyworth), Jack Palance (Boss Carl Grissom), Jerry Hall (Alicia), Tracey Walter (Bob the Goon), Lee Wallace (Mayor Borg), William Hootkins (Lt. Eckhardt).

Ta na na na na na na na Batman!! But brand spankin' new!

Bloopers

1. The old Jack Napier has brown eyes. The young Jack has blue-gray eyes. (00:09, 01:31)
2. Vicki Vale's name is spelled "Vicky Vale" on the front cover of *Time* magazine. (00:13)
3. Lt. Eckhardt is in the Axis Chemical Company handing out flyers, and he hasn't shaved for at least a couple of days. After a minute, as soon as Commissioner Gordon arrives, Eckhardt's face is smooth as a baby's behind. (00:24, 00:25)
4. After killing Tony Rotelli, Joker rubs part of the makeup off of his forehead. The shape of the white area changes when Joker talks to Tony's corpse. (00:43, 00:44)
5. Bruce places two roses on a sidewalk and then walks away. When Vicki gets to the roses, they have changed positions. (00:46, 00:47)
6. Vicki has five snapshots of Bruce Wayne on a table. She

picks one up, but when she is looking at it, through the back of the photo paper the snapshot looks different from the one she picked up. (00:52)

7. Vicki waits at the museum cafeteria, and "Fluegelheim Museum" is printed on the menu on her table. When she escapes with Batman, the sign at the front entrance of the building says "Flugelheim Museum." (01:00, 01:07)
8. Dancing in the art museum, one of Joker's goons ruins a painting with several red handprints of paint. In the next shot, when Joker mocks a tiny statue, the same painting is now untouched. (01:02)
9. When the Batmobile stops in front of Batman, who has called it via remote, he lowers the remote after saying "Stop!" In the next shot, the remote is close to his mouth again. (01:12)
10. Bruce pauses a tape of Joker when the evil man has his eyes closed. After being haunted by a memory from the past, Bruce looks back at the freeze frame of the Joker . . . who now has his eyes open. (01:29, 01:32)
11. During Joker's parade, the clown-shaped balloon is behind Joker, above his float, and then also behind it in a quick succession of shots. (01:35, 01:36, 01:37)
12. To protect herself from the smilex gas, Vicki jumps in a car and rolls the window up, then floors the gas pedal and

leaves. But just before hitting a pile of garbage, it's possible to see that the rear right passenger window is rolled down. (01:40, 01:41)

13. Joker literally spits his teeth, and some blood drips on his chin. But after he's plunged to his death, his chin is clean. (01:55, 01:59)

Question

Vicki wants to learn more about Bruce Wayne, so she quickly leaves the office to follow him. If she was in such a hurry, where did she find the time to change both her dress and her hairdo? (00:45)

BATMAN RETURNS (7)
1992, color, 126 min.

Director: Tim Burton

Cast: Michael Keaton (Bruce Wayne / Batman), Danny DeVito (Oswald Chesterfield Cobblepot / The Penguin), Michelle Pfeiffer (Selina Kyle / Catwoman), Christopher Walken (Maximillian "Max" Shreck), Michael Gough (Alfred Pennyworth), Michael Murphy (Mayor), Cristi Conaway (Ice Princess), Andrew Bryniarski (Charles "Chip" Shreck), Pat Hingle (Police Commissioner Gordon), Vincent Schiavelli (Organ Grinder), Steve Witting (Josh), Jan Hooks (Jen).

Batman, Catwoman, Penguin . . . let's start a zoo.

Bloopers

1. Bruce Wayne receives the projected bat signal while in his studio. As he stands up, the circle of light hits only the last shelf on the bookshelf behind the millionaire. In the long shot, the light circle is much, much lower and hits almost the entire bookshelf. (00:13)

2. When Penguin emerges from the sewer holding the baby, he starts rising through a manhole; then in the following shot he hasn't risen as far as he had already in the first shot—so he rises again. (00:35)

3. When Catwoman is doing the cartwheels in Shreck's store, her heels collapse as if made of rubber. The following shot reveals a close-up of the same heels, solid and unfoldable. (00:55)

4. While controlling the Batmobile, Penguin talks to Batman—who makes a CD copy of the speech ("Just relax. I'll take care of these squealing, wretched pinhead puppets of Gotham! . . . You got to admit: I've played this stinking city like a harp from hell [laughter]"). Later, when Bruce jams Penguin's sound and plays back the CD, the speech is slightly different ("Hey, just relax. I'll take care of the squealing, wretched pinhead puppets of Gotham! . . . You gotta admit: I've played this stinking city like a harp from hell [different laughter]"). (01:24, 01:29)

5. After opening the secret en-

trance to the batcave by pushing a button inside the fish tank, Bruce puts his right arm into his jacket sleeve, then starts with his left arm . . . but in the following shot he's still struggling with his right sleeve. (01:28)

6. Batman reveals his secret identity to Catwoman in Penguin's hideout. After he says "Split . . . right down the center," he takes off his mask. The black makeup he's wearing right around his eyes vanishes just before he rips off the mask. (01:53)

7. During his small funeral, Penguin is pushed down in his own pool by six penguins. As he hits the water, it's possible to see a rectangular black platform sinking fast (presumably it helped the penguins in pushing the body along the slide). (01:57)

BEETLEJUICE (6)
1988, color, 92 min.

Director: Tim Burton

Cast: Alec Baldwin (Adam Maitland), Geena Davis (Barbara Maitland), Michael Keaton (Betelgeuse [Beetlejuice]), Catherine O'Hara (Delia Deitz), Jeffrey Jones (Charles Deitz), Winona Ryder (Lydia Deitz), Glenn Shadix (Otho), Sylvia Sidney (Juno), Robert Goulet (Maxie Dean), Dick Cavett (Bernard), Susan Kellermann (Grace), Adelle Lutz (Beryl).

A newly dead couple calls a bio-exorcist to get rid of certain people. Then they have to get rid of the bio-exorcist.

Bloopers

1. Barbara only partially opens the wallpaper that Adam gives her—yet, when she says, "I'm gonna get started right away," the paper is completely unwrapped. (00:03)

2. As ghosts, neither Adam nor Barbara cast any reflection (as she shows him in front of a mirror). Yet, when they get home, she says, "I'll make some coffee," and they cast a reflection on a picture to the left. Also, when they cross the sixth door and he states, "This place just gets weirder and

---

Batman Returns Cameos

Straight from *Pee-wee's Big Adventure* (another Tim Burton movie) . . .

CAMEO	ROLE	TIMES
Paul Reubens	Mr. Cobblepot	00:00
Diane Salinger	Mrs. Cobblepot	00:00

weirder," there is a reflection of him on a glass pane in the background. (00:08, 00:09, 00:34)

3. The eccentric Otho makes his entrance through a window: he wears red shoes. When he walks with Delia ("Oh, look—an indoor outhouse!") he's wearing white sneakers. (00:15, 00:17)

4. Otho decides to get the show on the road; he produces two spray paint cans, removes the cap from one of them, and passes it to Delia . . . who removes the cap one more time. (00:16)

5. When Delia writes "Maurie" on a wall with the spray paint, in the following shot, the writing is different and much lower on the wall. (00:16)

6. Adam draws a door on the wall. He adds the knob, then knocks three times. By that point, the knob has vanished. (00:27)

Questions

1. According to the rule, if you say Beetlejuice's name three times, he'll appear. The first time Adam finds a Betelgeuse flyer, he says the name three and a half times, but nothing happens. So . . . ? (00:22)

2. When Adam and Barbara are in the model, they dig for Betelgeuse's grave. They remove pieces of cardboard with "Fragile" written on them. But, since they are in the model, this writing must be really microscopic. What's the point of writing "Fragile" on a box that nobody can read? (00:46)

BIG DADDY (13)
1999, color, 93 min.

Director: Dennis Dugan

Cast: Adam Sandler (Sonny Koufax), Joey Lauren Adams (Layla Maloney), Jon Stewart (Kevin Gerrity), Cole Sprouse (Julian), Dylan Sprouse (Julian), Josh Mostel (Mr. Brooks), Leslie Mann (Corinne Maloney), Allen Covert (Phil), Rob Schneider (Nazo, the Delivery Guy), Kristy Swanson (Vanessa), Joseph Bologna (Mr. Koufax), Steve Buscemi (Homeless Guy), Dennis Dugan (Sourpuss).

Slacker adopts kid and teaches him how to slack. Kid then teaches slacker how to love.

Bloopers

1. The first rollerblader Sonny trips at the park falls into the lake. The "rock" to the right floats and goes up and down after being hit by the waves. (00:13)

2. When Julian tosses the stick in front of the rollerblader, there's nothing on the ground by him. The following shot reveals a crushed soda can; nobody knows where it came from, but it stays there till the scene is over. (00:18)

3. Sonny spreads three news-

paper sections on Julian's bed after he wets it. When Julian is rolling on them and making noise later, the number of newspaper sections has increased. (00:19, 00:20)

4. When Julian tries to pour milk into his cereal, he drops the large jug on the floor, and the milk spills and flows toward Sonny. When we see the spill again, it hasn't flowed as far toward Sonny, and the puddle is different. (00:20, 00:21)

5. On the way to McDonald's, Sonny offers an Egg Mc-Muffin to a homeless man, but the bum requests a Sausage McMuffin instead, and Sunny agrees. When they return the homeless man asks where his Egg McMuffin is. They meet up with him later while scolding roller-bladers, and he reminds them that they owe him a Sausage McMuffin. (00:24, 00:25, 01:04)

6. After dancing to the "Kangaroo Song," Julian pukes on the floor. The shape of the vomit changes from a long strip to a roundish puddle. (00:28)

7. Julian takes off his backpack and goes by a puddle to play with his action figure. The backpack's position changes in almost every shot. (00:37)

8. Sonny shows Julian the "sleeper hold" on Nazo, who winds up fainting on the floor. Nazo's head keeps changing positions: it's on the floor, it's resting on his arm, it's on the floor again. Then, after Sonny moves him, his head leans to the right, to the left, then to the right again. (00:38)

9. Sonny demands that the sourpuss give Julian some stuff for trick-or-treat. The number of CDs in the guy's hands increases in the next shot. (00:40)

10. While Julian is showing off his spitting technique, Thomas is sitting on a bench with a bag of Lays potato chips. The bag keeps turning on his lap, but he doesn't move it. (00:41)

11. In the supermarket, Sonny teaches Julian how to make a dented can. The cans on the floor change position in every shot. (00:52)

12. To stop an itch on Julian's arm, Corinne places a bag of frozen vegetables on it with the label facing up. But after one cut, the bag has turned face down. (00:52)

13. After the trial, Julian runs to Sonny for a hug. In the first two shots, Sonny's right hand is above his left on Julian's back, but in the last shot they switch to left above right. (01:22)

Question
While Sonny is talking to his father on the phone, Julian can be seen answering to the person who's using the phone on the other side of Sonny's. Who the hell was he talking to? (00:35)

BLUE THUNDER (9)
1983, color, 108 min.

Director: John Badham

Cast: Roy Scheider (Frank Murphy), Warren Oates (Captain Jack Braddock), Candy Clark (Kate), Daniel Stern (Officer Richard Lymangood), Paul Roebling (Icelan), David Sheiner (Fletcher), Joe Santos (Montana), Malcolm McDowell (Colonel F. E. Cochrane), Ed Bernard (Sergeant Short), Jason Bernard (Mayor), Mario Machado (Himself), James Murtaugh (Alf Hewitt), James Pead (Policeman at Bridge).

An amazing police chopper is found to better patrol L.A. As if all the news choppers weren't enough.

Bloopers
1. After Captain Braddock says, "Is that right?" it's possible to see the crew reflected in his monumental sunglasses. (00:02)
2. During the presentation of the *Blue Thunder*, Colonel Cochrane fires at a few targets: his hands are bare, but when he yells "Damned bloody gun!" and lands, he's wearing black gloves. (00:32, 00:34, 00:35)
3. When Braddock tells Murphy, "They have $5 million invested in this aircraft," Murphy turns his head to his left. But when Braddock adds, "They don't wanna see it totaled," Murphy's head is turned to his right. (00:50)
4. Lymangood reads aloud the li-

 cense plate of a motorcycle: "2 − 21 − Bravo − 6." His face is reflected in the monitor, and his mouth begins to move after "Bravo." (00:55)
5. Cochrane goes to a window and moves a curtain. He freezes, staring at the *Blue Thunder*, and finally lowers the coffee mug from his mouth. The image on the chopper monitor acts a little sooner: the mug is lowered before Cochrane actually does it. (01:03)
6. Lymangood gets his hands tied behind his back. He manages to run away, but as he hits a biker, his hands are free−but they are tied behind his back again in the next shots. His hands are free again as he is run over by the car. (01:08, 01:10)
7. Speaking of the car, during the chase it collides with a parked car. As it backs up, only one front headlight is working; in the next shot, there are three working headlights, and in the final shot only two are doing their job. (01:10)
8. When Lymangood is run over by the car, he rolls on the ground, his arms over his head. When the paramedics reach him, his position has visibly changed (and his hands are tied behind him again). (01:10, 01:11)
9. When Kate is stopped on the bridge by two cops, the gun of the officer who gets out of the car changes between cuts: it switches back and forth from

being a Colt to a Smith & Wesson. (01:25)

Question

After the first night flight, Murphy and Lymangood enter the station: a clock on the wall says 05:44. Murphy gets home when it's almost dawn; but when Kate enters the house asking for her blender, he says: "At three o'clock in the morning?" So what time is it, exactly? (00:14, 00:18, 00:21)

BLUES BROTHERS, THE (16)

also Collector's Edition
1980, color, 133 min. / 148 min. (CE)

Director: John Landis

Cast: John Belushi (Joliet Jake Blues), Dan Aykroyd (Elwood Blues), James Brown (Rev. Cleophus James), Cab Calloway (Curtis), Ray Charles (Ray), Aretha Franklin (Soul Food Café Owner), Steve Cropper (Steve "The Colonel" Cropper), Donald Dunn (Donald "Duck" Dunn), Murphy Dunne (Murph), Willie Hall (Willie "Too Big" Hall), Carrie Fisher (Mystery Woman), Stephen Bishop (Charming Trooper), Henry Gibson (Head Nazi), Eugene J. Anthony (Gruppenfeuhrer), John Landis (Trooper La Fong).

Musically inclined duo manage to wreck enough cars to start their own salvage yard.

Bloopers

1. When Elwood decides to jump over the open East 95th Street Bridge, the two sides of the bridge change angles on virtually every shot, and are motionless during the actual jump. (00:08 / 00:09 CE)

2. Rev. Cleophus sings in the church and in the close-up he is on the right side of the microphone stand ("For the day of the Lord cometh . . . as a thief in the night! Amen!"). In the long shot he is on the left side. (00:17 / 00:19 CE)

3. Running away from the police, Elwood takes a curve and his car spins counterclockwise. From the inside, Jake is in a car that spins clockwise. (00:25 / 00:27 CE)

4. The police car that flips in the JCPenney's is seen skidding on the floor: in long shots the vehicle slides diagonally, while in the cops' close-ups it skids forward. Also, a piece of orange wood trapped beneath the car's roof vanishes in the close-ups. (00:28 / 00:31 CE)

5. The Mystery Woman uses a four-tube rocket launcher, yet she fires five rockets at Jake. (00:30, 00:31 / 00:34 CE)

6. Jake and Elwood avoid the rockets by falling to the ground. They stand up, clean themselves off, then enter the building—yet some rubble is still on their shoulders. (00:31 / 00:35 CE)

7. In the Soul Food Café, be-

hind the counter there's a pie cupboard with a glass sliding door. The sliding door keeps changing position, especially during the song "Think." (00:52, 00:53 / 01:01, 01:02 CE)

8. The Mystery Woman applies some red polish to her left middle fingernail. She blows on it, then as she grabs an M-79 Flame Thrower book, the hand has red polish on the ring fingernail, too. But she didn't apply the polish to that finger. (00:57 / 01:06 CE)

9. Bob, the owner of Bob's Country Bunker, shuts down the amplifiers of the Blues Brothers Band. Trying to solve the emergency, the Blues Brothers Band decides to play the "Theme from Rawhide," and so they do, beginning with a wonderful bass solo. With the amplifiers still turned off. (01:10 / 01:19, 01:20 CE)

10. During Steve Cropper's solo in "Rawhide," it's possible to see Jake walking to one side of the stage to grab the whip. He'll do the same thing again a few seconds later. (01:11 / 01:21 CE)

11. As he's entering the Palace Hotel Ballroom, Joliet Jake grabs a keychain in his right hand and makes it spin in the air. But as the Blues Brothers step onstage, the keychain is in Jake's left hand. (01:29 / 01:49 CE)

12. Jake and Elwood sing the fi-nale of "Everybody Needs Somebody to Love" kicking in the air and yelling "you, you, you!" The two micro-phones are either in front of or behind the two brothers, depending on whether the shot is in front of or behind them. (01:39 / 01:52 CE)

13. During the final car chase, before entering a subway, a police car is hit by another police car. The first car loses its front bumper twice. It also vanishes from the back-ground as we cut inside the Bluesmobile. (01:52 / 02:06 CE)

14. The Bluesmobile runs in front of an alley where the Illinois Nazis are waiting. The red car moves, but the close-up of the Head Nazi reveals a car that's still motionless. (01:54 / 02:08 CE)

15. When the Head Nazi says, "There they are," it's possible to see, in the rear wind-shield, a red White Power sticker with a swastika in the middle of it. As the red Nazi car takes off from the bridge under construction, the sticker is gone—in the inside-the-car shots. It's still there dur-ing the fall of the car. (01:54, 01:56 / 02:08, 02:11 CE)

16. When the army fires at a door labeled "11 Keep Door Closed," and then kicks it open, the bullet holes are dif-ferent in the alley shot from in the following room shot. (02:03 / 02:18 CE)

The Blues Brothers Cameos

Like almost any of John Landis's movies, *The Blues Brothers* abounds with cameos. A few of them are pointed out during the "Jailhouse Rock" number (Frank Oz, Aretha Franklin, et al.), but if you really want to know the rest . . .

CAMEO	ROLE	TIMES
Chaka Khan	Choir Soloist	00:16 / 00:18 CE
John Landis	Trooper La Fong	00:26 / 00:29 CE
Paul Reubens	Waiter (at Chez Paul)	00:43 / 00:51 CE
Steven Spielberg	Cook County Clerk	02:03 / 02:17 CE
Joe Walsh	Prisoner (he starts the dance)	02:05 / 02:19 CE

BRADY BUNCH MOVIE, THE (9)
1995, color, 90 min.

Director: Betty Thomas

Cast: Shelley Long (Carol Brady), Gary Cole (Mike Brady), Christine Taylor (Marcia Brady), Christopher Daniel Barnes (Greg Brady), Jennifer Elise Cox (Jan Brady), Paul Sutera (Peter Brady), Olivia Hack (Cindy Brady), Jesse Lee (Bobby Brady), Henriette Mantel (Alice Nelson), David Graf (Sam Franklin), Michael McKean (Mr. Dittmeyer), Jack Noseworthy (Eric Dittmeyer), Darion Basco (Eddie), Ann B. Davis (Trucker "Shultzy").

Here's the movie / of a lovely lady . . .

Bloopers
1. In the second shot of the movie (on Hollywood Boulevard), it's possible to see the whole crew reflected in the store windows (they are followed by a motorcycle cop, who appears later—intentionally—during the montage). (00:00)
2. Mr. Brady unfolds the morning paper . . . twice. (00:03)
3. Jan grabs a flour bag instead of her lunch; her Mom hands her the real lunch, but the fold of the brown bag turns 180° in Mrs. Brady's hands. (00:12)
4. Greg and Marcia are almost carjacked. Greg rolls down the window: a little if the shot is from the inside of the car, a lot if from the outside. (00:14)
5. Peter is threatened by Eric the bully, who grabs a slice of pizza—which bends at the end. When Eric is stopped by another student, the pizza slice is now straight again, and has turned in his hands. (00:23)
6. When Greg is "busy writing a song for Danielle," Cindy tells

him about the possible house sale. The guitar strap keeps jumping over and under Greg's shirt collar. (00:27)

7. A little later, while practicing guitar in front of the mirror, it happens again: while talking with Marcia, Greg's guitar strap keeps jumping over and under his shirt collar. (00:29)

8. At Sears, Mr. Dittmeyer loses his neck brace when charged by a group of fans. The collar falls to the ground, it's nowhere to be seen when Dittmeyer finds himself in front of all the TV screens, but is back (between the man and the toilet he's carrying) just before he drops the porcelain. (00:58, 00:59)

9. During what seems will be their last night in their home, Mr. Brady grabs Mrs. Brady's needlepoint and puts it on the floor on the right side of the bed. When Cindy enters the room, Mr. Brady grabs the needlepoint from the left side of the bed. (01:05, 01:06)

Questions

1. Mr. Dittmeyer is talking on his car phone, when Jan passes by, riding her bike. The first time we see Jan is through Mr. Dittmeyer's left side mirror, which says "OBJECTS IN MIRROR ARE CLOSER THAN THEY APPEAR." But isn't that line only on right side mirrors? Also, is it us, or is the detail shot of a different mirror? And, while we're at it, after seeming to get hit on the left side of his face, why does Mr. Dittmeyer rub his right cheek? (00:33)

2. While playing football in the backyard, Peter says, "Hey Greg: you're the Casanova of Clinton Avenue . . ." Later on, when Trucker "Shultzy" calls Mrs. Brady via radio, she says that she's dropped Jan "at 4222 Clinton Way." Did the Bradys move? (00:39, 01:11)

Fun Fact

Bobby pins a sign on a tree: "Attention! Missing School Supplies." But a small note says, "For moore information contact . . ." Good kid, bad speller. (00:31)

The Brady Bunch Movie Cameos

Here are the cameos / of a lovely lady . . .

CAMEO	ROLE	TIMES
Barry Williams (TV's Greg Brady)	Music Producer	00:31
Ann B. Davis (TV's Alice)	Trucker "Schulzy"	01:08
Florence Henderson (TV's Carol Brady)	Grandma Brady	01:23
The "Partridge Family" Bus	Itself	01:13

BRADY BUNCH 2, THE (SEE "VERY BRADY SEQUEL, A")

BREAKDOWN (7)
1997, color, 95 min.

Director: Jonathan Mostow

Cast: Kurt Russell (Jeff Taylor), J. T. Walsh (Red Barr / "Warren"), Kathleen Quinlan (Amy Taylor), M. C. Gainey (Earl), Jack Noseworthy (Billy), Rex Linn (Sheriff Boyd), Ritch Brinkley (Al), Moira Harris (Arleen), Kim Robillard (Deputy Len Carver), Thomas Kopache (Calhoun), Jack McGee (Bartender), Vincent Berry (Deke).

Kurt Russell's car breaks down in the desert, and it's all uphill from there.

Bloopers
1. Jeff stops at a gas station to change the oil; as he talks with Earl (".. . that you damn near killed us back there?"), a boom mike is visible in the jeep's left side mirror and again when Amy comes back from the store and asks, "What is that all about?" (00:04)
2. Amy changes her mind and decides to accept a lift from Warren. She gets close to the Jeep (the driver's door is open), opens the rear door, takes her purse, waves to the truck. Now the driver's door is closed. Neither she nor Jeff had ever shut it. (00:13)
3. Waiting in the car for the tow truck, Jeff holds his sunglasses by the right temple. When he steps out of the vehicle, he holds the glasses by the left temple. (00:13, 00:14)
4. Eventually, Jeff catches up with Warren's truck: when he brakes in front of it to make it stop, the shadow on the ground goes to the left of the Jeep. When Jeff calls his wife's name aloud and looks for her in the truck, the shadow goes to the right of the vehicles. When Warren leaves and Jeff goes to talk to the Sheriff, the shadow goes to the left again. (00:19, 00:20, 00:26)
5. Sheriff Boyd, holding a notebook in his left hand, tells Jeff to go to the town of Brackett. When he says, "If you wanna report that your wife's missing," there's no notebook to be seen. Right after that, the Sheriff reenters his car. With a notebook. (00:26)
6. After Jeff breaks in the "Caution—Road Closed Ahead" gate, and he gets chased by Earl, his rearview mirror vanishes in every exterior shot of the Jeep. The mirror will be back for good when Jeff aims for the river. (00:34, 00:35)
7. To find the keys of a yellow pickup, Jeff shatters the glass pane of a trailer door: the slivers that remain in the frame change size from the outside shot to the inside shot. (01:20)

Pan & Scan

Jeff and his wife are moving to San Diego from Massachusetts. They're driving through Arizona in their new Massachusetts-plated Jeep. When Amy comments about how fast Kurt's driving, the speedometer says 80 mph, but the odometer shows the Jeep has only gone 245 miles. From Massachusetts to Arizona!?? (00:02, 00:06)

Questions

1. When Jeff's Jeep misbehaves in the middle of the road, Jeff yells, "Hang on. I can't steer!" But when Warren helps him push the car, Jeff asks his wife, "Honey, you want to steer?" And she doesn't seem to have any problem. Huh? (00:07, 00:11)

2. Into Red's barn enters Arleen, Red's wife. Billy greets her with a warm, "Hey, Mrs. C." Red's last name is Barr. So . . . ? [NOTE: Both DVD subtitles and Closed Captions read "Mrs. B."] (01:12)

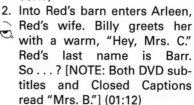

C

CASABLANCA (16)

1942, black & white, 102 min.

Director: Michael Curtiz

Cast: Humphrey Bogart (Richard "Rick" Blaine), Ingrid Bergman (Ilsa Lund Laszlo), Paul Henreid (Victor Laszlo), Claude Rains (Captain Louis Renault), Conrad Veidt (Major Heinrich Strasser), Dooley Wilson (Sam), Sydney Greenstreet (Senor Ferrari), Peter Lorre (Ugarte), S.Z. Sakall (Carl, the Headwaiter), Madeleine LeBeau (Yvonne), Joy Page (Annina Brandel), Wolfgang Zilzer (Man with Expired Papers).

"Play it Sam . . ." and again, and again. We won't complain.

Bloopers

1. Actor S.Z. Sakall is credited as S.K. Sakall. (00:00)
2. The man whose papers had expired three weeks earlier runs away from the police. He's shot in front of a large poster ("Je Tiens Mes Promesses, Meme Celles Des Autres" —Philippe Petain), close to an arch. As the man hits the ground, the statue of a woman has appeared in the archway, and a small stool is close to it. (00:03)
3. At the airport, the man behind Major Strasser gets off the plane twice. (00:05)
4. Sam's hand movements don't match the notes on the piano, most notably during "It Had to Be You" and "Knock on Wood." (00:07, 00:12)
5. At his table, Rick writes on a 1,000 franc loan request "OK. Rick," then underlines it. When he passes the loan request back, his name is no longer underlined. (00:08)
6. Rick stares at a chessboard, grabs a knight—but in the over-the-shoulder shot he's toying with a wine glass. (00:09)
7. Rick joins Renault at a table outside of Rick's Café. After two police officers (Captain Tonelli and Lieutenant Cas-

selle) pass by, a bottle has appeared on Renault's table, and a few pieces of paper have vanished. (00:15)

8. When Rick joins Renault, he has a lit cigarette. After sitting down, he brings an unlit cigarette to his mouth—but as the duo sees the plane taking off, smoke is coming from the cigarette that's now in Rick's hands—and he never lit it. (00:15, 00:16)

9. Rick waits for Ilsa at the train station, while it's pouring rain—and he's without an umbrella. Sam brings him a note from Ilsa, then pushes a destroyed Rick to the train. When Rick and Sam board, they're perfectly dry. (00:46, 00:47)

10. Captain Renault informs Lazlo he's filling out the report of Ugarte's death. Renault stops writing and flips one page—but in the over-the-shoulder shot, he's still writing. (00:54)

11. Ferrari makes a proposition to Rick while pouring himself a drink. Ferrari then places the cork back on the bottle—but the bottle is corkless after one shot of Lazlo and Ilsa. Needless to say, nobody seems to have touched the bottle in the meantime. (00:56)

12. Annina approaches Rick in his café and tells him how sad she is that her husband is losing money for their visa at the roulette table. Rick pours a drink and takes a long sip, leaving very little liquor in the glass. After a few seconds, much more liquor is in the glass. (01:05)

13. An indignant Lazlo asks the band to play "La Marseillaise." The band members obey, but the music erupts from the trumpets before they actually reach the mouths of the players. (01:12)

14. After Lazlo leaves the hotel, Ilsa pulls the blinds to watch him. From inside the room, the slats of the blinds are horizontal, leaving room enough for the light to get into the room. From the outside, the slats are vertical, completely obstructing the window. (01:18)

15. While checking on Rick's finances, Carl reassures him: "You are in pretty good shape, Rick." Carl's glasses are up over his forehead, but after the following cut, they are on his nose. (01:18)

16. While driving to the airport, Major Strasser is seen wearing a coat with bright epaulettes on the shoulders. As he reaches the airport, the epaulettes are gone, then back, then gone, back, gone, back ... (01:37, 01:39)

Question

When Rick and Ilsa remember the last time they saw each other in Paris, Rick recalls, "I remember every detail. The Germans wore gray, you wore blue." She confirms, "Yes. I put that dress away." But in a flashback she's wearing a suit, not a dress. Does his memory work better than hers? (00:34, 00:42)

Fun Fact

When Rick goes back in time to when he was in Paris with Ilsa, he remembers driving with her in Paris in his car . . . with the steering wheel on the right. How many British cars were there in Paris during the Second World War? (00:38)

DVD Blooper

While talking to Rick, Ugarte mentions that the letters of transit are signed by General Waygand. Both the DVD subtitles and the Closed Captioning say, "General De Gaulle." (00:11)

CASPER (7)

1995, color, 101 min.

Director: Brad Silberling

Cast: Christina Ricci (Kat Harvey), Bill Pullman (Dr. Harvey), Cathy Moriarty (Carrigan), Eric Idle (Dibs), Joe Nipote (Stretch), Joe Alaskey (Stinkie), Brad Garrett (Fatso), Garette Ratliff Henson (Vic), Jessica Watson (Amber), Amy Brenneman (Amelia), Malachi Pearson (Casper), Ben Stein (Rugg).

Teen ghost makes friends in our world, too.

Bloopers

1. Evil Carrigan extinguishes her cigarette on Rugg's table while hearing the reading of the will. As Rugg stands up, it's clear the cigarette is out—but in the following shot, smoke still comes from the table. (00:02, 00:03)

2. Casper pulls a prank on Kat's classmates: he ties their shoes together by the laces. The first shoelaces he ties are Amber's. In more than one of the subsequent shots, her tied-together legs are somehow crossed, and she even stands up to protest when Kat's house is picked over hers for the Halloween party. Yet, she still falls when the bell rings (like everyone else). (00:43, 00:44)

3. When the bell rings, every student stands up and falls because of their tied-together shoes. But keep an eye on the kid with a black shirt (fourth row to the left) and on the African American girl with the gray sweater, two seats behind Amber: their shoes are very free and not tied together—still, they fall at once with everybody else. (00:44)

4. Casper lifts his mom's dress out of the trunk and places it on Kat. She looks at herself in the mirror, and as he pulls her hair out of the dress, the top buttons of the dress are undone. Yet, when Kat passes through the secret passage in the wall and she hits the rail-

ing of the balcony, the dress is all buttoned up. (01:00, 01:02)

5. While riding on the red chair to go into the hidden room of the house, Kat gets squirted with toothpaste—which vanishes a few seconds later. (01:03, 01:04)

6. Kat looks for a switch to activate the resurrecting machine, and she finds a clean copy of *Frankenstein*—while moving a sheet of paper. One second later, the book is covered with dust. (01:06)

7. Then, Kat opens the book to find a dusty black button—a button that becomes shiny and clean after less than a second, without Kat touching it. (01:06)

Questions

1. Kat notices that ghosts don't cast a reflection in a mirror; still, when Amber and Vic are checking their costumes (in a mirror), Stretch, Stinkie, and Fatso appear to them in the reflection. How? (00:49, 01:24)

2. While riding on the red chair to go into the hidden room of the house, Kat finds herself in front of shaving cream, and her chair stops. But when Dibs and Carrigan ride on the same chair, he gets gallons of shaving cream in his face. Why did Kat's ride stop before the shaving cream? It can't be because Kat is a woman and Dibs a man, because in both cases the razors enter into action ... (01:03, 01:05)

CHARLIE'S ANGELS (12)
2000, color, 98 min.

Director: McG (Joseph McGinty Nichol)

Cast: Cameron Diaz (Natalie Cook), Drew Barrymore (Dylan Sanders), Lucy Liu (Alex Munday), Bill Murray (Bosley), Sam Rockwell (Eric Knox), Kelly Lynch (Vivian Wood), Tim Curry (Roger Corwin), Crispin Glover (The Thin Man), John Forsythe (Charlie), Matt LeBlanc (Jason

---

Casper Cameos

Ghosts, goblins and cameos ...

CAMEO	ROLE	TIMES
Don Novello	Father Guido Sarducci (the exorcist)	00:07
Dan Aykroyd	Dr. Stantz (the ghostbuster)	00:09
Clint Eastwood	Metamorphosis No. 1	00:30
Rodney Dangerfield	Metamorphosis No. 2	00:30
Mel Gibson	Metamorphosis No. 3	00:30
The Crypt Keeper	Metamorphosis No. 4	00:30

Gibbons), LL Cool J (Mr. Jones), Tom Green (Chad), Bob Stephenson (Red Star System Director One), Ned Bellamy (Red Star System Director Two), Sean Whalen (Pasqual).

"Good morning, Angels!"
"Good morning, Charlie!"

Bloopers

1. Pasqual, the bomber on the plane, has a black vest underneath his jacket. As he lands on the Angels' boat, the vest is gone. It'll be back when he yells, "You crazy bastard!" (00:02, 00:04)
2. The muffin Jason throws toward Alex's car lands upside-down. The detail shows it landed on one side. (00:11)
3. When Natalie tosses one of Alex's muffins into the door of the office, the muffin goes all the way through the door. When Bosley opens the very same door, half the muffin is sticking out of it. (00:12)
4. The Angels receive a color picture of the creepy Thin Man in the car; when they drive up to take their order at the drive-thru, the picture Natalie is holding ("And find out if he works for Corwin.") is in black & white and now has a white border. (00:17, 00:18)
5. Corwin offers Bosley some blowfish from a tray. Bosley has to dig through what seems to be cellophane to get one tart—although there

was no cellophane on the tray a few seconds earlier. (00:20)
6. When the Angels are checking the images coming from Corwin's microcamera on his briefcase, it's possible to catch the reflection of the cameraman pulling away from the TV screen. (00:34)
7. Director One sips his beer, holding the bottle with his right hand. Dylan makes a mold for the right hand. Yet in front of the Red Star security system entrance, she pushes her left hand in the gelatin-scanning plate to get in. (00:35, 00:36, 00:40)
8. The piece of glass that's holding Dylan's sheet changes shape in three different shots. (00:59, 01:00)
9. When Knox shows Dylan a picture of his father and Charlie, there is an extreme close-up on Charlie's name-tag. In the detail of the photo, a hand appears on Charlie's shoulder: but it wasn't there in the wider shot. (01:02)
10. Bosley meets a yellow-and-black bird, later identified by Natalie as a *Sitta pigmaea* or, for us laypeople, a Pygmy nuthatch, a breed of birds that "Only live in one place. Carmel!" Well . . . a Pygmy nuthatch is a gray-brown bird, and a common resident of montane pine forests, restricted only to the western part of the United States. (01:05)

11. After the Angels reach the beach below the mission, the cameraman can be seen reflected in Natalie's oxygen tank. (01:09)
12. Inside the mission, Natalie is about to set Bosley free, but she gets a call on her cell phone. She checks the Caller ID, and giggles, "It's Pete!" But he's calling from a pay phone. (01:12)

Questions
1. Is that a wire to trigger an explosion when a bullet hits a wall—the one on the close-up of Alex, after the Thin Man has shot the Angels in the alley? (00:24)
2. During a fight between Alex and the Thin Man, the mission bell's rope is cut and the bell plummets down. But when the Thin Man charges Alex, swinging his blade left and right, you can see a bell in the background. Was it a spare? (01:16)

Fun Fact
The CNN stock footage of Knox is flipped (check his "Boston" shirt). (00:13)

Charlie's Angels Cameo

The Asian guy who's talking to a couple of ladies in the plane is Cheung-Yan Yuen, the martial arts choreographer. (00:00)

CHASING AMY (7)
1997, color, 111 min.

Director: Kevin Smith

Cast: Ben Affleck (Holden McNeil), Joey Lauren Adams (Alyssa Jones), Jason Lee (Banky Edwards), Dwight Ewell (Hooper LaMont [Hooper X]), Jason Mewes (Jay Phat Buds / Chronic), Kevin Smith (Silent Bob / Bluntman), Ethan Suplee (Fan), Scott Mosier (Collector), Casey Affleck (Little Kid), Guinevere Turner (Singer), Brian O'Halloran (Exec No. 1), Matt Damon (Exec No. 2).

Guy falls for lesbian, pursues her, and gets her.
Science Fiction.

Bloopers
1. While talking on the swing to Holden, Alyssa pulls her sleeves up, revealing a wristwatch and a few bracelets while she's holding the chain of the swing. After Holden asks if "you're still a virgin," the wristwatch is visible only in Alyssa's close-ups—not in the long shots. (00:36)
2. When Holden comes back to his car after a fight with Alyssa in the rain, it's possible to catch a quick glimpse of the camera crew in the last two windows of the building in the background. (00:56)
3. Banky brings Holden the 1988 yearbook from Middletown North and urges Holden to "check out page forty-eight."

Holden flips through the pages, and stops on the indicated page. Or does he? He's staring at a picture on the right side of the book—which is usually an odd-numbered page. (01:06)

4. While at the hockey rink, Holden questions Alyssa about her past. On the ice, two hockey players start a fight: Number 12 removes his helmet, and so does Number 2, and they beat each other. A few seconds later, Number 12 is thrown against a wall—and his helmet is back on. A few more seconds go by, and the helmet is gone for good. (01:16, 01:17)

5. In the parking lot of the hockey rink, Alyssa and Holden fight for the second time. She bursts into tears, and eventually whispers, "I'm sorry" and buries her face in Holden's chest. He grabs her, says, "just don't do that," and pushes her away . . . twice (once in the close-up, once in the long shot). (01:21)

6. Silent Bob checks out the new issue of *Bluntman & Chronic* while sitting at the bar with Jay and Holden. He then places the issue down, and, after a handful of seconds, puts it down one more time. (01:24)

7. After Jay proclaims, "Life ain't nothing but bit**es and money," Holden has some ashes from the cigarette on the right leg of his pants. What follows is an intercutting sequence between Holden and Silent Bob and Jay, and the ashes vanish, come back, vanish again, come back again . . . (01:25)

Questions

1. During a discussion about love wounds with Alyssa, Banky moves his neck slightly to the right. He says that, because of a struggle with the father of one of his high school dates, "That's the farthest I can move my neck to the right." Later on, in their studio, Banky and Holden are on the couch and Holden rubs his friend's head, saying, "Aww, everyone bugs you!" Banky retracts, moving his head more than slightly to the right. Has he healed? (00:30, 00:44)

2. While Holden is driving in the rain, discussing with Alyssa her recently purchased painting, it sure seems like the speedometer needle is on 0 mph. Were they in a camera car, or were they simply driving super slow so that the special effects guy could hose water on the windshield? (00:50)

Fun Fact

In promotional posters, ads, laserdisc, and DVD covers for *Chasing Amy*, Ben Affleck is clean shaven. But his character Holden McNeil has a van dyke throughout the movie.

D

DEEP BLUE SEA (11)
1999, color, 105 min.

Director: Renny Harlin

Cast: Samuel L. Jackson (Russell Franklin), Saffron Burrows (Dr. Susan McAlester), Michael Rapaport (Tom "Scoggs" Scoggins), LL Cool J / James Todd Smith (Sherman "Preacher" Dudley), Thomas Jane (Carter Blake), Jacqueline McKenzie (Janice Higgins), Eyal Podell (Boy No. 1), Erinn Bartlett (Girl No. 1), Dan Thiel (Boy No. 2), Sabrina Geerinckx (Girl No. 2).

Dumb scientists fill remote sea lab with smart sharks. "Me Mako, you lunch."

Bloopers
1. Four kids are on a boat lis-

tening to music coming from a radio with a teddy bear on it. The first shot of the radio, it's facing left. When it gets pulled underwater by the shark, it's facing right. (00:01, 00:02)

2. Carter, after removing a license plate from a tiger shark's jaw, comes out of the lagoon, removes his gloves, and is introduced to Russell Franklin. When Carter was swimming, he was wearing flippers; on the pier he's now wearing sandals—but never changed footwear. Not only that, but he picks up the gloves and the license plate (which he passes to Franklin), and as he walks away, he's carrying the flippers with him. (00:08, 00:09, 00:10)

3. While arguing with Scoggs, who says "Look, I already told the doc: I locked the pen like I do every other night. The fish got out some other way," Carter replies with a "Ha!" without moving his lips at all. (00:12)

4. Carter swims in the underwater tunnel, under the surveillance of several cameras. But when he appears on Scoggs's monitor, one shot shows Carter being taped by a camera that moves in front of him while he swims. All the cameras in the tunnel are mounted and stationary. (00:25)

5. Right after Preacher gets

 frightened by his parrot in the flooded kitchen, he turns; he's wearing kneepads. (00:53)

6. One of the sharks rams the window of the oven where Preacher is hiding. The shark smashes the glass, but the mark of impact is different when seen from the inside than it is when seen from the outside. (00:55)

7. Carter snaps his knife in two while trying to pry open a door. Later on, when he dives in to save Susan, the knife seems to have returned to the holster on his leg. (01:05, 01:33)

8. In order to rescue his friends, Preacher creates a makeshift rope with clothes. After everyone is retrieved, Preacher pulls the rope up and the door gets locked. A few minutes later, when the same shaft is shown, the rope is dangling from outside the door. Then it is also seen another time, later on. Huh? (01:08, 01:12, 01:18)

9. Carter swims underwater to reach a flooded part of the lab. As he starts the journey, he has his left shoelace untied (which is floating in the water). When he reaches the lab, his shoes are both tied. (01:13, 01:14)

10. In order to get to her quarters and retrieve some research data, Susan puts one foot on the first step underwater, then the second foot. The shot goes underwater,

where she repeats the whole operation: first one foot goes underwater, then the second foot. (01:18)

11. To lure the shark with bait, Susan cuts her hand and jumps into the water. But despite the deep cut, when she's seen underwater there's no blood whatsoever. (01:32)

Deep Blue Sea Salutes *Jaws*

The license plate that Carter Blake (Thomas Jane) takes out of the tiger shark's mouth is the exact same license that Matt Hooper (Richard Dreyfuss) finds in the tiger shark he cuts open in *Jaws*. The only difference is that this time they got Louisiana's nickname right: "Sportsman's Paradise."

DETROIT ROCK CITY (12)
1999, color, 95 min.

Director: Adam Rifkin

Cast: Edward Furlong (Hawk), Giuseppe Andrews (Lex), James DeBello (Trip Verudi), Sam Huntington (Jeremiah "Jam" Bruce), Kiss (Kiss), Melanie Lynskey (Beth Bumsteen), Nick Scotti (Kenny), David Quane (Bobby), Lin Shaye (Mrs. Bruce), Joe Flaherty (Father Philip McNulty), Kevin Corrigan (Beefy Jerk #1), Steve Schirripa (Beefy Jerk #2).

How far would you go to see your favorite rock band?

Bloopers

1. In his room, Jam gets to the phone but, because his foot gets stuck in a chest expander, he's pulled back toward his bed. The phone is yanked and hits the kid right in the face, but no cable is attached to the base of it. Yet, Jam carries on a conversation with Hawk. (00:08)

2. Jam tries to retrieve the four tickets from the jacket pocket: he grasps his drumsticks, walks very close to the jacket, he's almost there . . . but then his mom turns and gives him a Kmart box—Jam no longer has the drumsticks in his hands. No sound of them dropping, either. (00:10, 00:11)

3. Mrs. Bruce waits for her son in the school hall, showing him the four Kiss tickets, fanned from the right to the left (the first one to Mrs. Bruce's right is on top of the stack, the other three are underneath it). When she sits and yells, "You want to reach out and touch pure evil!" the tickets are fanned from left to right (the one to her left on top). As she adds, "And in Detroit, no less!" they are fanned like they were earlier. (00:15, 00:16)

4. Mrs. Bruce has an unlit cigarette in her right hand, the tickets in the other. She

never lights the cigarette, yet she takes a brand new one from her packet before burning the tickets. (00:16)

5. To complete her "mission," Mrs. Bruce sets the Kiss tickets on fire and places them face down in an ashtray. When the tickets hit the ashtray, they are still fanned, but they are face up. (00:16)

6. During science class, Lex produces sparks that hit his left eye: he puts one hand over his eye, but in the following matching cut, he's fine and both of his hands are under the table. (00:20)

7. Father McNalty opens the mission box on his desk to take $10 to pay for a pizza, then he closes the box. Twice. (00:26)

8. On the highway, after Jam suggests he apologize to the other car, Hawk rolls his window up. But when Kenny, the driver of the other car, yells, "That motherf***er is dead!" Hawk's window is rolled down. Then it's up, then down, then up . . . (00:32)

9. When Hawk knocks down Kenny and walks back to his friends, Lex reaches for his belt buckle twice (wide shot, then close-up) before they beat the crap out of Bobby. (00:35)

10. Inside the "It's Raining Men" bar, Hawk asks for a man's drink. He's served a bourbon on the rocks with a slice of lime on the glass. When he pats his pockets to look for cash, the slice is gone, but when he makes a toast to the woman who bought the drink for him, the slice is back. (00:51)

11. Just before beginning his striptease, Hawk pukes into a pitcher. The level of vomit inside the pitcher decreases and increases from shot to shot. (00:59)

12. Kiss's drummer throws his drumstick into the crowd. Jam, who's holding one of his drumsticks in his right

---

Detroit Rock City Cameos

"I wanna rock 'n' roll all night . . ."

CAMEO	ROLE	TIME
Shannon Tweed	Amanda Finch	00:51
Director Adam Rifkin	Face on a muscle-man's body outside "It's Raining Men" bar	00:49

(Note: Shannon is the mother of Kiss bassist Gene Simmons's two sons.)

hand, jumps to get the stick. But he catches it with his right hand, which now is empty, as is his left. When he lands, he has both drumsticks (his and the drummer's) in his hands. (01:27)

Question
One of the two Beefy Jerks says, apparently about Lex's mom's car, "We can strip that Beemer in fifteen minutes." But earlier in the story, Lex says that his mom's car is a Volvo (which is what we see on the highway). So ... what car is he talking about? (01:14, 00:23, 00:25)

DIAMONDS ARE FOREVER (13)
1971, color, 119 min.

Director: Guy Hamilton

Cast: Sean Connery (James Bond 007), Jill St. John (Tiffany Case), Charles Gray (Ernst Stavro Blofeld), Lana Wood (Plenty O'Toole), Jimmy Dean (Willard Whyte), Bruce Cabot (Burt Saxby), Bruce Glover (Mr. Wint), Putter Smith (Mr. Kidd), Norman Burton (Felix Leiter), Donna Garratt (Bambi), Trina Parks (Thumper), Desmond Llewelyn (Q).

Bond is back after an "Australian" break, in his seventh adventure.

Bloopers
1. When Bond (as Peter Franks) boards the Slumber, Inc. hearse, the crew slams the rear door, the right door, and finally the driver's door. The right door makes no sound at all. (00:28)
2. In a Vegas sideshow, the owner of the attractions announces that inside the theater is Zambora, the "strangest girl who's ever lived," who was captured in Nairobi, South Africa. Actually, Nairobi is in Kenya. (00:47)
3. Tiffany finds a cadaver in her pool. Bond stands up, puts his right arm through the sleeve of his jacket, and in the following shot he's wearing the jacket. But he never put his left arm in its sleeve. (00:51)
4. During the moon buggy chase, one of the buggy's tires pops off and rolls away (when the third car hits a dune and flips over). Yet, in the next shot, the wheel is back in place. (01:01, 01:02)
5. Even before the car chase begins in Vegas, pedestrians are standing by, waiting to watch the cars (for instance near the Golden Nugget casino). Well, how the heck did they know a car chase was coming? (01:04)
6. In Vegas, 007 escapes the police by entering a narrow alley with his car tilted up on its two right wheels ... but comes out of the same alley with the car on its left wheels. (01:07)
7. Once back in the hotel, 007

turns to Tiffany, who is presumably naked on the waterbed, and she has a latex patch on her left breast. (01:08)

8. When Bambi and Thumper jump in the pool to fight with Bond, Thumper's hairdo has become much puffier and substantially different (stunt double, anyone?). (01:27)

9. In the same fight, 007 holds Bambi underwater with his right hand—but releases her with his left. (01:28)

10. Q hits a series of jackpots in Las Vegas, thanks to a special device he made. Yet not a single slot machine makes a sound. (01:30)

11. Standing next to a large globe, Blofeld shows 007 that his satellite is approaching Kansas. The light in the detail shot appears to be closer to the West Coast than it is in the master shot. (01:43)

12. When Blofeld shows the globe the first time and announces his plan to hit Washington, D.C., the globe spins at a certain speed. When they are at "Two minutes and counting," the speed of the globe has decreased substantially. (01:43, 01:50)

13. Mr. Kidd, disguised as a waiter, grabs two flaming kebobs with his bare hands and approaches Bond. 007 throws some liquor at him, setting the kebobs ablaze. Now Mr. Kidd is wearing protective gloves. (01:57)

Questions

1. 007 is nearly killed by a gangster who was in a mudbath. The gun the villain uses was in the mudbath, too. Did anyone realize that you can't rely on a gun that has been submerged in mud for a long period of time? (00:02)

2. 007 hides fake glass diamonds inside a body, which is then cremated. The fake diamonds are recovered later on among the ashes in the urn. Wouldn't glass have melted because of the high temperature? (00:29, 00:30, 00:33)

3. 007 imitates Burt Saxby's voice and receives instructions from Blofeld himself on where to kill Whyte. Later, the real Saxby shows up to kill Whyte. But since 007 got the directions, how did Saxby know about the whole thing? (01:23, 01:29)

4. On the radar image of Blofeld's hideout, five dots appear (indicating five choppers); yet, when the attack begins, there are six choppers. Did they buy the radar at a garage sale? (01:46, 01:47)

Scientifically Declined?

While explaining the voice box to 007 in *Diamonds Are Forever*, Blofeld says that science has never been his strong suit. (01:15) Yet, in *On Her Majesty's Secret Service*, he was introduced as a scientist. (01:04)

DIE HARD (21)
also "Extended Branching
Version"
1988, color, 131 min. / 132 min.
(EBV)

Director: John McTiernan

Cast: Bruce Willis (John
McClane), Bonnie Bedelia
(Holly Gennaro), Reginald
VelJohnson (Sergeant Al
Powell), Paul Gleason (Dwayne
T. Robinson), De'voreaux White
(Argyle), William Atherton
(Richard Thornburg), Hart
Bochner (Ellis), James Shigeta
(Takagi), Alan Rickman (Hans
Gruber), Alexander Godunov
(Karl), Bruno Doyon (Franco),
Andreas Wisniewski (Tony),
Clarence Gilyard Jr. (Theo),
Joey Plewa (Alexander),
Lorenzo Caccialanza (Marco).

*A gang of thieves holds an
entire building hostage.
Unbeknownst to them, a
cop has decided to give
them a really hard time.*

Bloopers
1. When John checks for Holly's
   name on the company's
   computerized directory, he
   finds it under her maiden
   name, "Holly Gennaro." As
   he presses the button, the
   name switches to "Gennero,"
   like it is on her office door. In
   the closing credits, it's "Gennaro" again. (00:09, 00:12,
   02:07)
2. John and Holly argue in the
   bathroom: a plant behind her

moves in and out of the shot.
(00:15)
3. In his wife's office, John
   holds the "dead" phone with
   his right hand. When he
   hears the shots, he drops it.
   From his left hand. (00:23)
4. When John runs up to the office door to check what's
   going on, a quick shadow (a
   crew member?) moves by
   the door in the opposite direction. Needless to say, at
   that moment John was alone
   in the office. (00:23)
5. When Takagi is asked for the
   code key of the main computer, he says he doesn't
   have it. Trees outside the
   windows shake in the wind.
   In the next, (mis)matching
   shot, they are suddenly standing still. (00:28)
6. Takagi is killed, and his blood
   hits a glass door. The amount
   of blood decreases when the
   terrorists run out to investigate some noise, but increases when John enters
   the office after crawling in
   the air duct. (00:31, 00:52)
7. John kills a terrorist named
   Tony, and then checks his driver's license. On the picture
   the terrorist is wearing sunglasses, which you can't
   wear in a driver's license picture. (00:38)
8. John sends Tony down the
   elevator. The pom pom on
   Tony's Santa hat moves from
   close to his ear to the back of
   his head. His being dead
   makes it a little hard for him
   to move it. (00:40)

9. Tony then blinks just before Hans moves his head. (00:40)

10. Under attack on the roof, John slides down some metal panels with the machine gun in his right hand. In the following shot, it's in his left. (00:45)

11. John enters the air duct with a white tank top and comes out wearing a green one, which he wears for the rest of the movie. And please don't tell us "it's stained from the air vent." The air vent is sparkling clean, and not covered in green dye. (00:49, 00:52)

12. In his radio transmission to the station, Sergeant Powell yells, "Police under automatic rifle fire at Nakatomi! I need backup assistance now! Now, goddammit, now!" Yet, when Thornburg intercepts a repeat of the same transmission on his scanner, he hears Powell yelling, "I'm at Nakatomi Plaza! They're turning my car into Swiss cheese! I need backup assistance now! Now, goddammit, now!" (00:57, 00:58)

13. Sergeant Powell backs his car into a ditch. He gets out of the car with a lot of blood on his forehead. A few minutes later, there's not a scratch. (00:57, 01:04)

14. John and Hans talk via walkie-talkie, interrupting each other several times. However, with a walkie-talkie only one person can talk at a time. (00:58)

15. Two terrorists obey Hans's order to fire on a tank, shattering a window. When they fire again, they reshatter the same window. (01:14, 01:15)

16. Holding the walkie-talkie with his left hand, John says to Powell that he has two kids, and he's looking at a picture of them in his wallet. He's holding the wallet with both hands, but he's still talking on the walkie-talkie—which he's still holding with his left hand. Hmmm... (01:21)

17. When Ellis is talking to John via a radio in Holly's office just before getting killed, one of the terrorists starts pouring a can of Coca-Cola into a glass. As Ellis talks, we hear at least 6 seconds of pouring. When the scene returns to Ellis, the glass has very little cola in it. (01:23)

18. All through the picture the characters mention that there are twelve terrorists, yet by the end, thirteen either die or get knocked out. In the credits, there are actually thirteen named terrorists. (01:31, 02:07)

19. When Karl and Hans are shooting at John, before Hans suggests he shoot the glass, John shoots at Karl. On the desk Karl is hiding behind there is a small Christmas tree lying on its side. After two shots, the Christmas tree is standing and then gets knocked down by John's shots. (01:36)

20. After sliding down the building using a hose, John crashes through a window and lands heavily on his back. As the camera follows the hose, John appears to be lying on his belly. (01:56 / 01:57 EBV)

21. When Hans is hanging on for his life, John tries to free his wife, and his bloody arm hits Holly's face, leaving a bit of blood on her left cheek. Despite this, in the following shot her cheek is clean. (02:02 / 02:03 EBV)

What's Her Last Name?

Holly's last name is listed as "Gennaro" in *Die Hard*, and "Gennero" in *Die Hard 2*. Go figure . . .

DIE HARD 2 (9)

1990, color, 124 min.

Director: Renny Harlin

Cast: Bruce Willis (John McLane), Bonnie Bedelia (Holly M. Gennero McClane), William Atherton (Richard Thornburg), Reginald VelJohnson (Sergeant Al Powell), Franco Nero (General Ramon Esperanza), William Sadler (Colonel Stuart), John Amos (Major Grant), Dennis Franz (Captain Carmine Lorenzo), Art Evans (Leslie Barnes), Fred Dalton Thompson (Trudeau), Tom Bower (Marvin), Sheila McCarthy (Samantha "Sam" Coleman), Vondie Curtis Hall (Miller).

Same as before, this time in an airport.

Bloopers

1. John uses a pay phone in Dulles Airport in Washington, D.C. The pay phone says Pacific Bell. With this phone, he calls his wife on a plane. Pacific Bell is in California, and you can't call a plane phone. (00:04)

2. The plane Holly's flying on has three engines. Yet in the cockpit, there are four fuel gauges (No. 1 main, No. 2 main, No. 3 main, No. 4 main). (00:04, 01:19)

3. In Dulles Airport, a TV reporter signs off as "Samantha Coleman." In the credits, her character is listed as "Samantha Copeland." (00:08, 02:01)

4. Miller, the African-American terrorist, picks up one of the gift-wrapped boxes from under a table. The detail shown is of a white-skinned hand (it's actually the detail of Cochrane's hand, who will pick up a box — with the same detail — a few seconds later). (00:09)

5. John fights with the guys in the luggage room and loses his gun. Suddenly, the black terrorist holds a gun that doesn't look like the one he had earlier, but suspiciously like John's. The terrorist runs away with the gun, but later on a cop gives John his gun back. Just a tad confusing . . . (00:13, 00:18)

Same Thing . . . Almost

In *Die Hard 2*, McLane says to himself following his banishment from the tower: "Oh, man—I can't f***ing believe this: another basement, another elevator . . . how could the same sh** happen to the same guy twice?" (00:39). But he was never in the basement in the first *Die Hard*.

---

6. Barnes turns around, holding a pencil with his right hand close to his head. Halfway through his twirl, the pencil vanishes. (01:04)
7. John crawls out of a grate on the runway where Esperanza is landing and rolls out of the way of the plane, which runs over the grate with the front wheels and closes it. Yet in the wide shot, the location of the plane's tracks in the snow indicate that none of the landing wheels could have run over the grate. (01:15)
8. While fighting with a terrorist outside of the old church, John is thrown into a few trash cans. The only trash can left standing has no lid; but in the next cut it does. (01:25)
9. During the battle on the jet's wing, Grant gets some blood on one side of his mouth—yet his mouth is clean as he says his last line. (01:47)

Questions

1. John sends a fax to Sergeant Powell; the fax is upside down—the image is face up, toward the sender—yet the document goes through just the same. Is there actually a fax that can work on both sides? (00:25)
2. John battles with Major Grant and Colonel Stuart out on the wing of the jet for some 10 minutes. Is Dulles's runway really that long? (01:45)

DOGMA (14)

1999, color, 123 min.

Director: Kevin Smith

Cast: Ben Affleck (Bartleby), George Carlin (Cardinal Glick), Matt Damon (Loki), Linda Florentino (Bethany Sloane), Selma Hayek (Serendipity), Jason Lee (Azrael), Jason Mewes (Jay), Alan Rickman (Metatron), Chris Rock (Rufus), Kevin Smith (Silent Bob), Bud Cort (John Doe Jersey), Alanis Morissette (God), Mark Joy (Mr. Whitland), Barrett Hackney, Jared Pfenningwerth, and Kitao Sakurai (The Triplets).

Celestial beings talk a little trash and kick a little ass.

Bloopers

1. John Doe Jersey is enjoying the sea at Asbury Park, New Jersey. The sun is behind him. When the Triplets arrive, though, the shadow on the ground indicates that the sun is now in front of John Doe. Then the sun moves again, first behind the Triplets, then in front of them. (00:01)

2. In order to join Bartleby, Loki has to jump over a row of seats: he places his right foot on the seat and lifts his left leg . . . but in the next shot, it's his left foot on the seat, and his right leg being lifted. (00:05)

3. At the airport, just before telling Loki they're going home, Bartleby produces a letter from his pocket and the address on the envelope faces the camera. But in the over-the-shoulder detail, the envelope has turned and now the address is toward Bartleby. (00:06)

4. While they're walking, Loki and Bartleby pass by a "Wisconsin Winter Magic" poster: it's possible to see the film crew reflected in the glass. (00:09)

5. When the Metatron enters Bethany's room, the phone on the nightstand is in place. After she's sitting on the bed, the phone is off the hook. It then begins to move all over the nightstand without anyone touching it. (00:14, 00:15)

6. Metatron says, "I am a Seraphim." Actually, he should have said, "Seraph." "Seraphim" (or the lesser used, "Seraphs") is plural. (00:16)

7. After the shooting on the bus, everyone runs away from the vehicle: the last person walking through the door is a chubby man in a blue-green striped shirt, followed by a guy with a hat.

But in the matching wide shot, only an old person with a yellowish sweater runs away. (00:35, 00:36)

8. Rufus falls from the sky and lands on a bridge, his legs spread. When everyone surrounds him, his feet are touching each other. (00:37)

9. The voodoo onion-doll that Loki places on the table changes shape just before being squashed. (00:49, 00:52)

10. Silent Bob gets rid of the Golgothan using a spray: when in the shot, Silent Bob presses on the spray can's nozzle with his index finger, but when the Golgothan is in the shot, it's Bob's thumb pressing on the nozzle. (01:00)

11. While Loki and Bartleby are talking with Azrael in a mall, there's an orange boogie board in the background, behind Bartleby. It changes positions all through the conversation ("So he's just gonna kill us?" and so on). (01:02)

12. It's the Centennial Celebration of St. Michael's Church, and Bartleby and Loki wreak havoc. Just after Bartleby snaps an officer's neck, he turns to the crowd and yells, "Ladies and Gentlemen . . ." The green banner behind him says "Centenial," with one *n*. (01:32, 01:33)

13. While Azrael is explaining his evil plan, Jay falls asleep ("Demons can't become hu-

man!"). He is wide awake when he exchanges looks with Rufus ("But fat lot of good that did, right?") and then he's asleep again. (01:35, 01:36)

> Admitting the blooper, Kevin Smith explained that other directors "waste money, go back, reshoot, and make a better movie. We just use all the footage we shot and somehow make it work."

14. Bartleby kills Loki and drops his body to the ground. A few minutes later, as Jay accidentally removes Bartleby's wings, from above the former angel it's possible to see Loki and the corpse that was close to him: they're now in different positions. (01:50)

Pan & Scan

1. In the Mexican restaurant, Bethany's robe goes from unbuttoned to buttoned, without her touching it. (00:17, 00:18)

2. In the Mooby board room, Loki works on his voodoo doll using a sharp knife. When Bartleby stands up, Loki accidentally beheads the doll—yet later on the doll looks fine. (00:47)

Questions

1. At the airport, Loki and Bartleby are wearing, respectively, a yellow highway T-shirt and a white T-shirt. On the bus, they're wearing a prune shirt and a gray shirt. Can fallen an-

gels change clothes at will, too? (00:03, 00:04, 00:33)

2. During his speech about Mooby the Golden Calf, Bartleby mentions "'The Mooby Fun-Time Hour,' two theatrical films, sixteen records, eight prime-time specials, a library of priced-to-own videos, and bicoastal theme parks dubbed Mooby World." Mr. Whitland adds that he forgot *Mooby* magazine. Did everyone forget about the Mooby fast food franchise where Rufus had an Egga Mooby Muffin? And what about the Mooby dolls, mentioned later by Bartleby? (00:41, 00:47, 00:50)

DVD Blooper

The putrid creature that comes out of the toilet is referred to as "The Golgothan," both in the movie subtitles and in the script. Chapter 16 of the DVD is titled "GolgAthan Demon." Whoops! [NOTE: they fixed this title in the *Dogma—Special Edition DVD*]

DR. NO (22)
1962, color, 110 min.

Director: Terence Young

Cast: Sean Connery (James Bond 007), Ursula Andress (Honey Ryder), Joseph Wiseman (Dr. No), Jack Lord (Felix Leiter), Bernard Lee (M), Anthony Dawson (Professor Dent), Zena Marshall (Miss Taro), John Kitzmiller (Quarrel), Eunice Gayson (Sylvia Trench),

ALL TIED UP

Here are a few necktie prop-blems.

Sean Connery in *Dr. No*	Blooper No. 14
Jack Nicholson in *A Few Good Men*	Blooper No. 9
Jack Nicholson (again!) in *Mars Attacks!*	Blooper No. 12
Richard Gere in *Pretty Woman*	Blooper No. 1
Steve Buscemi in *The Wedding Singer*	Blooper No. 1

Lois Maxwell (Miss Moneypenny), Peter Burton (Major Boothroyd), Yvonne Shima (Sister Lily).

The first Bond movie, featuring Ursula Andress in a bikini . . . need to know more?

Bloopers

1. As soon as they commit the crime, Strangways's killers jump in a black car, yelling "Get away, quick!" and the black driver stomps on the gas pedal. As the car bullets away, lights from the set are reflected in the window. (00:04)
2. Strangways's secretary (whose code name was W6N) removes her earpiece, checks her watch, lowers her left arm . . . and in the next cut, she lowers it again. (00:04)
3. 007 says his first line on camera, "Bond. James Bond," while lighting a cigarette. He removes it as Miss Sylvia says, "I suppose you wouldn't care to raise the limit," but when he answers "I have no objections," the cigarette is back in his mouth. (00:08)
4. The elevator that brings 007 to Moneypenny's office has doors that don't slide at the same time, and one of them doesn't slide all the way out. (00:09)
5. When 007 enters Moneypenny's office, he tosses his hat on the coat hanger. The hat faces the door. When 007 leaves M's office, he grabs his hat—which now faces M's door. Who moved it? (00:09, 00:14)
6. To kill Professor Dent, 007 doesn't use the Walther PPK, the new official gun that was given to him in M's office to replace his Beretta. 007 uses a Browning 1910 .32 (it is easier to screw a silencer on this kind of gun). (00:13, 00:57)
7. When Bond walks in, Sylvia raises her golf club in front of her. Then she raises the golf

club again from the opposite angle. 007 grabs the golf club near the top, but in the over-the-shoulder she's suddenly holding the club at the very top. (00:15)

8. 007 leaves the airport in a black car that has a red dashboard. As he notices that his driver is going very fast, a detail of the speedometer shows a black dashboard. Huh? (00:19)

9. In order to knock Mr. Jones down, 007 grabs him with his left hand, cocks his right fist to punch him ... but hits him with his left fist. (00:21)

10. Before leaving his hotel room, 007 places some fingerprint dust on his briefcase (to check if someone fidgets with it), then he leaves it on a table by the door, to the left of a round mirror. When he comes back, 007 checks on the briefcase and yes, he has the confirmation that someone tried to open it because the dust is smudged. Sharp eye, 007: when he picks up the briefcase, it has moved to the right of the mirror. (00:25, 00:42)

11. When 007 is visited in bed by a lethal tarantula, he freezes. But when the tarantula crawls over his shoulder, Bond moves a little—but the tarantula doesn't, because it's crawling on a glass panel put there to protect the actor. (00:43)

12. When Miss Taro gives 007 directions to her home, she tells him "Magenta Drive, 2391." Later, 007 calls for a taxi from Taro's house and gives the address "2171 Magenta Drive." And Miss Taro nods in agreement. (00:49, 00:54)

13. Miss Taro opens the door and finds a punctual Bond: all the shutters in the door are aligned at the same angle. As Bond steps into Miss Taro's apartment, one of the shutters is suddenly crooked. (00:51, 00:52)

14. 007 waits for Professor Dent, and in the meantime he screws the silencer onto his pistol. But the close-up shows that 007's tie has vanished. (00:57)

15. While inviting Professor Dent to sit down, 007 crosses his legs: his socks are first short, then long. (00:57)

16. While walking on the beach holding two seashells, Honey has her goggles around her right wrist—but when she says "Of course, I always do," the goggles are gone. (01:04)

17. From a boat patrolling Crab Key Island, a villain uses a megaphone to shout warnings to 007, Honey, and Quarrel. The villain's voice still sounds as if it's coming from a megaphone when he removes the bullhorn from his mouth and yells, "Full speed ahead!" (01:06)

18. Honey and 007 clean themselves in a waterfall: her shirt

is soaking wet—but when they go check the dragon's tracks that Quarrel is pointing out, her shirt is completely dry. (01:12)

19. 007 opens an electrified grate using one shoe; then he climbs into an airshaft—and his shoe is already on his foot. Fast, ain't he? (01:35)

20. While escaping from a cell on Crab Key Island, 007 almost drowns in a series of airshafts that get filled with water streams. He escapes by kicking the grillwork of a vent so that he can jump inside Dr. No's lab. But the vent, at the same level as the shafts, would have allowed the water to pour into the lab too—and of course this doesn't happen. (01:37, 01:38)

21. 007 brings the radiation level up to 38. Dr. No fights with him, as at the second punch, the indicator jumps to over 45—and then it's back at around 38. (01:44)

22. Right after tossing a rope to a boat to be towed, 007 sits to the right of Honey—but in the following shot, they've switched places. (01:48)

Fun Fact

United Artists Japan misinterpreted the title *Dr. No*, and made posters with the Japanese equivalent of "We Don't Want Doctors." The tiny little error was caught in the nick of time and corrected.

E

EMPEROR'S NEW GROOVE, THE (5)

2000, color, 78 min.

Director: Mark Dindal

Cast: David Spade (Kuzco / Kuzco Llama), John Goodman (Pacha), Eartha Kitt (Yzma), Patrick Warburton (Kronk), Wendie Malick (ChiCha / Pacha's wife), Eli Russell Linnetz (Tipo), Kellyann Kelso (Chaca), Bob Bergen (Bucky), Tom Jones (Theme Song Singer), Patti Deutsch (Waitress), John Fiedler (Old Man), Joe Whyte (Official).

Selfish emperor gets turned into a llama and befriends a peasant.

Bloopers

1. The first time the emperor's palace is shown, there's a single row of vertical banners on each side of the carpet leading to the entrance, and, except for the first two, all the banners are parallel to the carpet. But when Pacha walks to the entrance, the banners have all turned 90°, and are now perpendicular to the carpet. Also, in the background, there are now more banners than were displayed from the aerial shot of the building. (00:04)

2. While playing on the emperor's throne, Yzma's eyes have four long eyelashes. Then there are five on the right eye, six on the left, and then again four and four. (00:05, 00:06, 00:07)

3. Kronk lights two candles on a dinner table; the candelabra is facing the emperor's plate. But when he rushes to the kitchen to save his spinach puffs, the candelabra is now perpendicular to the plate. (00:12, 00:14)

4. When Pacha pulls the unconscious Kuzco Llama out of the water, he sets him down and his head is turned to the left with his tongue sticking out. In the next angle, no tongue. (00:30, 00:31)

5. After the first night outside with Kuzco Llama, Pacha washes his face in a pond; a bunch of

floating flowers appear in the pond as we cut closer to him. (00:36)

Question
Kuzco Llama, still wearing Pacha's hat and tunic outside of Mudka's Meat Hut, is abandoned and sad. He takes off his disguise and sleeps in the rain. When he meets Pacha again the next morning, the peasant is wearing the same tunic and hat. If he had spare clothes, where did he hide them? (00:53, 00:56)

ERASER (13)
1996, color, 115 min.

Director: Charles Russell

Cast: Arnold Schwarzenegger (U.S. Marshal John Kruger),

James Caan (Robert Deguerin), Vanessa L. Williams (Dr. Lee Cullen), James Coburn (Beller), Robert Pastorelli (Johnny C), James Cromwell (William Donahue), Danny Nucci (Monroe), Andy Romano (Harper), Nick Chinlund (Calderon), Michael Papajohn (Schiff), Joe Viterelli (Tony), Mark Rolston (J. Scar).

Arnold terminates a life . . . but only on paper.

Bloopers
1. Kruger snatches the gun from Benny twice when he surprises him at the refrigerator. (00:03)
2. When Lee talks with the agent while staring at herself in the mirror, the image they

CREW MEMBERS

A candid look at the people who work behind the scenes . . . and sometimes in the scenes themselves. Look for crew members in:

Dogma	Blooper No. 4
Eraser	Blooper No. 12
Ghost	Blooper No. 1
Jaws 2	Blooper No. 1
Jurassic Park	Blooper No. 46
Kentucky Fried Movie	Blooper No. 2
Speed	Blooper No. 19
Superman—The Movie	Blooper No. 4
The Talented Mr. Ripley	Blooper No. 6
10 Things I Hate About You	Blooper No. 5
Titanic	Blooper No. 12
Vertical Limit	Blooper No. 3
Wayne's World	Blooper No. 8

get on the monitor switches—first it's a reflected image as it should be, then it's not. Notice the pin she has on the right side of her jacket: it zaps to the left side. (00:13)

3. Lee enters the vault to make a copy of the file, a digital clock on the wall reads 10:23; in a wide shot two clocks appear, one on 10:25, the other on 10:24. The second clock switches to 10:25, but when Lee retrieves the CD, the clock is back to 10:24. A few seconds later, the clock goes to 10:26, then 10:25 again. (00:15, 00:17)

4. William Donahue commits suicide by shooting himself in the mouth: he falls backward on his chair, his eyes closed, some blood on his chin. The following close-up shows his eyes open and blood spurting out of one side of his mouth. (00:20)

5. John and Lee dive behind a refrigerator. The bomb explodes, and the walls and the refrigerator door are pierced by all the pointy thingies, leaving John's hand OK. In the next shot, he cries in pain because one of the pointy thingies has hit his hand. (00:29)

6. John gives Lee new IDs. Among these is a Master-Card that he swipes through a machine . . . with the magnetic strip not going through the machine, because the card is upside down. (00:36)

7. When they pass around the picture of the woman they have to protect, Agent Schiff stares at the picture (a waist-up portrait) holding it right side up. He then passes it to John, who takes it by the top, but in the next shot the picture has rotated 180° in his hand. (00:42)

8. As John lands on the car in the junkyard, his parachute lands after him . . . twice. (00:57)

9. John talks with Johnny C in a bar, who removes his vest. But in the following close-up, the vest is back. (01:10)

10. Kruger and Lee use Donahue's computer to locate off-shore banking deposits. When they come across "UBS," Lee says that that's the Union de Banques Suisses. But when Kruger opens the file, it reads "USB." (01:21)

11. As John and Johnny C park the Cadillac and the ambulance, it takes Johnny four steps to get from the ambulance to the car. But when he backs up the Cadillac, there's more than ten feet between the two vehicles. (01:25)

12. When they pass by the blue Cadillac, the boom mike is seen reflected in the car window. (01:25)

13. Kruger's van blows up with two large explosions, both of which knock down the police fence and a few cops. (01:46)

Question

Lee enters the elevator to go and meet her boss. We see her point of view—the same one that her friends see on a monitor. But they see the image of her entrance again, after she's entered. Did she get into the elevator car twice? (00:18)

EXORCIST, THE (9)

also The Version You've Never Seen

1973, color, 122 min. / 131 min. (VNS)

Director: William Friedkin

Cast: Ellen Burstyn (Chris MacNeil), Max von Sydow (Father Merrin), Lee J. Cobb (Lieutenant Kinderman), Kitty Winn (Sharon Spencer), Jack MacGowran (Burke Dennings), Jason Miller (Father Damien Karras), Linda Blair (Regan MacNeil), Reverend William O'Malley (Father Dyer), Barton Heyman (Dr. Klein), Peter Masterson (Barringer, the Clinic Director), Rudolf Schündler (Karl), Gina Petrushka (Willi), John Mahon (Language Lab Director).

Scary . . . very scary.

Bloopers

1. Father Merrin approaches an archaeologist who's kneeling before a box containing lamps, arrowheads, and coins. Merrin projects a very long shadow, but the box has a shadow that is much, much shorter. (00:02)
2. Talking about rats in the attic, Mrs. MacNeil pours herself some coffee, holding the cup with her left hand. As she spins to talk to Karl, the cup jumps into her right hand. (00:12)
3. Father Karras gets to his mother's home and removes the white collar from his shirt: he places the collar on a chest of drawers, and the collar is standing up against a picture frame. In the detail it's lying down, and in the following cut it's up again. (00:19)
4. To show her mom how the Ouija board works, Regan puts down her ping-pong racquet with the ball underneath it. When the board is placed on the table, the ball is gone. It'll be back a few seconds later, and then gone again. (00:22)
5. Lieutenant Kinderman meets Father Karras at the track. Karras wears a jacket and the collar is up. In the following shot, he pulls out the collar because it's tucked inside the jacket, and then it's up again. (00:58 / 01:03 VNS)
6. Mrs. MacNeil talks to Father Karras and she borrows a cigarette from him. She later drops it on the ground and extinguishes it with one shoe, but when he asks her, "I beg your pardon?" she has a lit cigarette in her hand—and of course she never lights a second one. Unless she has a lit cigarette dispenser in her coat pocket. (01:14, 01:16 / 01:19, 01:21 VNS)
7. After getting puked on, Father Karras checks a few drawings:

he holds them horizontally, but the detail shows him holding a vertical drawing of a tree. (01:20 / 01:25 VNS)

8. Karras decides to record Regan's session, so he moves his left hand to activate a tape recorder. But the detail shows his right hand pushing the button; then he pulls back his left hand again. (01:25 / 01:31 VNS)

9. When the language lab director listens to Karras's tape, the tape spins clockwise. The director says that it's English in reverse, so he plays the tape backward. The tape still spins clockwise. (01:29 / 01:35 VNS)

Question

When Regan slowly barfs on Father Merrin's stole, is that a tube below Regan's left ear, masked underneath the makeup, pumping the vomit out of her mouth? (01:40 / 01:48 VNS)

The Exorcist Cameo

The producer who asks Burke, "Is this scene really essential?" is *Exorcist* writer William Peter Blatty. (00:12 / 00:13 VNS)

F

FACE/OFF (15)
1997, color, 138 min.

Director: John Woo

Cast: John Travolta (Sean Archer), Nicolas Cage (Castor Troy), Joan Allen (Eve Archer), Alessandro Nivola (Pollux Troy), Gina Gershon (Sasha Hassler), Dominique Swain (Jamie Archer), Nick Cassavetes (Dietrich Hassler), Harve Presnell (Victor Lazarro), Colm Feore (Dr. Malcolm Walsh), John Carroll Lynch (Prison Guard Walton), CCH Pounder (Hollis Miller), Robert Wisdom (Tito Biondi), Chris Bauer (Ivan Dubov), Myles Jeffrey (Michael Archer), Lauren Sinclair (Agent Winters).

Detective and terrorist switch faces and bodies. It seems absurd, and it is.

Bloopers

1. When he's on the carousel with his son Michael, a bullet hits Sean in his back—but the spot seems higher in the detail than in the wide shot when Sean falls from the horse. (00:02)

2. Castor activates the bomb, which will blow up eleven days from that moment (246 hours). Later on, Hollis reminds Archer (already in Castor's body), "Six days until the 18th, the clock's ticking and so's the bomb." The next shot of the bomb shows the counter at 216 hours. But 216 hours is nine days—not six. (00:04, 00:38)

3. Castor gets close to a choir girl to whisper something in her ear, and he lifts part of her hair, leaving a long lock in front of the ear. In the following matching cut the lock is gone. (00:06)

4. During a chase on an airport runway, Castor pushes agent Winters (disguised as a flight attendant) through a plane doorway; then, staring at Sean ("One of yours, Sean?"), he shoots the woman. All during the sequence, the sky

is cloudy; in the shot after the BANG!, the sky is blue. (00:11)

5. In the same chase, Castor fires three shots at the chopper carrying Sean—yet the windshield has four holes. (00:12)

6. Sean eventually fires a few rounds and hits the engine to the far left on Castor's plane. An indicator light on the plane's console reads, "Fire 3 pull." The engine hit by Sean would be No. 1, not No. 3. (00:12)

7. Hollis hands Sean a zip disk: the labeled side is up. When Sean takes it, the labeled side is down. (00:21)

8. During a fight in Erewhon Prison, Sean (in Castor's body) hits Dubov with a metal tray: he charges right to left, but on the cut he hits the man left to right. (00:44)

9. Castor (in Sean's body) drives home and complains that his "new" neighborhood is blah. His window is rolled down. He then stops the car and backs up right in front of Eve, and at that point he rolls down the window. (00:54)

10. Castor (in Sean's body) lectures Sean's daughter, after giving her a cigarette. When he says, "This isn't you," he turns to sit. But he turns left to right, while in the matching over-the-shoulder cut, he's turning the opposite direction. (01:25)

11. Sasha grabs the two guns her son Adam is holding, then kneels down and tells him, "I don't want you to play with those things, they are very, very dangerous." Yet when she says, "they are very, very dangerous," her mouth isn't moving. (01:30)

12. Sean (in Castor's body) enters the church where they're celebrating Lazarro's funeral, and in front of a candle he makes the sign of the cross—with his *left* hand. (01:54)

13. Outside of the church, Castor (in Sean's body) grabs Sean (in Castor's body) by the neck. His hand alternates between being over and under Sean's shirt collar. (02:01)

14. After the white boat flies through the police boat, it emerges with many dark marks underneath its bow. After a close-up of Sean (still in Castor's body), a shot reveals an extremely clean bow. It'll be marked again after Sean jumps from his boat to the red boat. (02:05)

15. Sean (in Castor's body) finally kills Castor (in Sean's body). Castor's shirt collar is red with blood. Yet when Sean is placed inside the ambulance, he finds himself close to Castor's body, whose collar is as clean as a whistle. It'll be blood red one shot later, when Sean gets his ring back. (02:09, 02:11)

Questions

1. Eve comes home one night to a candlelight dinner with two

gigantic lobsters displayed prominently on the table. This is how Castor (in Sean's body) tries to get closer to Sean's wife. Later on, Sean (in Castor's body), to prove to Eve that he's really Sean, tells a story about when they were dating and he took her out for surf 'n' turf, not knowing that she was a vegetarian. Shouldn't the lobsters have tipped her off earlier, or is one detective in the family enough? (01:04, 01:49)

2. The Erewhon is a huge magnetic field, and the prisoners are tracked via their boots, which are provided by the same facility. When Sean (in Castor's body) decides to escape, he's about to get an electroshock—a procedure that Dubov has just undergone. Both the guys are bootless (that's the only time in the prison when the boots are removed). Yet, when they start a fight, on the computer the two are easily located by the tracking device. How? (01:08, 01:09)

FAST TIMES AT RIDGEMONT HIGH (5)

1982, color, 90 min.

Director: Amy Heckerling

Cast: Sean Penn (Jeff Spicoli), Jennifer Jason Leigh (Stacy Hamilton), Judge Reinhold (Brad Hamilton), Robert Romanus (Mike Damone), Brian Backer (Mark "Rat" Ratner), Phoebe Cates (Linda

Barrett), Ray Walston (Mr. Head), Scott Thomson (Arnold), Vincent Schiavelli (Mr. Vargas), James Russo (Robber).

Your average high school in the early 80s: sex, drugs & rock 'n' roll.

Bloopers

1. During his introductory speech to the class, Professor Hand underlines his name on the blackboard. The underlining changes in almost every take. (00:09, 00:10, 00:11)

2. Stacy reaches for the note in the middle of a bunch of red roses: she opens the small envelope and, in the detail, lowers it while reading the note. But in the following shot, she's still holding up the envelope with the note. (00:20)

3. In the mall, Stacy sells a slice of "mobile" pizza: in the close-up, the pizza's crust is parallel to the brim of the counter—in the matching wide shot, it has rotated 90° and now looks perpendicular to the counter. Needless to say, nobody touched it. (00:28)

4. Mike finds the word "Prick" spray-painted on the door of his car, and the "K" of the word reaches the door handle. As he drives to school, he has a large piece of cardboard taped over the word—but the cardboard is smaller than the painted portion of the door (the cardboard ends a couple of inches away from the handle). (01:07, 01:08)

5. An armed robber intimidates Brad with a gun and orders him to open the safe. While Brad fidgets by the safe, the robber hits a container of green chocolates, which scatter across the counter. One second later, the chocolates are gone ... but they'll be back in the last shot of the sequence. (01:24)

Question
Mike scalps two $20.00 Van Halen tickets. One of the buyers complains, "Those tickets were only $12.50!" Mike makes the sale anyway, and blows his own horn by telling Rat, "I just made sixteen bucks." Uh – no. He made only $15.00. Not exactly a math whiz, is he? (00:02, 00:03)

Fun Fact
The first appearance of Brad's Bud is when he places the "I am a homo" sign on the back of a nerd. He'll share a close-up later. Well, this dude is a certain Nicolas Coppola, in his movie debut. He'll soon after change his name to Nicolas Cage. (00:06, 00:30)

FERRIS BUELLER'S DAY OFF (8)
1986, color, 102 min.

Director: John Hughes

Cast: Matthew Broderick (Ferris Bueller), Alan Ruck (Cameron Frye), Mia Sara (Sloane Peterson), Jeffrey Jones (Edward R. "Ed" Rooney), Jennifer Grey (Joanie Bueller), Cindy Pickett (Katie Bueller), Lyman Ward (Tom Bueller),

Edie McClurg (Grace, the School Secretary), Charlie Sheen (Boy in Police Station), Ben Stein (Economics Teacher), Del Close (English Teacher), Virginia Capers (Florence Sparrow), Richard Edson (Garage Attendant), Larry Flash Jenkins (Attendant's Co-Pilot).

A day in the life of a class clown extraordinaire.

Bloopers
1. Ferris lies in bed, his parents worried sick. His mom tucks the blanket up to his chin, but as she leaves the room (wide shot), the blanket is up to the middle of Ferris's chest. In the following close-up, it's back up to his chin. (00:02)
2. Ferris fixes the equalizer of his stereo, but the placement of the sliders in the detail doesn't match with the master shot. (00:03)
3. In Ferris's kitchen, Cameron wears a brownish T-shirt with the American Medical Association logo on it. Later on, just before kicking his dad's Ferrari, Cameron's wearing the same T-shirt inside out—supposedly he hasn't had time to change. But the logo looks very different: it's even possible to see a parachute in the middle of the logo. (00:22, 01:23)
4. The garage attendant and his co-pilot take the Ferrari for a spin in town: as they "fly" above the camera to the accompaniment of the *Star Wars* theme, they do it in an almost

completely clear blue sky. When they land and zoom off, the sky is filled with clouds. (00:54)

5. Ferris is on a parade float, singing "Danke Schoen." Cameron and Sloane get closer, but a cop in a black jacket takes them and pushes them away. Only that when he pushes them, he's wearing a light blue shirt. (01:01)

6. When the trio is leaving town, Ferris checks the odometer. The car changes lanes, but he never turns the steering wheel. (01:11)

7. Joanie is driving her mom home in a station wagon. A rearview mirror can be seen inside the car. When Joanie's mom starts yelling at her daughter, the mirror is gone— but it's back soon after, when they run a stop sign and flee from the police. (01:30, 01:31)

8. As the station wagon reaches home, Joanie jumps out and slams the door. After a few seconds, when her mom gets out of the car, part of the seat belt is stuck outside the door Joanie just slammed. It wasn't there in the last shot. (01:33, 01:34)

Questions

1. Mrs. Bueller trusts her son very much and she's even more reassured when she peeks into his room and sees him (actually, a dummy) in bed, snoring. Is she so reassured that she doesn't notice the entire dummy arm very clearly sticking out from under the covers? (00:37, 00:38)

2. Mr. Rooney rings the doorbell at Ferris's house, but all he gets is a recording of Ferris on the intercom. Several shots indicate that the house is completely empty. So whose reflection moves on the fridge handle? (00:52)

3. Just before his parents enter his room, Ferris tosses the baseball to turn off the stereo. A nice shot using his left arm. Then the ball lands in a baseball glove for right-handers (presumably Ferris's). Is he ambidextrous? (01:37)

4. Mr. Rooney walks home when, to top off a really dreadful day, he's invited on to a school bus. It's after 6:00 P.M. (01:30), yet the bus is filled with students carrying school books. Did school let out really late, or did the bus get lost along its route? (01:39)

Fun Fact

When the aerial view of Chicago is shown for the first time, it's possible to see, reflected in a building, the chopper used for the shot. (00:31)

Polly Noonan, the young actress who plays the girl on the bus at the end of *Ferris Bueller's Day Off*, just might be the only actor who has been listed in the end credits before actually appearing on screen. (01:39, 01:40)

FEW GOOD MEN, A (9)
1992, color, 138 min.

Director: Rob Reiner

Cast: Tom Cruise (Lieutenant Daniel Alistair Kaffee), Jack Nicholson (Colonel Nathan R. Jessup), Demi Moore (Lieutenant Commander JoAnne "Jo" Galloway), Kevin Bacon (Captain "Smiling" Jack Ross), Kiefer Sutherland (Lieutenant Jonathan James Kendrick), Kevin Pollak (Lieutenant Sam Weinberg), James Marshall (Private First Class Louden Downey), J. T. Walsh (Lieutenant Colonel Matthew Andrew Markinson), Christopher Guest (Commander Doctor Stone), J. A. Preston (Judge Colonel Julius Alexander Randolph), Matt Craven (Lieutenant Dave Spradling), Wolfgang Bodison (Lance Corporal Harold W. Dawson).

Tom seeks the truth, and Jack tells him he can't handle it.

Bloopers
1. Jo meets with Captain West. She places her hat underneath her left arm, the gold symbol facing front. As she approaches the desk, the hat has spun underneath her arm, and now the symbol is facing the opposite direction. When she places the hat down, it spins 180° before landing on the desk. (00:05)

2. Just before Dan enters the meeting, Sam has his notepad flat on the desk. As the shot changes, he's holding and writing on it. One more cut, and it's back on the desk. (00:10)

3. Dan and Sam have a meeting with Jo. Dan is eating an apple, which keeps switching from his left hand (from the front) to his right (from the back), and again ("Have I done something wrong?"), and again ("They won't need a lawyer. They'll need a priest."). (00:12)

4. Jo approaches Dan while he plays baseball. She carries her briefcase with her right hand, but when she stops (cut), both hands are holding the handle. Dan in swinging the bat in front of his legs, but (cut) he's ready to hit the ball. (00:22)

5. After a plea of not guilty, court is adjourned. As everyone leaves, Jo and Sam, standing side by side, move to stare at Dan. In the next cut, they are still side by side—so they move again. (00:58)

6. Concluding a night of work, Dan moves to the door, opens it, and says, "You're a good man, Charlie Brown." Sam then opens the door again, and leaves. (01:03)

7. When the first witness, R. C. McGuire, is called by Captain Ross, Ross has just moved to the podium in between the counsels' tables. But when McGuire walks to the stand in

the wide shot, Ross has zapped back to his table. (01:08)

8. Dan finds Markinson in his car and the two begin to talk. Dan keeps steering the wheel left and right, yet the car keeps going straight. (01:27)

9. At the end of the sentence, right after Jessup has calmed down, Dan says, "The witness is excused." Jessup, his tie slightly crooked, turns to pick up his hat. His tie is now very, very messed up. (02:10)

FOLKS! (8)
1992, color, 108 min.

Director: Ted Kotcheff

Cast: Tom Selleck (Jon Aldrich), Don Ameche (Harry Aldrich), Anne Jackson (Mildred Aldrich), Christine Ebersole (Arlene Aldrich), Wendy Crewson (Audrey Aldrich), Robert Pastorelli (Fred), Michael Murphy (Ed), Kevin Timothy Chevalia (Kevin Aldrich), Margaret Murphy (Maggie Aldrich), Marilyn Dodds Frank (Mrs. Henney).

Guy is forced to house his semi-senile parents . . . and all the baggage that goes along with it.

Bloopers

1. As soon as he gets home, Jon passes his briefcase to his son Kevin, who grabs it with his left hand and walks toward the building entrance. One shot of Kevin shows the kid tangled in the dog's leash: he's now holding the briefcase with his right hand—but right after the shot, he's walking into the building carrying the case in his left hand again. (00:02)

2. Stepping out of the shower, Audrey dances to arouse her husband; she is wearing a large red towel. After Kevin exclaims, "I can't understand you!!" Audrey's cloth slides down a little too much and we can see her brownish slip. (00:03)

3. Harry races his car in reverse; after smashing through the first fence, there's a blue box on the windshield. The box flies away during the destruction of a verandah—but it is

---

A Few Good Men Cameos

You can't handle the cameos!

CAMEO	ROLE	TIME
Screenwriter Aaron Sorkin	Lawyer in a bar	00:56
Misery novels	Themselves, by the TV	00:46

(Note: *Misery* was another of Rob Reiner's movies.)

back in place almost immediately. (00:18, 00:19)

4. Jon pays a visit to his sister Arlene. When he breaks the news about their mom's "kidney stone" to her, the boats in the background appear and vanish. The same thing happens a few seconds later, when Jon meets Arlene's kids. (00:21, 00:22)

5. Jon and Harry go to Tom's office; a street clock reads 11:55, while in Jon's office another clock tells us it's 10:30. (00:45, 00:47)

6. While Jon and Harry are walking down a busy New York street, it's possible to see a large crowd gathered on the opposite sidewalk staring at the camera and the actors. (00:46)

7. Trying to save his folks, Jon winds up dangling out of a plane. It is easy to tell it's not Jon: it's a stunt double with differently colored hair. (01:31)

8. Harry is trying to tell about his stocks, but Arlene tosses away the piece of paper. Later on, Jon and Harry have a little chat in which Jon finds out they're rich, but Harry's shirt is not the same one that he was wearing a few minutes earlier. Same airplane pattern, but different shirt—check the large plane between the first two buttons. It's no longer there. (01:40, 01:43)

Question

To pay the clinic that's housing his mom, Jon passes Mrs. Hen-

ney a corporate American Express card. Shouldn't the card have a magnetic strip? (00:09, 00:10)

FORREST GUMP (10)

1994, color, 142 min.

Director: Robert Zemeckis

Cast: Tom Hanks (Forrest Gump / Nathaniel Bedford Forrest), Robin Wright (Jenny Curran), Gary Sinise (Lieutenant Daniel Taylor), Sally Field (Mrs. Gump), Mykelti Williamson (Benjamin "Bubba" Bufford-Blue), Michael Conner Humphreys (Young Forrest), Hanna R. Hall (Young Jenny Curran), Haley Joel Osment (Forrest Gump Junior).

A dim bulb gets picked for the spotlight.

Bloopers

1. Right after Forrest gets the feather, he looks ahead; the sky is gray and there's no light behind him. As the bus approaches (master shot), a very clear sunlight pervades the square where Forrest is sitting. (00:02)

2. While the principal is having intercourse with Mrs. Gump, Forrest sits on a swing, listening. His hands move up and down the ropes of the swing from the long shot to the medium shot. (00:08)

3. When Forrest is chased by the truck, the bumper is almost on his heels—but in the

following close-up, the truck is a few feet behind Forrest, then close again. (00:20)

4. Presenting a clip of the encounter between Governor George Wallace and General Graham at the University of Alabama, a newscaster says "here by videotape..." At that time, TV broadcasts were mainly using film—as it's shown, since all the cameras in front of the university are film cameras, not video cameras. (00:23)

5. While on his boat, Forrest dredges up some garbage, including a can of Mello Yello. The scene takes place during Gerald Ford's administration (1974–1977), yet Mello Yello wasn't introduced until 1979. (01:33)

6. Forrest receives a letter (dated September 21, 1975) from Apple Computer investments. Apple Computer, however, was founded in 1976 and didn't begin seeking investors until later. (01:41)

7. Forrest visits Jenny on the night of July 4, 1976. On the TV we see the New York Harbor Bicentennial Celebration, and the shot of the Statue of Liberty shows the torch as being gold. But the torch wasn't painted gold until after the 1986 restoration. (01:48)

8. Jenny shows Forrest a series of newspaper clippings. Among these is a *USA Today* photo (she wrote the name of the paper) and the date is 1978. *USA Today* hit the stands in 1982. (02:00)

9. As Forrest approaches his son, the iron on the ironing board behind Jenny stands up by itself. (02:02, 02:03)

10. Jenny's tombstone says "March 22, 1982." Forrest's voice says "You died on a Saturday." March 22, 1982 was a Monday. (02:09)

Question

When Forrest receives his discharge papers, he's playing ping-

---

DAYS, MONTHS, YEARS...

Millions of dollars are spent on a movie, yet they can't spare $5.99 for a decent calendar!

A tombstone in *Forrest Gump*	Blooper No. 10
Richard Attenborough in *Jurassic Park*	Blooper No. 37
O-Lan Jones in *Mars Attacks!*	Blooper No. 3
A cop in *The Terminator*	Blooper No. 1
Linda Hamilton in *Terminator 2*—Extended Spec. Ed.	Blooper No. 51

pong while standing on a basketball court that has a three-point line. Only the ABA had a three-point line at the time ... so was he playing on an ABA court? (01:25)

FRESHMAN, THE (9)
1990, color, 102 min.

Director: Andrew Bergman

Cast: Marlon Brando (Carmine Sabatini), Matthew Broderick (Clark Kellogg), Bruno Kirby (Victor Ray), Penelope Ann Miller (Tina Sabatini), Frank Whaley (Steve Bushak), Jon Polito (Chuck Greenwald), Paul Benedict (Arthur Fleeber), Richard Gant (Lloyd Simpson), Kenneth Welsh (Dwight Armstrong), Pamela Payton-Wright (Liz Armstrong), B. D. Wong (Edward), Maximilian Schell (Larry London).

Country kid goes to New York and receives an offer he almost can't refuse.

Bloopers
1. Dwight and Clark go hunting. Dwight fires a shot (Boom! Flash!) at another gunman. There's a second shot heard off camera, then a third shot (Boom! No flash!). (00:02)
2. Clark meets Victor in the metro station; after saying "Rule number one," Victor suddenly has a white T-shirt under his shirt. In the previous shots Victor wasn't wearing a T-shirt at all. (00:05)
3. Victor drives away, stealing Clark's luggage. Clark runs after him, turns a corner where there's a parked car, then throws his jacket to the ground. In the wide shot, the parked car has vanished. (00:08)
4. Carmine puts many teaspoons of sugar in Clark's coffee. He starts to stir the spoon in the coffee while holding the sugar bowl, but in the matching cut the bowl is gone. (00:19)
5. Clark sips his first espresso; he's holding it with his right hand in the long shot, and with his left hand in the close-up. (00:20)
6. Larry London holds a money bag in his hand; when he says, "If it is your nature to count it ..." the position of the bag changes: first it's pointing toward Larry, then toward Clark. (00:47)
7. The Dept. of Justice agents follow Clark in their car. There are two rows of parked cars in the road they're on (one on each side), but when Clark checks them in the rearview mirror, there's only one row of parked cars (to the right), then two rows when Clark turns his head, then one again ... (00:59)
8. The Italian passport that's given to Clark says "Palermo, Sicilia" (Italy never specifies the region after the town on their IDs); but it also has the month of "Febraio" with only one *b*—the correct spelling is "Febbraio." (01:24)

9. Larry wishes the crowd, "bon apetit" while holding the microphone in his right hand. When he turns to leave, the mike jumps into his left hand. (01:26)

Fun Fact

Clark's mom tells him that the Komodo dragon is an endangered species. Larry later presents the specimen as "One of only eight Komodo dragons left in the entire world," Well, thank God, the Komodo is not really that close to extinction. (00:49, 01:26)

FRIDAY THE 13TH (13)

1980, color, 90 min.

Director: Sean S. Cunningham

Cast: Betsy Palmer (Mrs. Voorhees), Adrienne King (Alice), Jeannine Taylor (Marcie), Robbi Morgan (Annie), Kevin Bacon (Jack), Harry Crosby (Bill), Laurie Bartram (Brenda), Mark Nelson (Ned), Peter Brouwer (Steve Christy), Rex Everhart (Truck Driver), Ronn Carroll (Sergeant Tierney), Ron Millkie (Officer Dorf), Walt Gorney (Crazy Ralph), Sally Anne Golden (Sandy), Debra S. Hayes (Claudette).

Simply one of the scariest and most clever movies of all time. Ch, ch, ch . . . ah, ah, ah . . .

Bloopers

1. Claudette leaves the group of counselors with her boyfriend: her socks are pulled up. When they reach the barn, her socks are neatly rolled down. (00:02)

2. On Enos's truck, Annie says that she'll "be cooking for fifty kids." Yet, later on, when she's in the car with the killer, she says, "I hate when people call them 'kids.' Sounds like little goats." Hypocrisy or blooper? You make the call. (00:10, 00:19)

3. Looking for a snake in one of the cabins, Bill lifts the skirt on one of the beds. Then in the shot from underneath the bed he lifts it again. (00:26)

4. Alice gets startled by Ralph, who's hiding in a closet. Behind Alice, it's possible to see the shadow of Marcie, who's approaching—but Ralph takes plenty of time to deliver his "message," and only then, finally, Marcie and Ned enter the kitchen. (00:30)

5. While playing Monopoly, Brenda's first dice roll is a 1 and a 2, yet she says, "Double sixes!" (00:40)

6. At the diner, Steve pays Sandy; she grabs the money with her left hand and pulls it back, but the following close-up briefly reveals the money still in front of Steve, and held by a right hand. (00:48)

7. Steve's car dies on him, and a police car approaches. After a few seconds, the emergency lights on the police car begin to twirl. As Steve talks to Sergeant Tier-

ney, the lights are off, then when he gets in the car the lights are on again, then turned off. (00:52)

8. During their drive together, Sergeant Tierney receives a call. He flicks the lights on (for just one frame), then he flicks them on again. (01:02)

9. Alice fixes some instant coffee but doesn't quite put the lid all the way back on the container. When she comes back after finding Bill's body, the lid is put on properly. Maybe the killer also has an obsessive-compulsive disorder. (01:08, 01:13)

10. While in the kitchen, Alice walks by the door: there's a blender and an egg carton on a table. When she runs back in, the two objects have switched places. (01:09, 01:13)

11. Brenda's dead body is thrown into the kitchen through a window: her head is tilted to the right. When Alice runs back and passes by the body, the head is tilted to the left. (01:14, 01:23)

12. Running away from Mrs. Voorhees, Alice slides open the huge door of the boathouse. A plank leaning on the right side of the door falls over onto a car tire. When Alice leaves the house through the same door, the piece of wood is still leaning against the door. (01:20, 01:21)

13. Mrs. Voorhees is clobbered with a pan: she falls down

with her arms outstretched — but when Alice pushes her, Mrs. Voorhees' left arm has moved to her chest. (01:25)

Friday the 13th . . . of What Year, Exactly?

The action is set on Friday, June 13th, which locates the movie in 1980 (00:06). Also, the trailer for *Friday the 13th Part 2* begins with, "On a June night, Friday the 13th, 1980 . . ." Yet, in *Friday the 13th: The Final Chapter*, Pamela Voorhees's tombstone says, "1930–1979" (00:18). But she died at the end of the first chapter of the saga. And just in case you're wondering, June 13, 1979 was a Wednesday, not a Friday. Now that that's all cleared up . . .

FRIDAY THE 13TH PART 2 (6)
1981, color, 87 min.

Director: Steve Miner

Cast: Amy Steel (Ginny Stevens), John Furey (Paul), Adrienne King (Alice), Kirsten Baker (Terri), Stuart Charno (Ted), Warrington Gillette (Jason Voorhees), Walt Gorney (Crazy Ralph), Marta Kober (Sandra), Tom McBride (Mark), Bill Randolph (Jeffrey), Lauren-Marie Taylor (Vicky), Russell Todd (Scott).

. . . and the saga begins, and keeps going on, and on, and on . . .

Bloopers

1. Scott raises his slingshot and winks at Terri, but when she turns, the slingshot is lowered. (00:19)

2. When Paul is in his office and tells Ginny he was starting to worry, he places his right arm around her neck—but in the following shot her neck has no arm around it. (00:22)

3. Just before Scott gets caught in the trap, Terri's sweatpant laces are not tied. As she enters her bungalow, the laces have been tied in a bow. When she leaves to return to Scott, the knot is tucked into her pants. (00:48, 00:49, 00:50)

4. Ted tries to hit on a female bartender; she carries a rug on her right shoulder, but when she gives him a snappy answer, the rug has snapped to her left shoulder. And then it moves back. (00:52)

5. Ginny and Paul leave the bar and get into her car. When he starts it, the left front parking light doesn't work. When they reach the camp, all the lights work fine. (01:03, 01:05)

6. When Paul stops the car at the camp, the windshield wipers are stuck halfway through their arc on the windshield. When Ginny reaches the car to escape from Jason, the wipers are in the horizontal position. (01:05, 01:10)

Questions

1. When Scott hits Terri with his slingshot, doesn't it seem like he hits her right buttock? Yet, she grabs her left. (00:19)

2. Jason slits Scott's throat very precisely with the machete. But doesn't Jason move the machete in a way that it couldn't possibly leave the cut it does? (00:50)

DVD Blooper

The trailer says that twelve people died on Friday the 13th, 1980. And adds, "The body count continues." But they start the count from fourteen. Are they superstitious?

JEWELRY PROP-BLEMS

A diamond is forever. But so is a blooper.

Tracie Savage's necklace in *Friday the 13th Part 3D*	Blooper No. 11
Blofeld's ring in *From Russia with Love*	Blooper No. 2
Karen Allen's medallion in *Raiders of the Lost Ark*	Blooper No. 4
Michael Douglas' necklace in *Romancing the Stone*	Blooper No. 7
Burt Reynold's ring in *Smokey and the Bandit*	Fun Fact No. 1

FRIDAY THE 13TH PART 3D (12)
1982, color, 96 min.

Director: Steve Miner

Cast: Richard Brooker (Jason Voorhees), Tracie Savage (Debbie), Paul Kratka (Rick), Jeffrey Rogers (Andy), Catherine Parks (Vera), Dana Kimmell (Chris), Larry Zerner (Shelly), Steve Susskind (Harold), Cheri Maugans (Edna Hatcher), Rachel Howard (Chili), Gloria Charles (Fox), Kevin O'Brien (Loco), Nick Savage (Ali), David Wiley (Abel).

. . . and on, and on, and on . . .

Bloopers

1. Edna yells at Harold, who's in the backyard. She slams the window shut, and the curtain gets caught in the window sill. But in the following shot from inside, the curtain is free. (00:08)
2. The hand Harold holds the fish food with rotates 180° from the master shot to the detail. (00:11)
3. Jason whacks Harold with a meat cleaver right in the middle of the chest. Blood runs all the way down from the wound to Harold's belt. But when Jason pulls him to the floor, he only has blood around the wound. (00:15)
4. As Chris's van stops and the kids jump out to go to Vera's house, the boom mike is reflected on the side of the vehicle. (00:16)
5. Andy, Shelly, Chris, and Debbie walk from the van to the house: the shadow of the trees is indicating that the sun is quite high in the sky. As the angle changes, it's almost sundown. (00:17)
6. While in the van, Chili passes a joint to Andy: the position of her hand changes from shot to shot. (00:19)
7. As they get out of the van when they reach the lake, Chris slams the driver's door twice (the first time it can be seen through the sliding door of the van, after Shelly and Chili jump out). (00:22)
8. Shelly stops Vera, who's going to town to shop. Shelly isn't wearing a wristwatch. In the store, he tosses Vera his wallet. He's wearing a wristwatch. When Shelly approaches Vera, who's holding his wallet, he has no watch again—and won't have it for the rest of the picture. (00:29, 00:31)
9. Once outside the store, Shelly turns the VW on. The camera pans around the car, and we can see a black flag used for shading the set reflected in the windshield. (00:32)
10. In the barn, Jason approaches Loco with a five-prong pitchfork. Yet, Jason stabs the poor sap with a four-prong pitchfork. (00:42)
11. Debbie takes a shower, still wearing her necklace. When she gets out she still has it, but as she enters her room

looking for Andy, the necklace is gone. (01:03, 01:04)

12. Hiding from Jason in the barn, Debbie spots an ax on the ground, the blade to the right. But when she picks it up, the ax has moved onto a saddle, the blade to the left. (01:26)

Questions

1. Debbie yells to stop the van, otherwise they'll run over a vagrant. Doesn't it seem like the van is empty, aside from the people in the front seat, even if there are four people in the back? (00:21)

2. Trying to stop Jason, who's attacking her in the van, Debbie rolls up her window. But . . . how? The window is completely rolled down, she cranks it one turn, and the window is completely up. Pretty fast, ain't it? (01:20)

"Nailed" for Continuity

After he dies at the end of *Friday the 13th Part 3D*, Jason Voorhees's fingernails look nice and trimmed (01:26, 01:31), yet at the beginning of *Friday the 13: The Final Chapter* (which begins on the same night where the previous movie ended), Jason's nails are very long and very dirty. (00:07)

Fun Fact

Shot in 3D, the "flat version" of the movie reveals more than one of the special effects created to achieve the three-dimensionality. Among these, the popping rattlesnake has a wire at the base of its head, the spear Jason shoots at Vera is guided by a wire, and so is Rick's eye. (00:13, 01:00, 01:12)

FRIDAY THE 13TH: THE FINAL CHAPTER (8)

1984, color, 90 min.

Director: Joseph Zito

Cast: Erich Anderson (Rob Dire), Judie Aronson (Samantha), Peter Barton (Doug), Kimberly Beck (Trish Jarvis), Tom Everett (Flashlight Man), Corey Feldman (Tommy Jarvis), Joan Freeman (Mrs. Jarvis), Lisa Freeman (Nurse Morgan), Thad Geer (Running Man), Crispin Glover (Jimmy), Wayne Grace (Officer Jamison), Ted White (Jason Voorhees).

. . . and on, and on, and on . . .

Bloopers

1. Paul dances with Tina, and she takes his cap and puts it on. After a few moments, he has the cap back on, and after a few seconds more, she has it on again. (00:39, 00:40, 00:43)

2. Jimmy gets one hand corkscrewed to the counter, and there's nothing else on the counter. When Jason grabs a knife later on, on that counter is a pot-holder stained with blood. (01:00, 01:03)

3. Sara walks down the hall from the bathroom to her room to

dry her hair, and back: there's a bench against one of the walls in the hallway. When Jason chases Trish through the same hallway, the bench has moved to the opposite wall. (01:06, 01:08, 01:21)

4. Jason shatters the glass door of a shower as well as Doug's head. The close-up of Jason reveals a hockey mask with three red triangles on it: one between the eyes, the other two under them. Yet when Jason breaks a window to grab Tommy, the two triangles under the eyes are gone. (01:07, 01:17)

5. Tommy and Trish are barricading Tommy's door: they push a large bookshelf, and one orange-and-white figure falls from the shelf, then it's back on it, then it's gone again. (01:18)

6. While moving away from the door, Tommy grabs a chair and holds on to it—but in the following shot the chair lies on the floor. (01:18)

7. When Jason smashes Tommy's door, one mask that is suspended by a wire begins spinning, then it's standing still, then it's spinning again. (01:19)

8. Jason drops the machete on the floor, and part of the handle lands on the rug. Yet when he picks it up, the weapon is not touching the rug at all. (01:24)

Question

Trish and Tommy are working on their broken-down car. The camera shows someone wearing gray pants approaching. Next, Tommy discovers a hiker named Rob Dire next to the car. But he's wearing black pants. So who was wearing the gray pants? (00:31, 00:32)

Fun Fact

When Trish and her mom are jogging, one tree branch moves as if someone has hit it—for example, a cameraman using a steadicam. (00:14)

Bondless Trailer

Both the American and the British trailers of *From Russia with Love* were missing one minor detail—Sean Connery's name. See for yourself on the DVD.

FROM RUSSIA WITH LOVE (15)
1963, color, 110 min.

Director: Terence Young

Cast: Sean Connery (James Bond 007), Daniela Bianchi (Tatiana Romanova), Pedro Armendáriz (Kerim Bey), Lotte Lenya (Rosa Klebb), Robert Shaw (Donald "Red" Grant), Bernard Lee (M), Eunice Gayson (Sylvia Trench), Walter Gotell (Morzeny), Francis De Wolff (Varva, Gypsy leader), George Pastell (Train Conductor), Nadja Regin (Kerim's Girl), Lois Maxwell (Miss Moneypenny).

The second Bond film, and SPECTRE starts to be a real pain in the ass.

Bloopers

1. In the main credits, actress Martine Beswick is listed as Martin Beswick. (00:04)
2. Blofeld chastises Klebb (a.k.a "Number 3") and waits for Kronsteen (a.k.a. "Number 5"). His SPECTRE ring, which is on his right pinkie when he strokes his cat, jumps to his left hand when he pushes a white button on his desk, and back again. It happens again toward the end, when Blofeld strokes his cat and calls another assistant. (00:08, 00:09, 01:44)
3. Tatiana Romanova enters Klebb's apartment. Klebb closes the door—but at the last second, a hand can be seen coming from the outside, grabbing the door handle (presumably to keep it shut). (00:15)
4. During the Gypsy fight sequence, it is possible to see 007 cocking his gun more than one time. But a real Walther PPK doesn't require this kind of operation, because it's an automatic pistol. The reloading operation is needed only if you fire blanks. (00:46)
5. 007 is getting ready for a relaxing hot bath and he removes his shirt. But then he's distracted by the entrance of Tatiana and eventually he ends up making love to her. While in bed, Tatiana reaches for 007's scar on his back—a scar that he didn't have a few minutes earlier, when he removed his shirt. (00:52, 00:55)

007: License to Lie?

While M and Miss Moneypenny listen to a tape 007 made with Tatiana, they hear him recalling a mission in Tokyo (01:02). Yet, in *You Only Live Twice*, Bond tells his contact Henderson that he's never been in Japan. (00:21)

---

6. When M turns a tape recorder off, he says, "Thank you, Miss Moneypenny. That's all, that's all." The secretary leaves, and M lowers his pipe—but in the following shot, he has it back in his mouth. (01:02)
7. During a wide shot of a fire truck reaching the Russian Consulate, one man (an extra) turns his son toward the camera, bends over, and points to the crew. (01:05)
8. The Orient Express stops in Belgrade, and one of Bey's sons is waiting to rendezvous with 007. Bey's son stares at the train: the handkerchief peeks out of his right jacket pocket. As he approaches 007, the handkerchief is in his left pocket. (01:17, 01:18)
9. 007 tries to bribe Grant by of-

fering him fifty gold sovereigns (coins Bond has hidden in his case). Grant tosses him the briefcase, and Bond produces the coins. He lowers his arms, but as Grant asks him, "Any more in the other case?" 007's hands are on top of the case. (01:33)

10. During the fight on the Orient Express, 007 is thrown on a seat: he kicks Grant with his right leg—but Grant receives Bond's left foot in his face. (01:34)

11. 007 is strangled by Grant's watch-wire. He reaches with his right hand (which is stained with blood) but he can't set himself free. So he reaches for the knife hidden in the case with the same hand (which is now clean), he stabs Grant, and finally he fixes his tie with his right hand (once again, stained with blood). (01:35)

12. After jumping off the train, 007 steals a flower truck. Clearly, the truck has no rearview mirrors. A few minutes later, Bond is driving the truck and finds himself under attack by a chopper. They toss grenades at the truck. Notice two extremely huge rearview mirrors that have appeared on the doors of the vehicle. (01:37, 01:40)

13. After the third grenade dropped from the chopper, the truck is almost hit: the windshield gets dirty and part of the hood gets burned and stained. However, when Bond reaches a pier to get a boat, the truck is squeaky clean. (01:40, 01:42)

14. Bond leaves the truck to attract the chopper: he carries a black case with him, holding it with his left hand. As the helicopter passes by him, Bond is seen holding the case with his right hand. Then again, he's holding it with his left hand. No no no, it's the right hand . . . (01:40)

15. When Bond and Tatiana get off the truck and move toward the pier, he says, "Tanya? Here, take this and cast the rope off." She whispers "Thank you," but her lips never move. (01:42)

Questions

1. Klebbs wants to meet Grant and she walks with Morzeny through a training area. As she passes by the area, machine guns, flame throwers, and other noises are heard. When she was on the outside, a few feet from the entrance, nothing was heard, even though the area doesn't seem to have a door. Did they all start at that exact moment? (00:12)

2. 007 is filling the bathtub in his hotel room when he hears a noise. Wrapped in a towel, he leaves the bathroom to investigate and finds that Tatiana has slipped into his bed. They flirt and make out and presumably spend the night together—but he neglected to turn off the faucet. So, did he flood the hotel? (00:52, 00:53)

G

GALAXY QUEST (5)
1999, color, 104 min.

Director: Dean Parisot

Cast: Tim Allen (Jason Nesmith / Commander Peter Quincy Taggart), Sigourney Weaver (Gwen DeMarco / Lieutenant Tawny Madison), Alan Rickman (Alexander Dane / Dr. Lazarus of Tev'Meck), Tony Shalhoub (Fred Kwan / Tech Sergeant Chen), Sam Rockwell (Guy Fleegman), Daryl Mitchell (Tommy Webber / Lieutenant Laredo), Enrico Colantoni (Mathesar), Robin Sachs (Sarris), Patrick Breen (Quellek), Missi Pyle (Laliari), Jed Rees (Teb), Justin Long (Brandon).

Star Trek *spoof with a metatheatrical twist.*

Bloopers
1. When Tommy is taking out the spaceship *NTE-3120* for the first time, he veers to the left and scrapes the bow of the ship against the wall—but the shape of the ship wouldn't allow a scratch on its bow without completely destroying its left "wing." (00:31, 00:32)
2. Jason is fighting with the rock monster Gorignak when he yells into his transmitter, "You could do this, Fred. I know in my heart, you're gonna save my life!" He's holding the transmitter in his left hand, up to his mouth—but when seen from behind, the transmitter is down. (01:00)
3. Throughout the movie, but mostly when Sarris is shown the historical document of "Galaxy Quest," the captain's last name is spelled "Taggart" (as in "Jason Nesmith as Commander Taggart"). That is, until the opening credits of the new movie at the end, where the captain's name is spelled "Taggert." (01:03, 01:36)
4. Gwen and Jason have to run through the chompers (metal presses that go up and down for no particular reason), and Jason yells, "Go!" at her several times, without moving his lips once. (01:17)

5. When the whole crew hold hands and take one final bow, Gwen's legs are crossed only in the shot from behind—and from no other angles. (01:36)

Question

 When the crew is flying to retrieve a beryllium sphere, Guy whines that his character doesn't have a last name. Jason admits that he actually doesn't know Guy's last name. However, while devising a plan on the planet, Jason says, "Flannigan, you set up a perimeter." How did he know Guy's last name? Guy never told him. (00:47, 00:52)

GHOST (9)
1990, color, 128 min.

Director: Jerry Zucker

Cast: Patrick Swayze (Sam Wheat), Demi Moore (Molly Jensen), Tony Goldwyn (Carl Bruner), Whoopi Goldberg (Oda Mae Brown), Rick Aviles (Willie Lopez), Vincent Schiavelli (Subway Ghost), Susan Breslau (Susan), John Hugh (Surgeon), Sam Tsoutsouvas (Minister), Armelia McQueen (Oda Mae's Sister), Gail Boggs (Oda Mae's Sister), Bruce Jarchow (Lyle Ferguson).

Patrick Swayze loves Demi Moore. Problem: he's dead.

Bloopers
1. Carl comments, "God, this place looks great!" while a worker moves a mirror. You can catch a quick glimpse of a C-stand and a lamp, reflected in the mirror. (00:08)
2. Sam and Molly work on a vase, then caress each other, and finally lie on the couch. But their hands, the same ones that erotically worked wet clay, are now perfectly clean (when did they wash?). (00:13, 00:14)
3. Willie is in Molly's apartment when she comes back. Sam desperately tries to warn her,

but can't. She walks upstairs in her jacket, holding a Reebok shoebox and a few pieces of mail. As the shot changes, she's got her jacket on one arm only. (00:33)

4. Oda Mae agrees to go downtown to help Sam and Molly. As she walks down the street, cussing and fussing, she's wearing black shoes. When she leaves the door because, according to her, nobody's home, Sam stops her again. She's wearing white sneakers. (00:46)

5. The subway ghost kicks a cigarette dispenser, and a lot of packs fall down. Actually, a whole lot. Both from the front and the following wide shot, there are sooo many more packs on the floor than actually fell from the machine. (01:16)

6. Sam tells Oda Mae that she has to deal with Lyle Ferguson. The plaque on Lyle's desk says "Lyle Ferguson." Yet in the closing credits, the character played by Bruce Jarchow is identified as "Lyle FUrgEson." (01:24, 01:26, 02:02)

7. Oda Mae hands her wallet to Lyle at the bank: the wallet is completely unfolded, but when he grabs it, it's folded. (01:28)

8. Sam, in Oda Mae's body, hugs Molly. She lays her head on his right shoulder but when she pulls back, she pulls away from his left shoulder. (01:51)

9. In the empty room above the apartment, Carl pushes Molly away from him, and she tumbles into two metal trash cans. The one on top falls over, then falls again in the following shot. (01:54)

Questions

1. Returning home, followed by Sam, Willie opens the door to the hallway that leads to his apartment. The door automatically closes. Later on, when Carl is "checking the place out," he opens the very same door. This time, it stays open. Should someone call the landlord? (00:36, 00:57)

2. Upset, Oda Mae leaves Molly's apartment, saying "Have a nice life," (and the kind tone suggests she's saying it to Molly). Then she says, "Have a nice death!" (presumably to Sam). Yet, Molly and Sam are in the opposite positions and it seems that Oda Mae had wished the wrong thing to both of them. What happened? (00:54)

3. Sam can jump from one train to another—and yet, he doesn't fall through the floor. Why not? (01:12)

4. While running away from Sam, Willie is killed by a car and his soul stands up from the middle of the road (but the body lies on the trunk of the car). What happened? You make the call . . . (01:42)

```
•••••••••••••••••••••••••••••••••••••••••
•                                         •
•               VANISHING                 •
•                                         •
•  Now you see it, now you . . .           •
•                                         •
•  A sticker in The Blues Brothers    Blooper No. 15  •
•  Art Evans's pen in Die Hard 2      Blooper No. 6   •
•  Boats behind Tom Selleck in Folks! Blooper No. 4   •
•  The Stay Puft Man's bow tie in Ghostbusters  Blooper No. 8  •
•  Randy Quaid in Kingpin             Blooper No. 13  •
•  Kate Capshaw's glass in The Love Letter  Blooper No. 9  •
•  James Caan's casts in Misery       Blooper No. 7   •
•  Whipped cream in Varsity Blues     Blooper No. 5   •
•                                         •
•••••••••••••••••••••••••••••••••••••••••
```

GHOSTBUSTERS (8)
1984, color, 107 min.

Director: Ivan Reitman

Cast: Bill Murray (Dr. Peter Venkman), Dan Aykroyd (Dr. Raymond Stantz), Sigourney Weaver (Dana Barrett / Zuul the Gate Keeper), Harold Ramis (Dr. Egon Spengler), Rick Moranis (Louis Tully / Vinz Clortho the Key Master), Annie Potts (Janine Melnitz), William Atherton (Walter Peck), Ernie Hudson (Winston Zeddemore), David Margulies (Mayor), Alice Drummond (Librarian), Slavitza Jovan (Gozer).

If there's somethin' strange in your neighborhood . . . you know the drill.

Bloopers

1. As the librarian pushes the book cart, she neatly places volume after volume, so that all the covers are one against the other. But in the wide shot, the books are in a totally different position—some of them are even laying flat. (00:00)
2. The eggs that pop out of the carton in Dana's kitchen change position from the master shot to the detail to the master shot again. (00:19)
3. During the "musical montage" with the Ghostbusters' theme playing, the first shot of the Ghostmobile (after the *USA Today* cover) is flipped: the antenna is on the right, as is the steering wheel, and the Ghostbusters logo is mirrored. (00:39)
4. In the same montage, one shot of the three heroes has, on a side, the cover of the *Atlantic* magazine. Right before the cover begins its slide to the left, the clip of the Ghostbusters moves backward, in reverse play—the smoke goes toward the trap, Spengler takes one step back . . . (00:40)
5. During the "biblical speech" in the Ghostmobile, Winston is

driving while Ray is checking a few blueprints. But as they arrive at their base, they get out of the car from the opposite doors—Ray from the driver's side, Winston from the shotgun side. Also, Winston is not wearing his uniform anymore. Did they stop at the dry cleaners? (01:03, 01:08)

6. The Ghostbusters reach Dana's building during the day; next, they're on the roof at sunset. The fight with the ghosts happens at night, and when they come down in the street it's day again. But it wasn't that long a fight! (01:19, 01:34, 01:38)

7. When the Ghostbusters get out of their car, the emergency lights on the roof are turned off. As the pavement cracks open, the car has all its lights on, and they stay on until the next morning ... boy that car sure has a long-lasting battery! (01:19, 01:20, 01:38)

8. The Stay Puft man walks through New York, and when he's hit for the first time by the Ghostbusters' rays, he doesn't have on his red bow tie. (01:32)

GOLDFINGER (23)
1964, color, 112 min.

Director: Guy Hamilton

Cast: Sean Connery (James Bond 007), Honor Blackman (Pussy Galore), Gert Fröbe (Auric Goldfinger), Shirley Eaton (Jill Masterson), Tania

Mallet (Tilly Masterson), Harold Sakata (Oddjob), Bernard Lee (M), Martin Benson (Solo), Cec Linder (Felix Leiter), Austin Willis (Simmons), Lois Maxwell (Miss Moneypenny), Bill Nagy (Midnight).

The third Bond, and a fight with a modern version of King Midas.

Bloopers
1. After she's come out of the bathtub, Bond passionately kisses Bonita and spots the evil Capungo reflected in her eyes. Well ... the reflection mismatches Capungo's lifted arm. From behind Bond, he lifts his right arm, while the reflection (which has not been flipped) shows Capungo with his left arm lifted. (00:04)

Impermanent Scar

007 introduces Dink (Margaret Nolan) to Felix while standing by the pool; then he sends the lady away. As he turns, he doesn't have the scar on his back (00:09), which was a very important detail in *From Russia with Love* (00:18). Did he get plastic surgery in between missions?

---

2. 007 stops Jill before she can tell Goldfinger the cards of his opponent, Mr. Simmons, with whom he's playing gin. Bond looks through the

binoculars and sees Mr. Simmons's cards from an over-the-right-shoulder shot. Then, without moving the binoculars, he sees Goldfinger's close-up from what should be an over-the-left-shoulder shot. Then he's back to the cards of Mr. Simmons, and then to another close-up of Goldfinger (different point of view, by the way). Bond also hears Goldfinger snapping a pencil. But Auric doesn't have a mike. (00:12, 00:13)

3. 007 is in M's office. When Bond says, "If I knew what it was about . . . sir," M has in his hands a pair of glasses—which are gone when the camera favors Bond. Then they come back. (00:18)

4. Moneypenny tosses Bond's hat on the rack. The hat lands on a hook far from the door, but when Bond retrieves it, the hat has moved to another hook. (00:19, 00:20)

5. In Q's lab, two technicians try a bulletproof vest. The tester opens the vest twice: once in his close-up, once in the master shot. (00:23)

6. Q shows Bond a transmitting device called "homer," as well as a smaller version of the same device. The larger homer is magnetic, and Q attaches the smaller one to one side of the larger. But as he passes it to Bond, the smaller homer has vanished. (00:23)

7. Bond apparently plays a golf match with a gold bar in his pocket; later on, he tosses one to stop Oddjob and he grabs two to open the atom bomb. A gold bar is way too heavy to be "casually" lifted with one hand. (00:26, 01:40, 01:43)

8. As a demonstration, Oddjob tosses his lethal hat and decapitates a statue. The hat flies away, but the detail of the sawn head shows the hat, too. (00:32)

9. Oddjob kills Tilly, using his powerful hat. But she falls to the ground with a small wound on her neck—even though Oddjob just used the same hat in the same way to decapitate a marble statue. (00:32, 00:46)

10. When in Geneva, Bond is driving his Aston Martin and is passed by a mysterious blond woman (Tilly Soames, a.k.a. Tilly Masterson). Her car drives by a valley with several small white columns as a guardrail. Bond, who is driving on the very same road, is driving by a small hill—no valley in sight whatsoever. (00:35)

11. During an effective demonstration of the power of lasers, 007 asks Goldfinger, "Do you expect me to talk?" Goldfinger stops, his right hand to his mouth—but then, in the close-up when he says, "No, Mr. Bond. I expect you to die!" he has both

his hands stuffed in his pockets. (00:52)

12. Oddjob drives Mr. Solo to the airport, but the poor Solo is killed and driven to a junkyard. The Lincoln Continental is then grabbed and crushed into a small block. But when the car is lifted by the claw, it's possible to see that there's no engine under the hood (we can see a piece of sky through the area between the front wheels). (01:15, 01:18)

13. In order to enter Fort Knox undetected, Goldfinger's henchman Kisch is disguised as an American army officer. But he has air force stripes on his uniform. (01:31)

14. The laser used to slice the door of Fort Knox is moved faster by the operator than the beam moves on the door. (01:34)

15. It's impossible to stack gold bars in the way they are shown in the Fort Knox depository. Gold is too soft a substance to be stored like that: the upper bars would have crushed the lower ones. (01:37, 01:40)

16. Oddjob tries to stop Bond from uncuffing himself, so the lethal hat flies across the Fort Knox vault. He misses Bond, and the hat falls over a grate. But when Oddjob retrieves it, he finds it on a platform. (01:39, 01:40)

17. The countdown on the atom bomb mismatches the ticking we hear. Most noticeably, it goes from 026 to 024 and we hear 19 clicks. It should be 005—instead it says 019. Not to mention the time that passes between 017 and 014!! (01:42, 01:43, 01:44)

18. After the atomic bomb in Fort Knox has been stopped, Bond comments "Three more ticks and Mr. Goldfinger would have hit the jackpot." The detail shows that the bomb has been stopped with the display reading 007. Huh? (01:44, 01:45)

Producer Harry Saltzman came up with the cool idea of the display reading "007" after Sean Connery had already completed the movie. And Sean wasn't available to replace his dialogue and fix this blooper. Oh well, more fun for us!

19. When 007's plane is hijacked, it is assumed that the only passengers on board are 007, Pussy Galore, and Goldfinger. Yet one of Goldfinger's henchmen (presumably one of the Korean guards) is visible in the background when Goldfinger says, "At the moment she is where she ought to be: at the controls." After a fight between 007 and Goldfinger—and no one else—the villain is sucked out of the plane and the henchman lies unconscious at 007's feet.

Who beat up the henchman? (01:46, 01:47)

20. After a bullet shatters one of the cabin windows, 007's plane plummets to the ground. In reality a cabin depressurization wouldn't cause that phenomenon in such a quick way. (01:47)

21. When the plane plummets to the ground, crossing the sky sideways from the left to the right, the two parallel wires that hold the airplane model can be seen. (01:47)

22. Felix searches for 007 from a chopper, coming out twice from the very same spot in between several trees; the first time the sky is cloudy and gray, the second time it's blue. (01:48)

23. To be picky, picky, picky, while Felix is flying through a cloudy sky at high speed, his close-ups show that the clouds in the background are motionless. (01:48)

Questions

1. Champagne Leader, while passing above Fort Knox with the five plane formation, does a countdown to the beginning of the operation Rock-A-Bye Baby. The countdown is "Five, four, three, two, zero!" What the hell happened to one? (01:28)

2. The fake deaths caused by the nerve gas Delta Nine (cars turned upside down, casualties all over the streets . . .) are staged way too quickly—there was no time at all to arrange

such elaborate scenery in such a brief time. How in the hell did they pull this off? (01:29)

GOOD WILL HUNTING (5)
1997, color, 126 min.

Director: Gus Van Sant

Cast: Robin Williams (Sean Maguire), Matt Damon (Will Hunting), Ben Affleck (Chuckie), Minnie Driver (Skylar), Stellan Skarsgård (Gerald "Jerry" Lambeau), Casey Affleck (Morgan), Cole Hauser (Billy), John Mighton (Tom), Jimmy Flynn (Judge Malone), Rachel Majorowski (Krystyn), Colleen McCauley (Cathy).

Blue collar kid is a genius, but he doesn't appreciate it.

Bloopers

1. Professor Jerry Lambeau concludes a demonstration; then he slides two parts of a blackboard close together and walks away. As he walks around his desk, the blackboard is open again. When Tom, the professor's assistant, walks to the desk, the blackboard is closed. (00:03, 00:04)

2. In the school corridor, Will sees the "advanced Fourier system" to be proven on the board. When the problem is solved and Professor Lambeau approaches the same board, the system is written totally differently. (00:04, 00:08)

3. While Billy, Morgan, Chuckie, and Will are seated at the

baseball game, someone asks, "Hey, Morgan, who's the girl with the striped pants?" Will takes a sip from his can (from behind), but from the front view, the can is lowered and he has to repeat the action. (00:09)

4. Will gives Skylar the spectrum for "ebogamine" while she's leafing through the pages of a book. As she sees him ("What are you doing here?") she stops on a page with three pictures. In the over-the-shoulder shot, she flips one more page, and when we see the book again . . . there they are, the same three pictures. Either the book is misprinted or this is a blooper. (01:00)

5. Jerry and Sean's discussion about Will escalates into an argument. Sean's boat painting is on the windowsill leaning against the window (close-up on Sean), laying flat on top of a stack of books (when Jerry moves away), and leaning again (Will is told by Jerry that he was about to leave) without anybody touching it. (01:44, 01:46)

Non-Blooper

Talking with Will at the Funland where they play baseball, Chuckie says, "Hey, uh, Casey's bouncin' up a bar at Harvard next week." He's not in fact referring to Casey Affleck (the actor who portrays Morgan, and Ben Affleck's real-life brother). Casey is a plump doorman who shows up later on, when the four kids go to his bar—

they even call him Casey. (00:07, 00:15)

GOONIES, THE (21)
1985, color, 114 min.

Director: Richard Donner

Cast: Sean Astin (Michael "Mikey" Walsh), Josh Brolin (Brandon "Brand" Walsh), Jeff Cohen (Lawrence "Chunk" Cohen), Corey Feldman (Clark "Mouth" Devereaux), Kerri Green (Andrea "Andy" Carmichael), Martha Plimpton (Stefanie "Stef" Steinbrenner), Jonathan Ke Quan "Ke Huy Quan" (Richard "Data" Wang), John Matuszak (Lotney "Sloth" Fratelli), Robert Davi (Jake Fratelli), Joe Pantoliano (Francis Fratelli), Anne Ramsey (Mama Fratelli), Jack O'Leary (Reporter).

They call themselves "The Goonies." Go figure.

Bloopers

1. Chunk sees a car chase and he's so excited he splatters his pizza on the window . . . but in the following shot, he has to do it again. (00:04)

2. When Chunk is at the gate of the Walsh's home, and they use all those gizmos to open it, the balloon that inflates changes from red to pink right before it pops. (00:07)

3. After the catastrophic entrance of Data, Chunk drops a statue from a table. Mikey, empty-handed, dives to get

it. When he picks it up, his inhaler is suddenly in his mouth. (00:09)

4. As they're entering the attic, Brandon fixes a flickering lightbulb. He smiles and walks away, but as the camera pans from the bottom up, Brandon is fixing the light again. (00:13)

5. When Chunk drops the treasure map, the frame shatters, so they brush off the glass. In the next shot, the glass has returned. (00:16)

6. When the Goonies ride their bikes toward the Fratelli hideout, Chunk asks everyone for a candy bar (among them, a Baby Ruth). However, later, when he's tied up with Sloth, Chunk produces a Baby Ruth from his pocket. (00:25, 01:07)

7. While Mouth tells Chunk about his mother's naked pictures, Data smiles with his teeth showing. In the next cut, he's dead serious. (00:37)

8. Stefanie asks, "Chunk, I hope that was your stomach" and next to her head is a lightbulb hanging from the ceiling. In the following cut, she's way below the same lightbulb, without taking a single step. (00:38)

9. In the basement of the Lighthouse Inn, Mikey tries to shatter the floor. Arguing with his brother, Mikey says, "There is something buried under there, Josh!" Mikey's brother's name is Brand (played by Josh Brolin). (00:40)

Mikey Tells All

When asked about this years later, actor Sean Astin replied, "I told Dick [Donner, the director] and everybody else that I said 'Josh,' but they didn't believe me!"

---

10. There's a water cooler with a clear bottle on top of it. The water level is about a quarter from the bottom. When Chunk hits the bottle, the level has risen to half. (00:40)

11. Chunk stops a car that is driven by Jake. He begins to sing, Chunk screams, and Jake is still heard singing . . . but in the side mirror we see Jake smoking a cigarette. (00:49)

12. Troy is sitting on the toilet when it explodes, sending him though the roof (literally). While skyrocketing up, Troy is wearing underwear. Who sits on the toilet bowl with their underwear on? (00:51)

13. The mole Chunk has above his lip on the left switches places when he says "Boy, you're hungrier than I am!" in the Baby Ruth scene. (01:07)

14. Pressured to play the right tune on an organ made of bones, Andy says that she's

not sure if a note is "A-sharp or B-flat." Actually, A-sharp is the same thing as B-flat. (01:21)

15. In One-Eyed Willie's ship, Andy kneels down to pick up a tiny doll. Then, when Mouth translates a map, she kneels down one more time in the background to pick up the same doll. (01:26)

16. The Fratellis bring the Goonies on the deck of the ship, but Mouth manages to hide a few jewels in his mouth (his cheeks are puffy). Yet, when Data shoots a suction cup dart at Mama Fratelli and he gets pulled to her, Mouth's mouth is open, with no jewels. After Mama drops the gun, Mouth's cheeks are puffy again. (01:31)

17. Andy's wrists get tied up and she's sent to walk the plank. When she falls in the water, her arms are actually crossed, but underwater her wrists are tied again. (01:32, 01:33)

18. While fleeing from the galleon at the end, Data dives from the plank three times in different shots. (01:34)

19. At the last minute, Rosalita finds the jewels and she pours them into Mrs. Walsh's hands. The first two shots of the hands show painted fingernails, but the last shot reveals unpainted nails. (01:46)

20. Mr. Walsh tears up the contract he doesn't have to sign anymore and tosses the pieces in the air. Suddenly there seem to be enough shreds of paper for a ticker-tape parade. (01:46)

21. A reporter asks Data about his adventure, and Data says, "the octopus was really scary." What octopus? (01:47)

The infamous "Octopus scene" was in fact shot, but didn't quite cut the mustard (check it out on the DVD). So it wound up on the cutting room floor, unlike Data's line.

Questions

1. In the attic, Chunk hits a framed page of a newspaper. The page is horizontal—so why is the wire on the back of the frame aligned to hang something vertically? (00:18)

2. The framed newspaper is the *Astoria Legend.* Later on, in the Lighthouse Inn, Stef finds a newspaper clipping from the *Astoria Ledger.* How many newspapers with strikingly similar names are there in the small town of Goon Dock? (00:18, 00:42)

Fun Fact

When Sloth swings like Tarzan to save Mouth and Stef who are on the plank, look at the two kids: they are actually two very, very still dummies. (01:33)

GREAT RACE, THE (10)
1965, color, 160 min.

Director: Blake Edwards

Cast: Jack Lemmon (Professor Fate / Prince Frederik Hapnick), Tony Curtis (The Great Leslie), Natalie Wood (Maggie Dubois), Peter Falk (Maximillian "Max"), Keenan Wynn (Hezekiah), Arthur O'Connell (Henry Goodbody), Vivian Vance (Hesther Goodbody), Dorothy Provine (Lily Olay), Larry Storch (Texas Jack), Ross Martin (Baron Rolfe Von Stuppe), George MacReady (General Kushter).

Laugh-a-minute race from New York to Paris.

[Note: the times listed don't include the 3 min. 43 sec. of the overture.]

Bloopers
1. A large hot air balloon is in a field ready to help the Great Leslie in his daredevil stunt. But when Hezekiah chops the rope and lets the balloon float away, only the basket of the balloon casts a shadow over the audience. Evidently, the basket was pulled up by a crane, not by a balloon. (00:03, 00:04)
2. The Great Leslie climbs into the hot air balloon (which is quickly plummeting) to get a parachute. The shot from up above shows the balloon being much, much closer to the ground than it is when Leslie actually jumps from it. (00:05, 00:06)
3. 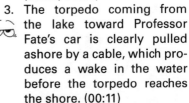 The torpedo coming from the lake toward Professor Fate's car is clearly pulled ashore by a cable, which produces a wake in the water before the torpedo reaches the shore. (00:11)
4. While hovering above the Leslie Special car on their flying bicycle, Max reminds Professor Fate that, once he arms the bomb, they'll "only have 10 seconds." It takes 19 seconds for the bomb to explode. (00:19)
5. Leslie sips champagne holding the glass from the bottom of the stem in the long shot, and from half the way up the stem in the close-up. (00:30)
6. While entertaining Miss Dubois, Leslie pours her a glass of champagne—the champagne is crystal clear in the long shot but tea-colored in the close-ups. (00:30)
7. Lily is onstage, sitting on a large half moon. As she sings "He oughtn't-a, shouldn't-a, hadn't-a feel so free," she lets the side ropes go and places her hands on her legs. In the following matching close-up, she's still holding on to the ropes. (00:59)
8. Professor Fate drinks a beer during Lily's performance. Fate's beer is almost without foam—but as Lily approaches him, the glass seems to be

filled only with foam: she blows on it, spraying the evil man with the foam. The glass will again be without foam as Fate slams it on the counter. (01:00)

9. When the crowd lifts them up, Miss Dubois kisses Professor Fate. In the close-up his arms are down, but in the wide shot his left arm is stretched out, holding his top hat. (01:37)

10. During the 2,357 pie fight, the Great Leslie remains immaculate until Miss Dubois hits him. Well—not exactly: after Prince Hapnick's remark that he never mixes his pies, there are five shots (two of Leslie, two of pie throwers, and one of Miss Dubois). In the last of these it's possible to see a brown spot appearing close to Leslie's shirt button. It'll be gone the next time we see him. (02:18, 02:19)

H

HALLOWEEN (9)
1978, color, 91 min.

Director: John Carpenter

Cast: Donald Pleasence (Dr. Sam Loomis), Jamie Lee Curtis (Laurie Strode), Nancy Kyes (Annie Brackett), P. J. Soles (Lynda), Charles Cyphers (Sheriff Leigh Brackett), Kyle Richards (Lindsey Wallace), Brian Andrews (Tommy Doyle), John Michael Graham (Bob), Nancy Stephens (Nurse Marion Chambers), Arthur Malet (Graveyard Keeper), Mickey Yablans (Richie), Nick Castle (The Shape), Will Sandin (Michael Myers, age 6), Sandy Johnson (Judith Myers), David Kyle (Judith's boyfriend).

Murderer skips the looney bin and comes home to roost . . . among other things.

Bloopers

1. Little Michael Myers spies on his sister and her boyfriend. They go in her room to make out, and the following steadi-cam shot happens in real time. So, since the lights go off and then the boyfriend gets dressed again and leaves, they make out for only 65 seconds. Too quick for practically anyone. (00:03, 00:04)

2. Nurse Chambers is in the car with Sam, smoking a cigarette. Halfway through the speech, she lights a second cigarette (without ever extinguishing the first). (00:07, 00:08)

3. While walking home, Laurie spots The Shape behind a bush. Annie steps closer and mocks Laurie: "He wants to take you out tonight." In that shot, a puff of smoke crosses the screen from left to right. (00:24)

> It was John Carpenter himself who admitted that the floating smoke "was from the director who was smoking too near the camera."

4. Once alone, Laurie bumps into Mr. Brackett and then keeps walking home. Even if it's the same day and a few seconds

later, the sidewalks and streets go from dry as a bone to completely drenched. (00:25)

5. Laurie steps out of her home carrying a pumpkin; red leaves are falling from the trees, giving the feeling of a cold Halloween night. As Laurie looks at the houses on the other side of the street, the trees look as green as they can be, and there's not one leaf on the ground. (00:28)

6. Laurie and Annie smoke a joint in Annie's car. The lock button on Laurie's side keeps going up and down by itself. (00:30)

7. Dr. Loomis says that fifteen years ago he met this six-year-old child—hence, Michael Myers is twenty-one. Yet, in the closing credits, actor Tony Moran is credited as "Michael age 23." (00:38, 01:28)

8. Just after having sex, Bob puts his glasses back on and puts his hands on his belly. In the following cut, he has one hand on his belly and the other behind his head. (01:03)

9. Laurie stabs Michael Myers in the closet upstairs, then she drops the knife (fool!!) by her bed. After Michael vanishes, a few shots of the house reveal the knife's now somehow downstairs, by the couch. (01:24, 01:28)

Question
Tommy spots The Shape in front of Lindsey's house—the front porch light is off. But when Laurie checks the house a minute later, she sees no one—except that the porch light is now on. Did Michael really care enough to turn it on? (00:41, 00:42)

Fun Fact
After talking on the phone to Laurie, Lynda and Bob get up from the couch and walk upstairs. Lynda trips on something, which was the dolly track. (01:01)

VANISHING (PART 2)

More mysterious disappearances . . .

Some chocolate in *Fast Times at Ridgemont High*	Blooper No. 5
A rearview mirror in *Ferris Bueller's Day Off*	Blooper No. 7
A toy car in *Happy Gilmore*	Blooper No. 2
H. B. Warner's pipe in *It's a Wonderful Life*	Blooper No. 2
Glenn Close's papers in *Jagged Edge*	Blooper No. 2
The powder on Julie Andrew's nose in *Mary Poppins*	Blooper No. 8
A white phone in *Scream*	Blooper No. 16
A piece of cake in *The Wedding Singer*	Blooper No. 4
A sign on the doorknob in *Zero Effect*	Blooper No. 4

HAPPY GILMORE (11)
1996, color, 92 min.

Director: Dennis Dugan

Cast: Adam Sandler (Happy Gilmore), Christopher McDonald (Shooter McGavin), Julie Bowen (Virginia Bennett), Frances Bay (Grandma), Carl Weathers (Frederick "Chubbs" Peterson), Alan Covert (Otto), Robert Smigel (IRS Agent), Richard Kiel (Mr. Larson), Dennis Dugan (Doug Thompson), Joe Flaherty (Donald, the Jeering Fan), Ken Camroux (Coach), Rich Elwood (Assistant Coach), Jessica Gunn (Signed Chest Woman), Mark Lye (Mark Lye), Helen Honeywell (Crazy Old Lady).

Hockey player wannabe becomes golf champion.

Bloopers

1. Happy shatters the glass of the coach's office with a hockey puck, but the glass is back in place after two shots. (00:04)

2. Happy reaches his grandma's house while movers are piling up the furniture in the yard. A yellow toy car is in front of the steps but is gone when Happy throws the IRS agent out of the house. The yellow car is back when Happy tries to golf for the first time with the movers. (00:07, 00:09, 00:11)

3. While driving his grandma to Silver Acres Rest Home, a picture of Grandma is hanging from Happy's rearview mirror. But when a lady jumps on the hood begging him to take her away, the shot from inside the car reveals no hanging picture. (00:09)

4. In her room at the rest home, Happy stores his grandma's suitcase underneath the bed. When he points the lady to one of the custodians, the suitcase has vanished. (00:09, 00:10)

5. The air conditioner in Grandma's room has a large frame that fills the window. Still, when Happy drops the machine down and it lands on a screaming lady, the frame seems to have shrunk. (00:30)

6. At the golf club, Happy meets with Mark Lye. In between is Shooter, who takes a sip from a glass he's holding with his left hand—followed immediately by a second sip from the glass . . . that he's holding with his right hand. (00:31)

7. Mr. Larson grabs one golf club out of Shooter's bunch and bends it, holding it from the handle with his right hand (from the front) or with the handle in his left hand (from behind). (00:44)

8. The players join the Michelob Invitational. But when Shooter sinks his putt (complaining about the crowd noise), his caddy wears the Visa Everglades Open shirt—

and so does the flag on the hole. The Visa Everglades Open will be played later on by these same players. (00:44, 00:45, 00:47)

9. Happy signs the chest of a young woman. When he's signing the chest of an older woman, we can see that his signature on the young woman's chest has changed. (00:45, 00:46)

10. During the "happy place" sequence, Grandma plays at a Rol-a-top slot machine. She gets a triple cherry—but only in the detail. In the master shot, the symbols are different. Yet she wins anyway. It's a happy place, after all. (01:06)

11. At the beginning of the Tour Championship, a wide shot reveals a yellow Volkswagen Beetle stuck in a metal TV structure. That Beetle will hit Happy on the golf course a few minutes later—then will crash into the tower and get stuck. (01:09, 01:14)

Questions

1. Happy uses a ball thrower to get ready for hockey. Chubbs pulls the plug of the machine from the outside of the fence. Later, a kid switches places with Happy, and turns on the machine—but from the inside he couldn't have plugged the machine back in. How did he do it? (00:15, 00:16)

2. On the first hole that Happy

plays, one of his usually powerful hits reveals that he's not wearing any undershirt. Later on (still playing the same day), he'll hit another ball because Grandma wants him to be happy. This second shot reveals Happy's now wearing a gray undershirt. Did it get cold during the round? (01:13, 01:19)

HERBIE RIDES AGAIN (7)
1974, color, 88 min.

Director: Robert Stevenson

Cast: Ken Berry (Willoughby Whitfield), Stefanie Powers (Nicole Harris), Helen Hayes (Mrs. "Grandma" Steinmetz), Keenan Wynn (Alonzo Hawk), Raymond Bailey (Lawyer), Dan Tobin (Lawyer), John Zaremba (Lawyer), John McIntire (Mr. Judson), Huntz Hall (Judge), Liam Dunn (Doctor), Richard X. Slattery (Traffic Commissioner), Vito Scotti (Taxi Driver), Herbie (Himself).

The bug with a heart helps a sweet old lady.

Bloopers

1. Willoughby rides in Herbie with Nicole; they stop and switch places. Willoughby walks around the car in a street crowded with pedestrians; but from inside the car we see an empty road. (00:16)

2. Alonzo Hawk talks to his lawyers just outside the office;

he's on a blue screen. The close-up that was inserted for his speech is awkward because the blue screen doesn't change perspective. (00:31)

3. Mrs. Steinmetz goes to the mall and is chased by three treacherous cars. Herbie takes a U-turn and runs away . . . yet the hands of Mrs. Steinmetz's stunt double are steering the wheel. But, of course, Herbie only steers himself. (00:38)

4. As they're chasing Herbie on the Golden Gate's suspension cable, the five lawyers run in between two red steel cables, which are approximately at chest height. As the car starts to roll down, the Lawyers—seen from behind—stop . . . and the cables are gone. (00:41)

5. When he smashes the Alonzo Hawk Van & Storage door, Herbie has a new light on his front trunk. This light is gone in the warehouse as he runs up to push off furniture to trap the two cops and then he has it again once back on the street. (00:49, 00:50, 00:55)

6. Willoughby grabs the exterior elevator to reach Mrs. Steinmetz and Herbie; the blue screen reveals a different building (there are plants now, too). (01:03)

7. Mr. Judson uses an ax to smash one pane in Mrs. Steinmetz's front door. The old lady hands him a fireman's hat, and when he proclaims he's mighty proud to wear it, the door behind him clearly shows all the panes intact. (01:22)

Fun Fact
The first time Herbie shows Willoughby what he's able to do, there's an aerial shot of the car running on a desert road and passing by an area in the shadow to a sunny area (00:17). It's stock footage from the first movie, *The Love Bug.* (01:36)

INDEPENDENCE DAY (29)
also Special Edition
1996, color, 145 min. / 153 min.
(SE)

Director: Roland Emmerich

Cast: Will Smith (Captain
Steven "Eagle" Hiller), Bill
Pullman (President Thomas J.
Whitmore), Jeff Goldblum
(David Levinson), Mary
McDonnell (First Lady Marilyn
Whitmore), Judd Hirsch (Julius
Levinson), Robert Loggia (U.S.
Space Command General
William Grey), Randy Quaid
(Russell Casse), Margaret Colin
(Constance Spano / Levinson),
James Rebhorn (Secretary of
Defense Albert Nimzick),
Harvey Fierstein (Marty
Gilbert), Adam Baldwin (Major
Mitchell), Brent Spiner (Dr.
Brakish Okun), Giuseppe
Andrews (Troy Casse), Vivica A.
Fox (Jasmine Dubrow Hiller).

*UFOs try to destroy the
world in order to conquer it.
Pretty pointless, huh?*

Bloopers
1. Earth is shown as the alien
    ship gets closer. The rotation
    of Earth is visible, and it's
    about 2 or 3 degrees per sec-
    ond. If Earth rotated that fast,
    we would have days lasting
    2 minutes. (00:01)
2. When Constance, the presi-
    dent's assistant, is waiting
    for him she's reading a sec-
    tion of *USA Today*. A weather
    map is visible with blue and
    green areas, the colors for
    cold in *USA Today*. But in
    July? (Not to mention that a
    radio station states that in
    Central Park it's 95°.) (00:06,
    00:07 / 00:06, 00:08 SE)
3. David plays chess with his
    dad Julius, who puts a cigar
    in his mouth, moves a pawn,
    and the cigar has zapped into
    an ashtray on the table.
    (00:07 / 00:08 SE)
4. In his trailer, young Troy
    Casse is mad at the TV and
    whacks it with his right hand.
    Meanwhile, his left arm is
    first down, then resting on
    the table, then down again.
    (00:09 / 00:10 SE)

5. Every alien ship casts a very sharp shadow on buildings and towns. However, all the ships emerge from a gigantic cloud, so what's making the sharp shadow? (00:20, 00:21, 00:22 / 00:21, 00:22, 00:23 SE)

6. The shadow from the spaceship hovering over Washington, D.C., hits the Lincoln Memorial, the Washington Monument, and the Capitol Building, in that order. The shadow falls over Lincoln's statue from the face going to the back of its head. First of all, this statue is under a dome, so that shadow's not gonna happen. Also, the statue faces the Washington Monument and the Capitol, so the shadow wouldn't be moving in that direction anyway. (00:21 / 00:22 SE)

7. Leaving home, Steven argues with Jasmine. His left epaulette is under his jacket collar, then over it, then under it, then over it again. (00:28 / 00:30 SE)

8. Julius and David are driving toward Washington, D.C. The lock button on David's side is down, then up, then down again. (00:32 / 00:33 SE)

9. After being turned down by NASA, Steven opens his locker. His jacket, which he's wearing, instantly zaps into the locker in the following shot. (00:35 / 00:37 SE)

10. Jasmine comes backstage and collects her stuff, then she steps out of the scene for less than 5 seconds, and—in real time!—she comes back fully dressed. (00:36 / 00:38 SE)

11. David and Julius reach Washington, and the ground is wet as if it's raining. But if the ship is "over fifteen miles in width" and doesn't move, how can rain hit the ground? (00:37 / 00:40 SE)

The Strange Streets of *Independence Day* (Special Edition only)

When David is looking for his ex-wife's phone number on a CD-ROM, he displays two listing pages. A very sharp eye (or better yet, a hit on "pause" at the right moment), will reveal some amusing street names, such as "5367 Asif Av.," "28934 Upndown Rd," "6849 Allfun Way," of course back-to-back "63892 Donald, 9827 Fagen Dr," (as in Donald Fagen of the group Steely Dan) and also "397 Windowjump," "10028 Onthe Rd" and "234 Guesswho Blvd." (00:41)

---

12. David's laptop is open on the president's desk, then closed as David stands up, then open, then closed. (00:40 / 00:44 SE)

13. The laptop shows a countdown to the alien attack. When David sits on the chopper, while evacuating the White House, the top bar of

the countdown reads, "Remain Time." When he sits on Air Force One, the top bar reads, "Time Remaining." (00:43, 00:46 / 00:47, 00:50 SE)

14. When Marty is stuck in traffic, he slams his car horn three times. We only hear two honks. (00:44 / 00:48 SE)

15. When the aliens blow up the Empire State Building, the shot is from an avenue in front of the building. That avenue doesn't exist. (00:45, 00:47 / 00:49, 00:51 SE)

16. When Jimmy's and Steven's planes are being chased through the desert by the alien fighters, Steven's speed indicator reads something in between Mach 2 and Mach 2.2. There's no way an F-18 can go anywhere even close to Mach 2. Their maximum speed is between Mach 1.3 and 1.8. Unless it's crashing. (00:59 / 01:03 SE)

17. While Steven is dragging the alien in the desert, clouds in the sky disappear and reappear all through the scene. (01:07 / 01:13 SE)

18. Once the president enters the "clean room" of Area 51, all the workers are wearing masks over their mouths . . . except the dude to the right, emerging from behind a desk, who puts it on quickly. But still . . . he's in the shot. (01:09 / 01:15 SE)

19. David opens a fridge to look for some ice. He doesn't find it. However, when Constance opens the door to put a bottle back in the fridge, the food that was on the shelf of the door (a Coca-Cola can, some milk, perhaps a yogurt) has vanished. (01:24, 01:25 / 01:32, 01:33 SE)

20. Proposing a toast to the end of the world, David stands close to a bottle that turns about 45° all by itself. (01:25 / 01:33 SE)

21. While he's talking to his ex-wife, David slams the bottle down on a table: a little liquor spurts out of it. She walks away, and David picks the bottle back up, but for some reason he needs to unscrew the cap, which had been lying next to the bottle. (01:25 / 01:33, 01:34 SE)

22. A bomber fires a nuclear missile at an alien ship, then veers to the left. On the radar signal, it is shown veering to the right. (01:28 / 01:36 SE)

23. David is drunk and mad and he trashes an office. When he kicks a green wastebasket, it is possible to see (painted on its bottom) "Art Dept." In Area 51? (01:35 / 01:43 SE)

24. In the cockpit of the alien ship, Steven holds up a cigar, to be given to David. Steven's fingers are together in his close-up and separated in the over-the-shoulder shot. (01:52 / 02:00 SE)

25. Missiles and engines on a plane are numbered 1, 2, 3, and so on, starting from the

pilot's left. President Thomas says, "Eagle One. Fox three." and fires the first missile to his right (fox three). However, for the next try he says, "Eagle One. Fox three." Again?! Yet, he fires missile No. 2 (the first missile to his left). Later on, he goes, "Eagle One. Fox two!" but the missile that is shot is the farthest to the right—Fox four, that is. (01:59, 02:00 / 02:97, 02:08 SE)

26. Not to mention that President Thomas fires a missile at the starship, then a second one (which goes through), then a third one. With a fourth missile he destroys a smaller spacecraft, then he fires one last missle at the primary weapon of the spacecraft. Wait a second . . . didn't his plane carry only four missiles? (01:59, 02:00, 02:04 / 02:07, 02:08, 02:09 SE)

27. The last missile that Russell is about to fire is Fox one (first to the left of the pilot). But he says, "Fox two!" (02:05 / 02:14 SE)

28. Steven and David light up their cigars in the Mothership. They escape, fly back to Earth, crash-land, and when they're found by the rescue crew . . . they're still smoking pretty long cigars. (02:09, 02:14 / 02:17, 02:22 SE)

29. The countdown of the detonator of the missile fired into the hull of the Mothership goes from 00:30 to 00:00 . . .

in about 1 minute and 35 seconds. (02:10 / 02:19 SE)

Questions

1. As the starship approaches, the moon's gravel vibrates. How did the shockwave from the alien ship spread? Last time we checked, there's no atmosphere in space or on the moon. (00:01)

2. When the starship arrives over Washington, D.C., it casts a shadow over the Capitol and over the White House. How come there are people frolicking by the Capitol and in front of the White House, oblivious to what's happening? Can you say "stock footage?" (00:21 / 00:22 SE)

3. In the morning, Steven grabs the newspaper, which is tied up, yet opens it without breaking the ribbon. How'd he do that? (00:25 / 00:26 SE)

4. Jasmine survives through the fireball that exploded inside the tunnel. How? A fireball of that size would either burn up all the oxygen in the tunnel or raise the temperature to such an extent that Jasmine would've become Velveeta. (00:49 / 00:53 SE)

5. How come the fire truck Jasmine finds didn't blow up when the fireball hit the ground? It did have gas in the tank (she drives it). So . . . ? (01:02 / 01:06 SE)

6. How come PCs and Macs are like apples and oranges, yet David somehow manages to

give a Mac virus to an alien computer? (01:37, 01:58 / 01:45, 02:06 SE)

7. With an "oops!" Steven claims the instructions sheet was just upside down. When he turns it, everything's oriented correctly. But wouldn't turning the instructions sheet reverse forward and backward, as well as left and right? Not in this case . . . (01:53 / 02:01 SE)

8. If the ship was precisely over the base when it was blown up, how could it not land on the base? It was fifteen miles in diameter, after all . . . (02:03, 02:07 / 02:12, 02:16 SE)

IT'S A WONDERFUL LIFE (14)
1946, black & white, 129 min.

Director: Frank Capra

Cast: James Stewart (George Bailey), Donna Reed (Mary Hatch / Mary Bailey), Lionel Barrymore (Henry F. Potter), Thomas Mitchell (Uncle Billy), Henry Travers (Clarence Odbody), Beulah Bondi (Mrs. Bailey), Frank Faylen (Ernie), Gloria Grahame (Violet Bick), H. B. Warner (Old Man Gower),

Todd Karns (Harry Bailey), Samuel S. Hinds (Peter "Pa" Bailey), Sheldon Leonard (Nick), Bobbie Anderson (Little George Bailey), Tom Fadden (Tollhouse Keeper), Frank Hagney (Potter's Bodyguard).

Holiday favorite is aired at least fifty times a year, and we can still watch it over and over . . . unless it's colorized.

Bloopers
1. When young George enters Mr. Gower's pharmacy, we can see on the wall a "Silhouette Girl" Coca-Cola thermometer. The year is 1919. That particular Coca-Cola image was introduced in the late 1930s. (00:06)

2. While young George is talking about diptheria to Old Man Gower, the cigar the poor man has in his mouth vanishes, comes back for a quick close-up ("Yes, George . . ."), and vanishes again—just before Mr. Gower sends George out of the room. (00:08)

3. While in Peter Bailey's office,

ID4 Cameos

CAMEO	ROLE	TIME
Visual Effects Supervisor Volker Engel	Man filing in office	00:46 / 00:51 (SE)
Writer / Producer Dean Devlin	"I'm on it" voice	02:04 / 02:13 (SE)

Mr. Potter's codger is standing behind the wheelchair, to its left. In a close-up of Mr. Potter, the codger has zapped to the right of the chair. He comes back to the left in the following wide shot. (00:09)

4. Harry's graduation party happens in 1928. When we find George and Uncle Billy at the train station, we learn that George is "four years older." But when George gets married, the stock market crashes. That would place the crash in 1932, when it actually happened in 1929. (00:19, 00:35, 00:54)

5. While waiting for Harry at the train station, Uncle Billy rests his hands by a bag of peanuts—but in the following matching shot, he's digging in the bag and chewing, too. (00:35)

6. When George and Uncle Billy are introduced to Harry's wife, Ruth, she steps down from the train . . . twice. (00:36)

7. Just before letting George in, Mary puts "Buffalo Gals" on the phonograph. The old record has a dark label—but the detail shows a record with a white label (so the viewer can read the title better). (00:43)

8. George enters his office with a wreath around his arm; when he starts to talk to his brother Harry on the phone, George tosses the wreath on a table—but in the following

shot, the wreath is back. (01:17)

9. Holding a pipe in his mouth, George gives Violet a loan. As he stands up, the pipe vanishes. (01:21)

10. Furious at Uncle Billy, George flees. Billy, desperate, puts his head in his crossed arms: the right one over the left in the wide shot, the left one over the right in the close-up. (01:24)

11. Clarence jumps in the river before George can. Clarence yells "Help, help! Heeeeelp!" at the top of his lungs, but his mouth barely moves. (01:39)

12. The man who has Clarence and George in his shack after the river incident is about to spit. Clarence says that he's from heaven, and the man freezes, his hands by his sides. In the matching wide shot, his left arm is leaning on the desk. (01:40)

13. While recovering from saving Clarence, George is taking a sip from a cup. Clarence says, "Your lip's bleeding, George." In the matching close-up, the cup has vanished and George is holding one hand over the wound. (01:40)

14. George and Clarence are thrown out of Nick's bar (formerly Mr. Martini's): the man who throws them out grabs George with his right hand and Clarence with his left, but when they fly through

the door, their positions have switched. (01:50)

Question

Bailey Bros. Building & Loan Association is an office on the second floor of a building. The only entrance has a large flight of stairs. How could Mr. Potter and his heavy wheelchair ever make it up there? (00:08, 00:09)

J

JAGGED EDGE (4)
1985, color, 108 min.

Director: Richard Marquand

Cast: Glenn Close (Teddy Barnes), Jeff Bridges (Jack Forrester), Peter Coyote (Thomas Krasny), Robert Loggia (Sam Ransom), John Dehner (Superior Court Judge Clark Carrigan), Leigh Taylor-Young (Virginia Howell), Karen Austin (Julie Jensen), Lance Henriksen (Frank Martin), James Karen (Andrew Hardesty), Michael Dorn (Dan Hislan), Louis Giambalvo (Fabrizi), Marshall Colt (Robert "Bobby" Slade).

Did he do it? Did he not do it? Or did he? Or didn't he? Or...

Bloopers

1. During the first day of the trial, Teddy goes to court wearing a gray dress; when Thomas Krasny delivers his opening statement, Teddy is wearing a a dark-blue *tailleur* with a white shirt, and during Krasny's first witness interrogation, she wears a brown dress. When Virginia Howell is called, Teddy is wearing the blue *tailleur* with a similar shirt—all in the same scene. And apparently, all in the same day. (00:48, 00:49, 00:51)

2. When Eileen Avery, the reluctant witness, is called, both Krasny and Teddy approach the bench. Teddy carries a list with her. When she returns to her desk, she's holding nothing—but as she reaches her seat, she hands the list to her assistant. (00:59, 01:00)

3. In the garage, Slade threatens Teddy, who honks the horn of her car using her left hand. The honking keeps going, even when she grabs the door handle with her left hand, and shuts it. Hmmm... (01:19)

4. Teddy uses a gun in self-defense against the killer: the third shot puts a large blood stain against a footstool behind the killer. The fourth shot, probably sponsored by Mr.

Clean, reveals a spotless footstool behind the killer. (01:44)

Question

Sam enters Teddy's house and exclaims, "What the f*** are you doing, sitting in the dark?" Didn't he see the two lit lamps on the wall, just above Teddy? (01:10)

JAWS (25)

1975, color, 125 min.

Director: Steven Spielberg

Cast: Roy Scheider (Martin Brody), Robert Shaw (Quint), Richard Dreyfuss (Matt Hooper), Lorraine Gary (Ellen Brody), Murray Hamilton (Larry Vaughn), Carl Gottleib (Meadows), Jeffrey Kramer (Hendricks), Susan Backlinie (Chrissie Watkins), Ted Grossman (Estuary Victim), Chris Rebello (Michael Brody), Jay Mello (Sean Brody).

A big white shark has a rousing vacation on the shores of Amity, New York.

Bloopers

1. Amity is crowded with people partying on the 4th of July—a date seen for instance on the sign that publicizes the regatta. But there are no leaves on the trees (the scene was shot in March–May). (00:07, 00:50)
2. When we see the rest of Chrissie on the beach covered by crabs, it's hard not to notice one crab falling from above. Where from, since there's nothing above? (00:08)
3. Brody types the report on Chrissie's death: it states, "Date/Time Original Ill./Inc. 7-1-74, 11:50 PM" and "Date/Time Deceased Discovered 7-2-74, 10:20 PM." Later on, by the council chamber, a

---

SHOES THAT "SHINE"

These folks get a little fancy with their footwear:

Michelle Pfeiffer in *Batman Returns*	Blooper No. 3
Glenn Shadix in *Beetlejuice*	Blooper No. 3
An entire class in *Casper*	Blooper No. 3
Thomas Jane in *Deep Blue Sea*	Blooper No. 9
Whoopi Goldberg in *Ghost*	Blooper No. 4
Ted Grossman in *Jaws*	Blooper No. 11
Keith Gordon in *Jaws 2*	Blooper No. 7
Ariel in *The Little Mermaid*	Blooper No. 11

sign offers a reward to capture the shark that killed Alex M. Kintner on Sunday, June 29th. But Alex was killed after Chrissie. Hmm . . . And while we're at it, June 29, 1974 was a Saturday—not a Sunday. (00:09, 00:18)

4. When Brody hands Hendricks a bunch of signposts, the posts point to Hendricks's right. But when he meets Mayor Vaughn, they point to his left. (00:11)

5. Brody sits on the beach, keeping one eye on the swimmers. He's wearing a wristwatch; but as he startles from the first false alarm (the old man swimming underwater with a black skullcap), his wristwatch is gone. And so is his wife. (00:14, 00:15)

6. As Brody confiscates some sticks of dynamite, he asks Hooper to tell a few fishermen they're overloading a boat. A chubby man in a light blue jacket gets on the boat twice—while the man close to him and bent over simply vanishes between cuts. (00:28)

7. Hooper measures the mouth of the tiger shark that has been captured; when he's asked to move because they're taking a picture, he puts away his tape measure—twice. (00:33)

8. While questioning Matt Hooper, Brody "works" on a bottle neck, to remove the black covering. From one angle he's working on the middle of the neck, from another he's working on the top of it. (00:42)

9. Hooper cuts the tiger shark open to examine what the fish ate in the last 24 hours. Hooper tosses Brody one half fish, one full fish, then (reverse angle) one metal can. But the can lands among two halves of fish, and an entire fish—which, if it's the one he threw a few seconds ago, has moved back a few feet. (00:43)

10. The Louisiana license plate retrieved from inside the shark says, "Sportsmen's Paradise." The actual Louisiana nickname is, "SportsmAn's Paradise." (00:44)

11. A future victim sits on a small boat in the estuary. He's asking three kids if they have any problem with their boat, when the shark turns the man's boat upside down. As he dives into the water, he is barefoot—but as one of his legs falls to the sea floor, there's a shoe on the foot. (01:02)

12. Quint tosses a bag to Hooper; the bag rotates midair and lands with its opening toward Quint—but in the following cut, the opening has rotated 180°. (01:07)

13. Quint is sitting in his fishing place and he has no socks on; later on, in the same scene, he's wearing gray socks. (01:12, 01:14)

14. After telling Quint, "You're

gonna need a bigger boat," Brody is holding a cigarette in his mouth and is wearing gray gloves. When Quint steps on the deck to take a first look at the shark and corrects Hooper, "Twenty-five [footer]," Brody has no cigarette in his mouth. As Hooper jumps down onto the deck, Brody's cigarette is back in his mouth—but the gloves are gone. (01:21)

15. The poignant speech Quints delivers about his experience sinking on the USS *Indianapolis* concludes with him stating the day that it happened: June 29, 1945. Ahem, we beg to differ: the USS *Indianapolis* was first sighted by the Japanese submarine *I-58* on July 29, 1945, and torpedoed a few minutes past midnight on July 30, 1945. (01:32)

16. When Quint harpoons the shark for the second time (attaching the yellow barrel to the fish), the shadow over the shark is not Quint's—it's the cameraman's (the camera's shadow is visible, too). (01:39)

17. When Brody fires his gun at the shark, Quint attaches a second barrel to the animal. There are two barrels left on the *Orca*—but then as the boat turns to approach the two floating barrels, there are three yellow barrels on the deck. (01:41, 01:42)

18. The shark pulls the ropes so hard that one cleat is ripped off before Quint can use his machete. A few minutes later, when the *Orca*'s engine blows up, the cleat is back. (01:44, 01:45, 01:48)

19. After Quint cuts one of the ropes with his machete (the sea is pretty rough), he swings and the machete sticks in the wood (the sea is completely calm). Then Quint walks back to the cabin (and the sea is choppy again). (01:45)

20. Brody gives up trying to use a water pump to clean the deck, which looks to be entirely covered with at least one inch of water. Brody heads to a metal ladder, but as he starts moving up, the whole boat rocks to the right. The following shot, from the outside of the boat, reveals a thoroughly dry deck. (01:46)

21. As Matt enters the cage, he's wearing a wristwatch over the arm of his blue wet suit. As the cage is lowered underwater, the watch has slipped underneath his sleeve. (01:51, 01:53)

22. Before putting his scuba mask on, Matt gives his glasses to Martin, who holds them by the right side in his mouth; in the following shot, he's holding them by the left side. (01:52)

23. Once underwater, Hooper has an innocuous first encounter with the shark. Hooper puts his spear down and grabs the cage, but in the following shot the spear is back in his hands. (01:53)

Jaws Cameos

CAMEO	ROLE	TIMES
Jaws Writer Peter Benchley	TV news reporter	00:55
Steven Spielberg	Voice calling from Amity	
	Point light station	01:22

24. When the shark attacks the underwater cage, he has no barrels attached whatsoever (in this case, it was a real shark off the coast of Australia). (01:54)
25. The shark attacks and bends the bars. However, when Hooper flees and the shark goes on a rampage on top of the cage, the bars all look fine. (01:54, 01:55)

Bloopers

The Healing Waters

In *Jaws*, the shark shatters the left window of the *Orca*, enters the cabin, and gets hit by an oxygen tank (01:58). But when two scuba divers reach the submerged *Orca* in the beginning of *Jaws 2* (00:01), the boat's left side is perfectly intact.

JAWS 2 (13)
1978, color, 116 min.

Director: Jeannot Szwarc

Cast: Roy Scheider (Martin Brody), Lorraine Gary (Ellen Brody), Murray Hamilton (Mayor Vaughn), Joseph Mascolo (Peterson), Jeffrey Kramer (Hendricks), Collin Wilcox Paxton (Dr. Elkins), Ann Dusenberry (Tina Wilcox), Mark Gruner (Mike Brody), Barry Coe (Andrews), Marc Gilpin (Sean Brody), David Elliott (Larry Vaughn), Keith Gordon (Doug), G. Thomas Dunlop (Timmy), Gigi Vorgan (Brooke), Donna Wilkes (Jackie).

Another big white shark has a rousing vacation on the shores of Amity, New York.

1. Brody takes the "Amity on time" raft with his Police truck. As he boards it, the shadow of the crew is visible on the truck itself. (00:03)
2. Once at the Amity Scholarship Fund benefit, Brody parks his truck close to another one. But the following shots reveal that his truck is parked much farther back. (00:05)
3. Hendricks drags the bottom of the ocean, nabbing a powerline by mistake. When the hooks surface, the bar that holds them is on top; in the shot at sea level, the bar is on one side. (00:25)
4. To retrieve a piece of wood from the sea, Brody starts removing his right shoe. In the

following shot, he's already removed the left and is starting to remove his right sock. (00:35)

5. Talking to a few potential investors, Ellen comments about the sunset and winds up spotting her husband on the shark tower. The boom mike is reflected in her sunglasses. (00:42)

6. Sitting at the bar, Mike has a full glass in front of him. When they ask him if he'd like to go sailing, and he replies "Yeah, why not?" the glass is gone, but it's back in the following shot. (00:55, 00:56)

Good Old . . . What's-His-Name

In *Jaws*, both Mayor Vaughn (after Brody drives away from the hardware store [00:11]) and Brody himself (commenting on something Hooper just said [00:29]) call Hendricks "Lenny." Yet, in *Jaws 2*, after Hendricks is made Sheriff, both Mr. and Mrs. Brody (00:58) call him "Jeff" (The actor's name: Jeffrey Kramer).

7. Doug inflates his rubber dingy: he's wearing sneakers. When he's chased by the shark, he's barefoot—but as he gets on another boat, the shoes are back. (01:22, 01:23)

8. Larry also has a shoe problem: he doesn't have them on when he's trying to leave the scene of the first attack on the boats, but he does have them on when the shark vanishes after Mike has been rescued. (01:24, 01:25)

9. When Timmy struggles to pull Mike on board the boat, he has his right foot on the edge of the boat, inside of it, on the edge again, inside . . . (01:25)

10. Mike is rescued just in time when he floats, unconscious, from the shark's jaws. Well, not exactly "unconscious." Pay attention, he retracts his legs just in the nick of time! (And take a good look at the piston and gears inside the mouth of the shark.) (01:25)

11. Larry tosses a rope to the helicopter pilot. Jackie is sitting in the back of the catamaran, to the right, and her cousin Brooke is crouching in front of her. But when the pilot catches the rope, Jackie has moved to the left side of the boat and now she's sitting in front of Brooke. (01:31)

12. Brody's boat rams into Cable Junction and gets stuck. The boat appears to be level with the water, but after a couple of shots it's listing to one side. (01:44, 01:45)

13. After the shark's last attack on the boats, while the kids are swimming to Cable Junction, a shot shows a real shark underwater. To the left (in only a few frames) is a propeller. But these sailboats don't have motors . . . (01:47)

Fun Fact

As the shark aims at Mike, right after the second shot of Timmy grabbing the kid, there's a shot of a real shark that will be used again toward the end of the movie, when Andy yells to Brody, "He's gonna take hold of the wood!" (01:25, 01:51)

Burying the Survivor

In *Jaws*, Matt Hooper meets Mrs. Brody and mentions his boat, the *Aurora* (00:39, 00:42). Yet, in *Jaws 2*, Mrs. Brody says to her husband that "a certain Matt Hooper" was on the phone (00:39) as if she doesn't recognize his name. Can't she remember the only other survivor (besides her husband) from the boat that tracked down the first shark?

JURASSIC PARK (50)

1993, color, 126 min.

Director: Steven Spielberg

Cast: Sam Neill (Dr. Alan Grant), Laura Dern (Dr. Ellen "Ellie" Sattler), Jeff Goldblum (Dr. Ian Malcolm), Richard Attenborough (John Hammond), Bob Peck (Robert Muldoon), Martin Ferrero (Donald Gennaro), B. D. Wong (Dr. Henry Wu), Joseph Mazzello (Tim Murphy), Ariana Richards (Alexis "Lex" Murphy), Samuel L. Jackson (Ray Arnold), Wayne Knight (Dennis Nedry), Cameron Thor (Lewis Dodgson).

The dinosaurs are back; and they're mean, lean, and computer generated.

Bloopers

1. A man is knocked down from the steel cage he just opened and has his fall broken by a hand that pops out from the lower right (but none of the other workers appears to be there). (00:02)

2. The amber that was found in the Dominican Republic and that contains the dinosaur DNA is 20 million years old. According to scientists, the dinosaurs became extinct 65 million years ago. (00:05)

3. Ellie leans against the computer desk in one of the back corners. In the following shot, she's moved to one of the front corners. (00:07)

4. Dr. Grant enters his trailer by opening a door with hinges on the left—but from the inside, they are on the right. (00:10)

5. The amount of dust on Grant's face changes while he's talking to Hammond. (00:10)

6. The white cloth Hammond uses to clean the glass ("Make the one I've got down in Kenya look like a petting zoo.") suddenly becomes pink. (00:11)

7. The café in San Jose, Costa Rica, is shown to be facing

the sea. Unfortunately, the real San Jose, Costa Rica, is inland. (00:13)

8. At the café, Nedry is given a bag filled with money; the bag vanishes from under his arm while Dodgson shows him a fake shaving cream can. (00:14)

9. When Nedry is done with the shaving cream, he elegantly places it on top of a slice of pie; then he cleans his hands using a napkin he never picks up. (00:14)

10. On the helicopter, Hammond switches places: he was sitting in front of Malcolm, close to the left door; but when they all get out of the chopper, Hammond is the first one to get out—from the right door. (00:15, 00:18)

11. When they land on the island, the transport jeeps are already in position for loading. However, the next shot of the area shows the jeeps backing up quickly. There was no room at all: if they would have backed up any more they surely would have gone into the water. (00:18)

12. Dr. Grant and Ellie walk from the jeep to the brachiosaurus, passing by an open space. When the dinosaur stands up on its hind legs, three tall trees have appeared on one side (they'll vanish when the paleontologists stare at the lagoon). (00:21)

13. While touring in the moving theater, the guests see a woman scientist walk along the glass and then vanish as the camera moves inside the lab. (00:27)

14. Dr. Grant stands in front of a velociraptor egg, which is delicately held by a computer-controlled arm—which proceeds to vanish before the next shot. (00:28)

15. A cow is lowered into the velociraptor cage: there's a rope around its neck. The last cut shows no rope at all. (00:31, 00:32)

16. When the group of visitors observes the feeding of a raptor, they approach a platform that surrounds the beast's cage. The platform is concrete, but when Muldoon reaches the gang, a red pad appears on part of the platform. (00:31, 00:32)

17. During lunch, one of the waiters seems to be waiting for his cue. He's between the screen behind Hammond and the one to his right. (00:34)

18. Malcolm moves around the jeep; in the following cut, he moves around it one more time. (00:39)

19. At the latitude of the Island Nublar, storms move westward; not eastward, as is shown on one of the computers. (00:40)

20. While waiting for the T-rex to appear, a shot reveals that Dr. Grant's jeep is already wet—but it hasn't started raining yet. (00:46)

21. Dr. Ellis's left arm disappears as she examines the triceratops' eye with a small flashlight. (00:51)

22. Nedry tries to buy some time by talking to the ship captain on the pier via computer videolink. It's not a live picture, but clearly a videoclip being played back from the hard drive (there's a progress meter on the bottom). (00:54)

23. Nedry steals several embryos from the frozen chamber. On the stand, Tyrannosaurus is spelled "TyraNosaurus," and Stegosaurus is spelled "StegAsaurus." (00:57)

24. Trying to get access into the system, Arnold types (and says) "access main program." On the screen we see "access security." He then says "access main security," but on the screen we read "access security grid." Finally, he says "access main program grid," but he types "access main security grid." (00:59)

25. Tim looks through the windshield with the lit goggles. Lex is looking in his direction. From the outside, she's looking in a completely different direction. (01:01)

26. When Gennaro runs from the jeep toward the restrooms, he leaves the car door open. When the T-rex walks toward the jeep, the door is closed. But it's open again when little Tim reaches out to close it. (01:03, 01:04)

27. Trying to get to the kids via the sunroof, the T-rex's mouth smashes the glass and the roof snaps in two. In the next shot, the roof is intact; then it's in two pieces. Then it's in one piece again. (01:05)

28. Tim and Lex switch places under the sunroof during the T-rex attack. (01:05)

29. The T-rex flips the car over. As the car rolls, it's possible to see, far in the distance, something that looks like a tree inside a pot (?) and a stage light (!). (01:06)

30. Dr. Grant holds his hand over Lex's mouth while they kneel in the mud close to the overturned car. When the T-rex spins the jeep, Grant and Lex are now crouching, but they haven't moved at all during the scene. (01:08)

31. Nedry tries to reach the dock but loses control of the jeep and slams into a big embankment that is as high as the headlights. In the following shots, the embankment is no longer in front of the car, but rather we find a waterfall. (01:10)

32. Right after this incident, Nedry spots the East Dock sign on the road below: there's an arrow pointing up at first, then (after the man's fall) left. (01:11)

33. As the car falls down the tree toward Dr. Grant and Tim, the front left headlight gets smashed—but in the following shot appears OK. (01:17)

34. Dr. Grant and the kids fall asleep on a barren tree; in the morning, there are vines and leaves all around them. Did they grow overnight? (01:22, 01:28)

35. When asked to shut down the system, Arnold flicks breakers C-3, C-2, C-1, and Main. Then he turns Main on. Surprisingly enough, C-1, C-2, and C-3 are on, too. (01:32, 01:33)

36. The gallimimus that gets eaten by the T-rex, a few seconds before meeting its maker, jumps through the T-rex's neck. (01:35)

37. Hammond says that when they opened Disneyland in 1956, nothing was working properly. Wrongo! Disneyland was opened on July 17, 1955. (01:36)

38. When she steps out to reinstall the power, Ellie puts her headphones on; but the headphones are coiled on her side in the following shots. (01:37)

39. At the fence, Dr. Grant tests whether or not there's electricity by tossing a branch against it. Wind messes up his hair. But when he grabs the wires, his hair is neatly combed. (01:40)

40. Dr. Grant pulls the kids' legs by faking his own electrocution. However, he grabs the fence between only two vertical wires. A few seconds later, he's holding a piece of fence with four vertical wires.

The "Danger 10,000 volts" sign has moved from below his face to above it. (01:40)

41. After a walk in the mud, the soles of Dr. Grant's shoes are squeaky clean as he climbs the electric fence. (01:41)

42. When the alarm lights begin to flash, Tim skids down the fence and stops—but in the close-up of the light, he is still climbing down in the background. (01:42)

43. A lightbulb seems to be burning the skin (or latex?) of the velociraptor that attacks Ellie in the power room. (01:43)

44. Muldoon spots a velociraptor hiding among the foliage. He brings up his gun; then . . . he brings up his gun again. (01:45)

45. Tim's hair is a mess after he's electrocuted; but after eating, he runs into the kitchen and his hair is perfectly combed. (01:46, 01:48)

46. Dr. Grant and Ellie push a door to prevent a velociraptor from entering the control room. The raptor sneaks its claws in the door one time, then a second time; behind them, it's possible to see the head of a man (probably the puppeteer). (01:53)

47. When the part of the dinosaur skeleton she's hanging on drops down, Lex (actually her stunt double) lets go. In the following shot, she's still hanging on to it. (01:56)

48. The T-rex has made her final entrance and is killing the first velociraptor. For some bizarre reason, the raptor vanishes from the T-rex's mouth for just one frame. (01:57)

49. On the chopper leaving the island, Hammond sits by the left window. Yet, there is a man dressed in white (same colors as Hammond's) who sits by the right window when the chopper is seen from the outside. Who's that guy? (01:58, 01:59)

50. While flying away from Isla Nublar, the helicopter heads into a breathtaking sunset. And probably on to Japan, since the island is 120 miles west of Costa Rica. Alert the pilot! (01:59)

Questions

1. Hammond states that he knows his "way around a kitchen," yet he serves champagne in tumblers. Didn't he see the champagne glasses on top of the electric oven? (00:11, 00:12)

2. Nedry is required to steal fifteen embryos from the lab. Yet, when he concludes his mission, it seems the fake shaving cream dispenser is holding only ten vials. Did they drop five species at the last moment, or . . . ? (00:14, 00:57)

3. When Dr. Grant, Ellie, and company enter the lab, everything suggests that it is a sterile room. Yet, Dr. Wu erases something from his clipboard and casually brushes the shavings on the floor. Huh? Also, while we're at it, does he or doesn't he stare right into the camera as soon as he turns his head after greeting Hammond? (00:28)

4. The cars used for touring the park are computer-controlled electric vehicles (at least this is what Hammond says). Then why do they have ignition keys and a stick shift? (00:38, 00:39)

5. As the Jurassic Park gate closes, is that an arm that appears briefly in between the doors, to secure them? (00:41)

6. When the T-rex pushes the jeep over the wall and into its pen, the jeep falls some fifty feet. Yet when the T-rex stepped out of its pen a few minutes earlier, it seemed to be stepping out from level ground. (01:04, 01:09)

7. One of the electric cars is flipped by the T-rex. So why do we see an exhaust pipe but no hook to connect the car to the electrical track that guides the cars across the park? (01:06)

8. As the jeep flees from the T-rex, we see the "OBJECTS IN THE MIRROR ARE CLOSER THAN THEY APPEAR" label in the driver's side mirror. Isn't the "objects" warning only on the passenger's side mirror? (01:20)

9. During Hammond's "roman-

tic" dinner all by himself, candles are lit everywhere because the power is out. So how come the ceiling fans are still spinning? (01:25)

10. To justify why he's having ice cream, Hammond says, "They were all melting." And why were they melting? Did someone take them out of the freezer? Later on, Tim finds a freezer with enough ice to create his own hockey rink. (01:25, 01:51)

11. As the raptors open the kitchen door, one second before Lex asks, "Timmy, what is it?" tell us: is that an arm that pops out and seems to hold down the rear part of the beast, or not? Discuss amongst yourselves. (01:49)

12. The velociraptor is inside the headquarters, and the computer projects DNA sequences on its body. Since when does a computer project what's on its screen? Or if it's a reflection, why isn't it reversed? (01:55)

13. When everyone is in the air shaft, the velociraptor lifts one of the panes and stays there until Dr. Grant kicks it in the face. It seems the raptor was standing on a table; yet when the opening to the lab is seen, there's nothing there but the floor. So . . . ? (01:55)

Fun Fact

In Michael Crichton's novel, John Hammond is proud to mention that the narrator for the tour of the park is Richard Kiley. The voice of Richard Kiley in the movie was . . . well, Richard Kiley. . . . One of the few cases in which a role in a book and a role in a movie are played by the same person. (00:41)

K

KENTUCKY FRIED MOVIE, THE (7)

1978, color, 90 min.

Director: John Landis

Cast: Mallory Sandler (Joyce the Astrologer), Jeff Maxwell (Man [Feel-A-Round]), Michael Alaimo (Usher), Joe Medalis (Paul Burmaster), Barry Dennen (Claude LaMont), Evan C. Kim (Loo), Master Bong Soo Han (Dr. Klahn), David Zucker (Various Roles), Jerry Zucker (Various Roles), Jim Abrahams (Various Roles).

[**Note:** the actors listed are only the ones in our bloopers. Too bad for the others.]

A potluck of hilarious skits.

Bloopers

1. During the astrological report, it's hard not to notice the pad underneath Joyce the Astrologer's shirt, which will "help" the arrow kill her later. (00:04)
2. The Man at the Rialto Cinema, as he's leaving the ticket booth, passes in front of a glass door: the camera and crew are reflected in the glass. (00:11)
3. Inside the theater, there are many inconsistencies between wide shots and close-ups, most noticeably the "knife" moment. (00:13, 00:14)
4. During the "High Adventure" segment, Claude Lamont and Paul Burmaster kiss; Paul knocks over a glass of water. A few seconds later, during the "heart attack" moment, the glass is up and empty. And a few seconds later, it's up and filled with water. (00:17, 00:18)
5. In "A Fistful of Yen," Loo and his men walk on the Isle of Lucy: Loo moves right to left, and when he sees an elephant, the stock footage shot travels in the wrong direction. It should have been right to left, too. (00:30)
6. During the fight with Klahn, Loo traps his four-blade metal hand and detaches it from Klahn's arm. Klahn's metal hand still has the black, circular attachment connected, but

in the close-up the attachment has vanished. (00:53)

7. The "Cast in order of appearance" during the closing credits does not match with the sequence of the movie. (01:20)

Fun Facts

1. When Loo is by the elevator, a second group of warriors charge. After the first warrior is knocked out, it's possible to hear John Landis (the director) screaming, "Go! Go! Go! Go! Go!" (00:42)

2. The gongman hits the gong the second time, and the head of his mallet flies away. This was not supposed to happen. But the filmmakers liked it and left it in the movie. (00:48)

KING KONG (4)
1933, black & white, 100 min.

Directors: Merian C. Cooper and Ernest B. Shoedsack

Cast: Fay Wray (Ann Darrow), Robert Armstrong (Carl Denham), Bruce Cabot (Jack Driscoll), Frank Reicher (Captain Englehorn), Sam Hardy (Weston), Noble Johnson (Native Chief), Steve Clemente (Witch King), James Flavin (Briggs, the Second Mate), King Kong (Himself).

Oversized gorilla is captured and shipped to New York, where it escapes, climbs the Empire State Building, and plunges to its death.

Bloopers

1. When the tribe on Skull Island spots Denham's crew, the chief points to Ann and mumbles, "Sita. Malem. Malem Ma Pakeno!" Ann hugs Jack's shoulders—but in the following shot of Captain Englehorn beside Mr. Denham, she's in the background and she's not hugging Jack at all. She will be a few seconds later, though. (00:30)

2. Kong goes berserk when Ann escapes from his hideout, and he trashes the village. The natives scatter everywhere, and one of them jumps from his hut, trips over a cage that contains a few chickens, falls back . . . and his wig gets caught on the cage and ripped off. (01:14)

3. During the presentation of Kong in NYC, Carl says that "twelve of our party met horrible death [on Skull Island]." (01:23) Close . . . Only ten of the men died on Skull Island: three were killed by the dinosaur that flipped the raft (00:51), one was killed by the same dinosaur that followed him up a tree (00:53), and six were killed by Kong while they were crossing a gorge on a log. (00:55)

4. Kong escapes from the chains that were holding him center stage. One of the wristbands is still on his right wrist—but occasionally vanishes, such as when he goes up on a roof after two fire trucks go by, or when he destroys the monorail. (01:29, 01:32, 01:34)

KING KONG (9)
1976, color, 134 min.

Director: John Guillermin

Cast: Jeff Bridges (Jack Prescott), Charles Grodin (Fred Wilson), Jessica Lange (Dwan), John Randolph (Captain Ross), Rene Auberjonois (Bagley), Julius Harris (Boan), Jack O'Halloran (Joe Perko), Dennis Fimple (Sunfish), Ed Lauter (Carnahan), Jorge Moreno (Garcia), Mario Gallo (Timmons), King Kong (Himself).

Same old, same old. Only new.

Bloopers

1. Wilson shows his crew a slide of a fog bank, then he moves to a second, more recent slide. As he talks, the slide projector advances one more slide, but the image behind Wilson doesn't change. (00:09)
2. Dwan whines that she's been promised to go on land with the first boat. As she does, Jack is facing the sea; but in the next shot he's combing his hair and checking his cam-era—now with his back to the sea. (00:26)
3. As the group reaches the barri-cade, Bagley takes off his hat and grabs his binoculars. In the following shot, he grabs his binoculars again. (00:33)
4. When they come back ashore to look for Dwan, Jack jumps off the boat: his pants are al-ready wet (Take 2, anyone?). (00:51)
5. After taking Dwan from the sacrificial altar, Kong turns twice before leaving. (00:54)
6. When Wilson falls into the footprint, his ascot alternates between being tied and loose around his neck. (00:57)
7. When he jumps from one tower of the World Trade Cen-ter to the other, Kong lands on one corner of the tower. The cables that help Kong perform this feat are visible. (02:04)
8. As he plummets from the World Trade Center, Kong sud-denly appears in midair two frames after they cut to the shot from the ground. (02:09)
9. After the plunge, Kong turns his huge head to look one last time at Dwan. He smiles, re-vealing blood all over his teeth. But as soon as he dies and the photographers run over his chest, his teeth are pearly white. (02:10)

KINGPIN (14)
also Director's Cut
1996, color, 113 min. / 117 min. (DC)

Directors: Peter Farrelly and Bobby Farrelly

Cast: Woody Harrelson (Roy Munson), Randy Quaid (Ishmael Boorg), Vanessa Angel (Claudia), Bill Murray (Ernie McCracken), Chris Elliott (The Gambler), William Jordan (Mr. Boorg), Richard Tyson (Owner of Stiffy's), Lin Shaye (Landlady), Zen Gesner (Thomas), Prudence Wright Holmes (Mrs. Boorg).

Former bowling champ fosters career of Amish bowler savant.

Bloopers

1. Roy is a great bowler in 1979. He has a golden Rhino ball. Rhinos weren't made until 1991. (00:02)
2. Following Roy's victory, Ernie sips from a Coca-Cola bottle that he slams down on a table. In the over-the-shoulder shot, he slams it down again. (00:05)
3. Roy and Ernie are setting a trap, telling their victims they're selling dictionaries. Ernie lifts a glass of beer, but in the following shot the glass is still on the counter. (00:09)
4. Frightened by a vision, Roy adjusts the rearview mirror of his car until it's crooked, then backs up to pick up Ishmael. When he backs up, the mirror is no longer crooked. (00:37 / 00:38 DC)
5. Claudia and Roy are having a dinner in which he's eating a salad and she's munching some fries. A plastic ketchup bottle stands, sealed, screen right. After a few moments, the same bottle has not only moved to the left with nobody touching it, but the lid has popped up by itself. (00:51, 00:52 / 00:52 DC)
6. Roy is flossing his teeth. When Ishmael says, "Never saw a man pick his nose with a hook before," it's possible to catch a glimpse of Roy's now-intact hand holding the hook underneath his bathrobe. (00:56 / 00:58 DC)
7. Claudia and Roy are arguing in the parking lot, and after her "knee-in-the-crotch" stunt, they circle around. Roy's nose is already bleeding, but he has yet to receive her punch. (00:59 / 01:00 DC)
8. While fighting in the parking lot of the motel, Roy is thrown to the ground. He grabs Claudia's leg to bite it. The fingers of his rubber hand flex and bend to hold the leg. (01:00 / 01:01 DC)
9. Roy and Claudia set Ishmael free from his "lap dance" job at Stiffy's. Once in the car, Ishmael (still dressed as a ballerina) has a tattoo on his upper left chest. The same tattoo he's so shocked about the morning he wakes up in Reno and—apparently—notices it for the first time. (01:06, 01:09 / 01:08, 01:12 DC)
10. During the Reno bowling tournament, Ishmael encourages Roy by showing him a white sign that says, "Go Roy." But after one close-up of Roy and one of his hallucinations, the sign says "Will Work for Food." (01:23 / 01:26 DC)
11. Roy bowls his ball and we see it approaching the pins

from behind them. The ball bowls a strike ... but instead of going into the return device, the ball bounces back and stays in the lane, apparently having hit a protective shield for the camera. (01:24 / 01:27 DC)

12. Ernie bowls the ball and is cheered on by the crowd. Evidently, nobody (neither players, audience members, directors, nor the script supervisor) noticed his left foot crossing the foul line. That roll would have been disqualified. (01:24 / 01:27 DC)

13. During a musical montage, Ernie gets closer to the crowd and to the seats where Ishmael and Roy are following the game. On the following cut, Ishmael has vanished. (01:33 / 01:36 DC)

14. Roy loses the Reno tournament and collapses in a chair. In the following shot, maybe it's possible to see the actor's real hand before he places the hook in position. You be the judge. But in the same shots, a towel definitely appears in Roy's hands seemingly from nowhere ... (01:39 / 01:42 DC)

L

LIFE LESS ORDINARY, A (1)
1997, color, 103 min.

Director: Danny Boyle

Cast: Holly Hunter (O'Reilly), Delroy Lindo (Jackson), Dan Hedaya (Gabriel), Cameron Diaz (Celine), Ewan McGregor (Robert), Ian McNeice (Mayhew), Frank Kanig (Ted), Mel Winkler (Frank), Stanley Tucci (Elliot), Anne Cullimore Decker (Ms. Gesteten), K. K. Dodds (Lily), Ian Holm (Naville).

Kidnapping, love, and the grace of God . . . lots of fun.

Blooper
As Celine and Robert prepare to drink, and also as they drink during their tequila contest, the levels of tequila in the glasses vary from different angles and in different shots. (00:44, 00:45)

Non-Blooper
O'Reilly climbs up the front of a moving pickup truck, and she's wearing her signature skirt, nylons, and boots. After Celine and Robert jump out of the truck, in a brief shot from the front, it looks as if O'Reilly is wearing pants. But it's an illusion: the slit of her skirt is aligned almost perfectly with the space between her legs. (01:02)

LIMBO (1)
1999, color, 126 min.

Director: John Sayles

Cast: Michael Laskin (Albright), Leo Burmester (Harmon King), Hermínio Ramos (Ricky), Dawn McInturff (Audrey), Vanessa Martinez (Noelle De Angelo), David Strathairn (Joe Gastineau), Tom Biss (Baines), Mary Elizabeth Mastrantonio (Donna De Angelo), Jimmy MacDonell (Randy Mason), Kathryn Grody (Frankie), Casey Siemaszko (Bobby Gastineau), Kris Kristofferson (Smilin' Jack).

Stranded in Alaska . . . isn't that redundant?

Blooper
At the beginning of the wedding

reception scene, the father of the bride is talking to Phil about themes for Alaska: "Kingdom of the Salmon, Lumberland . . ." In the background, a red-haired lady in a suit hugs a lady in a print dress . . . twice. (00:05)

LITTLE MERMAID, THE (11)
1989, color, 82 min.

Directors: John Musker and Ron Clements

Cast: Jodi Benson (Ariel), Christopher Daniel Barnes (Prince Eric), Pat Carroll (Ursula), Jason Marin (Flounder), Samuel E. Wright (Sebastian), Kenneth Mars (Triton), Buddy Hackett (Scuttle), Rene Auberjonois (Louis), Paddi Edwards (Flotsam & Jetsam), Edie McClurg (Carlotta), Will Ryan (Seahorse), Ben Wright (Grimsby).

The classic fairy tale that resurrected Disney animation.

Bloopers
1. Ariel and Flounder go "shopping" in a shipwreck. When the mermaid approaches the boat, she has no red bag under her arm. Then she has one while she's in the ship; but when Ursula checks on her, the bag is gone. (00:05, 00:06, 00:10)
2. Inside the ship, Ariel finds a fork: the utensil has four prongs when Ariel sees it for the first time, but only three when the mermaid picks it up. (00:07)
3. Sebastian makes an entrance into Ariel's private realm and he winds up with his legs stuck in a thimble—but in the over-the-shoulder shot, the thimble is gone. (00:18)
4. Ariel takes a peek at the sailors dancing on the ship. Max the dog spots her and licks her right cheek—but Ariel wipes off her left. (00:19)
5. On the ship, Grimsby quiets everyone down by saying, "Silence, silence." Then, as he continues . . . "It is now my honor . . ." the shirt of a sailor behind him turns from blue and white stripes into blue and azure stripes. (00:20)
6. Once again, an eating utensil problem: during her first dinner with Eric and Grimsby, Ariel sees a four-pronged fork (the detail), but by the time she gets it, the fork has only three prongs. (00:51)
7. Louis the cook goes after Sebastian with a mallet: Sebastian hides between the pots, but Louis's reflection is not right. He raises his right arm in the air, but in the pots' reflection he appears to be raising his left. (00:54)
8. To save his life, Sebastian tiptoes away from Grimsby's plate, passing by a few slices of lemon. But when Grimsby realizes the crab is gone . . .

the lemons are gone too. (00:54)

9. On the first night Ariel spends at the castle, she lies on top of the bed and falls asleep. When Sebastian blows out the candle, Ariel is under the sheets. (00:55, 00:56)

10. While Scuttle spies on her, Ursula (in disguise) dances and sings in front of the vanity on the ship. As she steps on the furniture, she shatters a round bottle that wasn't there before. Also, another round bottle vanishes as we return to the wide shot. (01:06)

11. Ariel, barefoot, jumps into the sea to reach Prince Eric's ship. The former mermaid, barefoot, jumps on the ship and, after a small disturbance, regains her voice. When she speaks her first words again, she's wearing black shoes. (01:07, 01:09)

Fun Facts

1. When King Triton arrives at the arena, after the extreme close-up of the trident, it is possible to briefly spot Goofy, Donald Duck, and Mickey Mouse in the crowd of sea-people. (00:03).

2. The diminutive minister who's about to perform the marriage between Prince Eric and Ursula appears to have an erection. Those naughty, naughty Disney animators! (01:08)

LOVE BUG, THE (10)

1969, color, 107 min.

Director: Robert Stevenson

Cast: Dean Jones (Jim Douglas), Michele Lee (Carole Bennett), David Tomlinson (Peter Thorndyke), Buddy Hackett (Tennessee Steinmetz), Joe Flynn (Haversham), Benson Fong (Mr. Wu), Andy Granatelli (Association President), Joe E. Ross (Detective), Iris Adrian (Carhop), Herbie (Himself).

Race car driver and small VW Beetle with a heart form a winning team.

Bloopers

1. Just after purchasing Herbie, Jim takes him out for a spin and turns from an arterial on to a two-lane street. A sign on the street on to which Jim turns says, "Left lane must turn left," meaning that Jim has just started traveling the wrong way on a one-way street. (00:12)

2. As Herbie reaches Seabreeze Point, it can be seen how the film was cranked to make Herbie stop suddenly: the heads of the actors in the car are bobbing very rapidly. (00:19)

3. A police officer stops Jim and Carole (and Herbie) while they're walking at Seabreeze Point. The officer then turns to find his car in the lake "head first." But

when we saw his car parked, it was parallel to the lake; so it would have been impossible for it to end up in the water this way. (00:21, 00:22)

4. Herbie's license plate vanishes halfway through the picture, only to reappear later on. (00:28, 01:02)

5. Thorndyke and Jim are ready to start the third race at Riverside. They signal the starter and we see behind Thorndyke a purple car to screen left and a dark red car with black tape on the headlights to the right, as well as a group of some five people behind Jim. Later on, the two drivers are ready to start the Monterey Grand Prix. Behind Thorndyke are the same two cars, and behind Douglas are the same five people! (00:33, 00:36)

6. As the Big Road Race starts, there's mayhem among the cars. Herbie drives by in the background and his right door looks completely smashed in. A few seconds later, the door is as good as new. (00:38)

7. Just after destroying Thorndyke's window, Herbie vanishes around a corner in San Francisco. Watch the car's roof: the matte painting will "cut" it away because Herbie is too tall for the painting. (01:04)

8. As the judges follow the race on a map, we see a woman placing a model of Herbie

and one of Thorndyke's cars on the red road between "Chinese Camp" and "El Dorado." As we cut away, not only have the cars changed positions, but the map looks slightly different from the one we just saw in the detail. (01:18)

9. Thorndyke bumps into Herbie, knocking one of the VW's wheels off. Herbie spins on the street, smashes a small fence, and ends up hanging on for his life on the edge of a cliff with the trunk open. In the following cut, before anybody can do anything, the trunk appears to be closed. (01:25)

10. As Herbie snaps in two and Tennessee is overtaking Thorndyke, a close-up of Tennessee shows his eyes wide open with fear, his arms close to his body. But in the long shot, he (actually, his stunt double) looks much more relaxed and he's holding onto the sides of the car. (01:44)

LOVE LETTER, THE (9)
1999, color, 88 min.

Director: Peter Ho-Sun Chan

Cast: Kate Capshaw (Helen MacFarquhar), Blythe Danner (Lillian MacFarquhar), Ellen DeGeneres (Janet Frank), Geraldine McEwan (Mrs. Constance Scattergoods), Julianne Nicholson (Jennifer

McNeely), Tom Everett Scott (Johnny Howell), Tom Selleck (George Mathias), Gloria Stuart (Eleanor MacFarquhar), Bill Buell (Officer Dan), Alice Drummond (Postal Clerk), Lucas Hall (Garbage Man), Christian Harmony (Garbage Man), Christopher Nee (Garbage Man).

A small-town love story of affectionate misunderstandings.

Bloopers

1. A postal clerk asks Johnny to place his finger on a map, over Prague. Johnny moves his left arm but places his right finger on the map. (00:02)
2. In her daydream, Helen sees a few garbage men simultaneously reciting part of the letter she found a few moments earlier. Too bad the part they say ("When I'm close to you, I feel your hair brush my cheek when it does not. I look away from you sometimes, then I look back. When I tie my shoes, when I peel an orange, when I drive my car . . .") wasn't said aloud by Helen when she had the letter (she zapped from " . . . unless they're thoughts of you. When I peel an orange . . ."). Maybe she was using the Cliffs Notes. (00:11, 00:13)
3. The first time Helen reads the letter (00:11) it says, "Dearest, do you know how in love with you I am?" Still, when Johnny repeats it in Helen's dream

(00:14), as well as when Johnny reads it for the first time (00:19), when Janet reads it (00:34), when Mrs. Scattergoods reads it (01:23), and when we see it for the second time (01:24), the letter says "do you know how MUCH in love with you I am?"

4. Johnny juggles three oranges, then puts two down and begins to peel one. The two oranges change positions on the fruit plate, while in the close-up, the orange is much more peeled than it is in the master shot. (00:20)
5. Johnny tears off most of his clothes and jumps off a dock into the water. What he's wearing when he jumps are his boxers and, for some strange reason, his socks. Thankfully, when he pulls himself out of the water the socks are missing (otherwise he'd be squishing around while he walks). (00:29, 00:30)
6. Helen doesn't stop at an intersection and gets pulled over by Officer Dan. She leans against the door, placing her left elbow by the rolled-down window—but only when the camera is on her. The view of Officer Dan shows that the window has no elbow on it. (00:35)
7. During a lobster dinner, Jennifer places a large bib around Johnny's neck. He then leans forward to kiss her, and she retracts her hands—but in the next close-up, her hands are

once again around Johnny's neck. (00:42)

8. During an almost romantic dinner after the opera, George proposes a toast, "To Tosca. He died for love." But Tosca was a she. If there's any doubt, just check the DVD subtitles. (00:52)

9. While she's discussing a Bicentennial trip to New York and postcards, Helen's wine glass appears and vanishes depending on whether the shot favors her or is over-the-shoulder. (00:53)

M

MARS ATTACKS! (13)
1996, color, 106 min.

Director: Tim Burton

Cast: Jack Nicholson (President Dale / Art Land), Annette Bening (Barbara Land), Pierce Brosnan (Donald Kessler), Martin Short (Jerry Ross), Sarah Jessica Parker (Natalie Lake), Michael J. Fox (Jason Stone), Rod Steiger (General Decker), Lukas Haas (Richie Norris), Jim Brown (Byron Williams), Lisa Marie (Martian Girl), Sylvia Sidney (Grandma Norris), Pam Grier (Louise Williams), Ray J (Cedric), Brandon Hammond (Neville), O-Lan Jones (Sue Ann Norris).

Little martians with big heads come to Earth to kick a little tail.

Bloopers

1. Art places a cigarette in his mouth to reach in his pocket and give Barbara some coins. However, in the following cut, the cigarette has flown into Art's left hand. (00:09)

2. When Jason passes the cell phone to his wife, Natalie, they yell at the dog, so it lays its head on the table. As they keep talking, the dog's head is mostly up, but when they mention the dog again its head is lying on the table, ready to pop up. (00:13)

3. As Richie reaches his home, a superimposed line tells us it's Perkinsville, Kansas, and it's Thursday, May 11. Once inside the trailer, he asks if anybody wants some donuts, "fresh baked Monday." His mom replies, "Monday?! That's six days ago!" No. It's four. (00:14)

4. While driving her bus, Louise passes by her two sons playing in a video arcade. With the bus still moving, she tells her passengers, "Excuse me, folks, but we got to make an unscheduled stop!" Finally, she hits the brakes . . . and the bus stops right in front of the video arcade it already passed. (00:15)

5. While Natalie is interviewing Donald, her dog lies on one

side of her chair. In one cut right before the Martians' interference, the dog has jumped onto Natalie's lap. (00:19)

6. The "Today in Fashion" van is knocked down by one explosion caused by the Martians, and Natalie and her cameraman fall from the van. As Jason runs for her, the van is back up on its four wheels. (00:41)

7. General Decker hands President Dale a red clipboard with a paper to sign. On his side, Decker holds the clipboard with the plastic up and the paper down; on the president's side, the clipboard is upside down. (00:55)

8. Jerry flips JFK's head in a bust to reveal a red button. Jerry presses it and a door slides open. He moves to the door, leaving the head flipped. Later, when the Alien Woman passes by the same bust, the head has reset itself. (01:01, 01:04)

9. The Martians break into the White House and blast away almost everything. The first alien that gets shot in the helmet collapses to the ground on its knees, suffocating. One minute later, another alien gets shot by the two kids, and it collapses, too. The animation of the two aliens is exactly the same, reversed. (01:09, 01:10)

10. While trying to reach Byron, Barbara bumps into the same extra twice—a woman dressed in silver with blue earrings. (01:13)

11. When the Martians enter the room where the president is at his desk, the aliens shoot around and knock Africa and Australia from the world map on the wall. When one of the president's bodyguards gets vaporized, Australia is back on the wall. (01:27)

12. President Dale straightens his tie while talking with three Martians, but after a few shots (as he says "... or we can smash it all!") the knot is loose, then straightened again. (01:28)

13. The mariachi band has their trumpets down, but in the background of Grandma's close-up, the trumpets are up. (01:37)

Question
The Martians show Natalie's detached head what they've done to her dog. Natalie's head is underwater in a jar, and as she sees the result, she screams, causing air bubbles to rise from her mouth. If she's just a head, her lungs are gone, so where do the bubbles come from? (00:48)

MARY POPPINS (9)
1964, color, 139 min.

Director: Robert Stevenson

Cast: Julie Andrews (Mary Poppins), Dick Van Dyke (Bert /

Mr. Dawes Sr.), David Tomlinson (George W. Banks Esquire), Glynis Johns (Winifred Banks), Hermione Baddeley (The Domestic— Ellen), Reta Shaw (The Domestic), Karen Dotrice (Jane Banks), Matthew Garber (Michael Banks), Elsa Lanchester (Katy Nanna), Arthur Treacher (Constable Jones), Reginald Owen (Admiral Bloom), Ed Wynn (Uncle Albert).

The perfect nanny is not of this Earth—but she sure can sing!

Bloopers

1. Bert performs his one-man-band show, the silver trumpet is lowered away from his mouth, but as he finishes . . . he lowers the trumpet again. (00:03)

2. Saying that "what he's famous for is punctuality," Bert introduces us to Admiral Bloom, late of His Majesty's Navy, who's standing on the roof of his house, ready to announce with his cannon that it's eight o'clock. He checks on his watch and declares that it's 3 minutes and 6 seconds to the hour. But he fires the cannon after 5 minutes. Talk about punctuality . . . (00:06, 00:11)

3. George tears a letter into eight pieces, and throws the pieces into the fireplace. The pieces take off up the chimney, but when they get out, there are many, many more pieces. (00:21)

4. When Mary reads the letter made out of eight ripped pieces, she holds it with a white-gloved hand. But the detail shows a gray glove. (00:24, 00:25)

5. Mary, Bert, and the kids jump into Bert's drawings and come out when the rain erases them. When they get out, Bert has his hat on his head—but when he entered the drawings, his hat was left on the sidewalk, with a couple of coins in it. (00:38, 00:41, 00:59)

6. Mary, Bert, and the kids (in the

cartoon world) race on four merry-go-round horses. The poles of the horses leave a trace on the ground only every now and again and not always, like they should—for instance, when they go over the bridge. (00:52)

7. While singing "Supercalifragilisticexpialidocious" at the end of the horse race, Mary and Bert say, "You summon up this word and then you've got a lot to say," then they move to the right. The cartoon background moves before they do. (00:58)

8. When they decide to go exploring the roofs of London, Mary powders her nose black. After a few seconds, her nose is clean again. (01:44, 01:45)

9. Michael is out, flying a kite. His father places both hands on his shoulders—but in the following wide shot, only one hand is on the kid's shoulders. (02:15)

MASK, THE (9)
1994, color, 97 min.

Director: Charles Russell

Cast: Jim Carrey (Stanley Ipkiss /The Mask), Peter Riegert (Lieutenant Mitch Kellaway), Peter Greene (Dorian Tyrrell), Amy Yasbeck (Peggy Brandt), Richard Jeni (Charlie Schumaker), Orestes Matacena (Niko), Tim Bagley (Irv), Nancy Fish (Mrs. Peenman), Johnny Williams (Burt), Reg E. Cathey (Freeze), Jim Doughan (Doyle), Cameron Diaz (Tina Carlyle).

Magical mask transforms a normal guy into a zoot-suited maniac.

Bloopers

1. When the scuba diver spots the mask box underwater, the detail reveals only one corner of the box emerging out of a few rocks—but in the following shot, one whole side of the box is free from the rocks. (00:00)

2. Charlie spots Tina as she enters the bank, so he says to Stanley, "Killer at three o'clock." But they both look in front of them—which would be twelve o'clock. (00:03)

3. Tina and Stanley are discussing his tie; after the discussion ends, it suddenly flips over Stanley's shoulder. (00:06)

4. Outside of Ripley Auto Finishing, Peggy introduces herself as a reporter from the *Evening Star*. But when she meets Stanley for the first time, she says she's from the *Tribune*. (00:26, 00:28)

5. While talking to Peggy, Stanley asks if she is the writer of "Ask Peggy." She says yes, but a few seconds later she says that her column, "'*Dear* Peggy' pays d*ck." (00:29)

6. When in jail, Stanley places three strips of toilet paper on the seat, but after he gets Milo the dog, the paper has vanished. (01:03)

7. The evil Mask (Dorian) crashes Niko's party at the Coco Bongo. Niko hides behind a table and fires at the intruder.

His gun flashes every time a bullet leaves the barrel . . . but more than once we hear a bang without a flash ("bang, bang, bang"—only the first bang has a flash). (01:21)

8. Tina kicks the mask from Dorian's hand. The mask flies away, rotating clockwise in the air. While everyone is running for it in slow motion, the mask is rotating counterclockwise, and when Milo the dog grabs it, the mask is rotating clockwise again. (01:26)

9. When Milo jumps and grabs the mask, he grabs the mask by its chin. When Milo lands, he's holding the mask by its forehead. (01:26)

DVD Bloopers

1. Mr. Dickey, in the back, says to Stanley, "You're 40 minutes late." The subtitle says, "50 minutes." (00:26)

2. Checking the mask, Dr. Neuman says, "This is an interesting piece." The subtitle says, "This is an interesting place." (00:52)

MATRIX, THE (25)
1999, color, 136 min.

Directors: Andy and Larry Wachowski

Cast: Keanu Reeves (Neo / Thomas A. Anderson), Lawrence Fishburne (Morpheus), Carrie-Anne Moss (Trinity), Hugo Weaving (Agent Smith), Joe Pantoliano (Cypher Reagan), Gloria Foster (Oracle), Marcus Chong (Tank), Julian Arahanga (Apoc), Matt Doran (Mouse), Belinda McClory

---

FRONT & BACK

What happens in front sometimes changes from another perspective.

Jim Carrey and a book in *Ace Ventura: Pet Detective*	Blooper No. 5
Jack Nicholson's glasses in *As Good As It Gets*	Blooper No. 1
A picture of Michael Keaton in *Batman*	Blooper No. 6
Humphrey Bogart in *Casablanca*	Blooper No. 5
Sean Connery's cigarette in *Dr. No*	Blooper No. 3
Sigourney Weaver's legs in *Galaxy Quest*	Blooper No. 5
A hanging picture in *Happy Gilmore*	Blooper No. 3
Kate Capshaw's arm in *The Love Letter*	Blooper No. 6
Keanu Reeve's hand in *The Matrix*	Blooper No. 5
Keven Costner's hand in *Robin Hood: Prince of Thieves*	Blooper No. 4
Arnold Schwarzenegger in *Terminator 2*	Blooper No. 5
A landing plane in *The Usual Suspects*	Blooper No. 6
Judy Garland in *The Wizard of Oz*	Blooper No. 9

(Switch), Anthony Ray Parker (Dozer), Paul Goddard (Agent Brown).

Mind-boggling, eye-popping adventure about a "real" reality of which Keanu is aware.

Bloopers

1. Police officers are chasing Trinity on the rooftops, and they all jump the short gap between two buildings. One of the officers doesn't quite make the jump and he hits the brick wall with his legs. The wall wobbles. (00:04)

2. Trinity escapes by crashing through a window and rolling down a flight of stairs. When she shatters the glass, the lamp fixture above the window barely moves. When she stops rolling and aims at the window, the lamp swings noticeably. Then (even if the lamp's squeaking is still audible), the shadow and the light by the window are still once again. (00:05)

3. Neo sleeps in front of his computer, the images reflected on his face. Computers don't project images . . . must be a "glitch" in the matrix . . . (00:06)

4. The building where Neo works is called Metacortex; but when he ducks into an empty cubicle and then runs to the office at the end of the hall, a green banner in the background says, "Meta Cortechs." (00:12, 00:14, 00:15)

5. When Mr. Rhineheart is lecturing Neo about his attitude, Neo's arms are crossed in front of him when Rhineheart's in the shot, and behind him when he's in the shot. (00:12)

6. Neo receives a FedEx envelope. He begins to open it, the courier leaves, and he begins to open it again. (00:13)

7. When Neo takes the cell phone out of the FedEx package, the envelope rotates in his hands: first the logo faces the camera, then, as he tosses it on his desk, the logo faces up again (a little product placement, maybe?). (00:13)

8. When he's outside the Metacortex building, Neo looks down: a road perpendicular to the avenue below him looks empty. When Neo drops his cell phone, the road is crowded with what seems to be a parade, then it's empty again. (00:16)

9. Agent Smith opens a green file in front of Neo. He lifts half a page; yet, in the following shot there are a lot of pages flipped onto the back cover—and he hasn't been leafing through it. (00:17)

10. Underneath the Adams Street bridge, a limo arrives to pick up Neo. The rear door is opened by Trinity twice. (00:22)

11. Neo meets Morpheus for the first time; they both stretch hands to shake. Morpheus' left hand is folded behind his back when the shot is from

behind but is to his side when the shot is in front. (00:25)

12. While on a stretcher, Neo is covered with acupuncture needles, including a few in his face. But in the close-up, the needles on his face vanish. (00:35)

13. Morpheus tells Neo that "The Matrix is a computer-generated dream world . . ." with the purpose of turning humans into batteries. Neo leans on an easy chair—yet in Morpheus' mirrored sunglasses, he's reflected as standing up straight. (00:43)

14. Fighting in the virtual gym created by the sparring program, Morpheus jumps high in the air and lands hard on Neo—missing him. As a result, the floor is dented. But a few seconds later, instead of a dent, there's something that looks like a hole in the floor. (00:50, 00:51)

15. The piece of steak Cypher cuts at the restaurant changes shape and color just before he eats it. (01:03)

16. On the way to the Oracle in the car, Neo's sideburns suddenly grow longer, then change shape even more when the car stops. (01:08)

17. The camera lens is reflected in the quick shot of the doorknob at the entrance to the Oracle's apartment. (01:10)

18. When reflected in the doorknob, Morpheus is still wearing his glasses; in the following shot, he already has them in his hand. (01:10)

19. In the bathroom, Morpheus stops Agent Smith by head-butting him: Smith's shades fly away, but they're still on when the Agent grabs Morpheus's throat. (01:23)

20. Still during the fight, Smith punches a hole in a brick wall. The hole vanishes a few seconds later when Smith pulls Morpheus to the ground. (01:24)

21. While interrogating Morpheus, Agent Smith holds the poor man's head, his hands over Morpheus's ears. From the front, Smith's fingers are over the right ear, from the back they're not. (01:40)

22. Neo and Trinity enter the building where Morpheus is kept and raise hell. A guard backs behind a column, radioing for backup. The guard is wearing kneepads under his pants. (01:41)

23. The lobby attack leaves almost every column destroyed, riddled with bullets. Yet, when the bomb explodes in the elevator and flames erupt into the same lobby, it seems the columns have somehow been restored. (01:44, 01:45)

24. On the roof of the building where Morpheus is kept, Neo and Trinity are under attack by a half dozen soldiers. They kill them all and the soldiers' bodies lie on the ground. But when Neo dodges the bullets a few seconds later, it seems that all the bodies

have been removed. (01:45, 01:46)

25. Just before the train in the subway arrives, Neo back-flips on the platform. His hands briefly hold on to the cables, which allow him to perform this jump, and the actual cables become visible very briefly as Neo lands. (01:58)

Questions

1. When a phone call gets intercepted, the computer monitor displays, "2-19-98." But when Morpheus talks to Neo in the real world, he says, "You believe it's the year 1999." So . . . what year is this? (00:00, 00:37)

2. Tank tries to locate a structural drawing of a building, to guide his friends who are in a trap. As he displays the drawing, "Eleventh Floor" is written on the corner of the map. Agent Smith, who was tracing the call, communicates to his team, "Eighth floor." Where are they really? (01:20)

3. Morpheus is chained to a chair. He seems helpless—but when Neo cleans up the room, it seems that Morpheus has no problem ripping off the chain. Was the drug they gave him spinach? (01:32, 01:49)

4. During the battle in the lobby, Trinity runs over a wall: the marble tiles wobble and move as she runs over them. Were the tiles not well fixed? (01:42)

5. Neo fires several shots at

Agent Brown, who dodges every single bullet. Shouldn't the window of the building behind the agent have been shattered by the flying bullets? (01:46)

6. While on a chopper, Neo gets close to a window and unloads a massive number of bullets, destroying all the glass in sight, not to mention furniture and people. But Morpheus is completely unharmed. How?? (01:47)

MISERY (8)
1990, color, 107 min.

Director: Rob Reiner

Cast: James Caan (Paul Sheldon), Kathy Bates (Annie Wilkes), Richard Farnsworth (J.T. "Buster" McCain, Elridge County Sheriff), Frances Sternhagen (Deputy Virginia McCain), Lauren Bacall (Marcia Sindell, Paul Sheldon's Publicist), Graham Jarvis (Libby, Manager of Silver Creek Lodge), Jerry Potter (Pete), Thomas Brunelle (Anchorman), June Christopher (Anchorwoman).

Fan of a novelist collects all his books, all his articles . . . what the heck—even the novelist himself.

Bloopers

1. The snow begins to fall; Paul turns the windshield wipers on, but they are faster in his

close-up than in the long shot of the car passing by. (00:03)

2. The note the sheriff places on the board behind him moves from one shot to another. (00:12)

3. The snow under the sheriff's jeep melts in one second—the car stops over a white area, but in the following shot Annie drives by and the asphalt underneath the jeep is wet but clear. (00:20, 00:21)

4. Annie burns Paul's manuscript; one page, on fire, lands on the curtain rod; nobody does anything, yet the curtain doesn't catch fire. (00:37)

5. When Paul is having dinner in bed, the detail shows the painkillers closer to the plate, even if in the long shot they are quite far from it—on the tray. (00:40)

6. A long shot of Annie's house shows her car in the driveway. Yet, in the following shot, Paul is hit by the lights of her car, which is arriving. Huh? (01:18)

7. When the Sheriff reaches Annie's house, Paul (who had two casts on his legs) turns in the wheelchair and the casts are gone. (01:25, 01:27)

8. Annie sets a tray with a cigarette to the right side of the screen, a bottle of champagne in the middle, and a glass to the left. She picks the tray up, but as she enters Paul's room, the glass has moved to the right side of the screen. (01:38)

Question
Lauren says that James has published eight *Misery* novels. Yet, when Paul enters Annie's living room, she has nine *Misery* books. Oops . . . (00:50)

MISSION: IMPOSSIBLE (6)
1996, color, 110 min.

Director: Brian De Palma

Cast: Tom Cruise (Ethan Hunt), Jon Voight (Jim Phelps), Emmanuelle Béart (Claire Phelps), Henry Czerny (Eugene Kittridge), Jean Reno (Franz Krieger), Ving Rhames (Luther Stickell), Kristin Scott Thomas (Sarah Davies), Vanessa Redgrave (Max), Dale Dye (Frank Barnes), Marcel Iures (Alexander Golitsyn), Ion Caramitru (Zozimov), Ingeborga Dapkunaite (Hannah Williams).

It's easier to learn a new language than to figure out the story of this movie.

Bloopers

1. Ethan checks Job 3:14 "who built for themselves places" but he types on the keyboard "who built for themselves palaces." (00:35, 00:36)

2. max@job 3:14" is not a proper e-mail address. (00:36)

3. Claire leaves her yellow firefighter's uniform in the closet in the Langley building and doesn't have it as she leaves the building (disguised as one

of the victims). But she's wearing it as the team drives away. (00:56, 01:11)

4. When copying the NOC list, Ethan is holding a disk in his mouth. He "bites" it by the corner but after one cut he's holding it by one side. (01:10)

5. Ethan climbs on top of the train and the wind blows in his face. The way the train is going, the wind should be against his back. When he flips to turn around, the wind is still blowing in his face. (01:38)

6. The TGV goes through the Channel Tunnel. The TGV never goes into that tunnel: only EuroStar and other trains that take cars do. (01:40)

Question
Ethan sends some e-mails to Max. At first, Max's address is "max@job 3:14," and then later it's "max@job 3:15." Huh? (00:36, 01:12)

MUMMY, THE (9)
1999, color, 124 min.

Director: Steven Sommers

Cast: Brendan Fraser (Rick O'Connell), Rachel Weisz (Evelyn "Evie" Carnahan), John Hannah (Jonathan Carnahan), Arnold Vosloo (Imhotep, High Priest of Osiris), Kevin J. O'Connor (Beni), Jonathan Hyde (The Egyptologist), Oded Fehr (Ardeth Bey), Erick Avari (The Curator), Stephen Dunham (Mr. Henderson), Corey Johnson (Mr. Daniels), Ohid Djalili (Warden).

Indiana Jones *and* George of the Jungle *meet* The Mummy.

Bloopers
1. Rick tries to stop an army of Tuaregs who are charging his post. As he tosses away his rifle and grabs the two guns he has in his belt, the shadow on the ground changes directions many, many times—in almost every cut. (00:09)

2. Before being hanged, Rick kisses Evie—then he's attacked by two guards. The chain that theoretically is doubling as handcuffs snaps after the first hit, prompting one of the guards to immobilize Rick by twisting his arm behind his back. Good thing they don't make chains like they used to, eh? (00:21)

3. While Rick is hanging, he's suspended a few feet from the ground. The tight knot of the rope moves to the left, to the right, then to the left of his neck. (00:22)

4. When inside the lost city of Hamunaptra, Rick faces a group of Americans whose guide is Rick's old friend Beni, who says, "Your odds are not so great, O'Connell." Rick crosses his arms to point one gun at Beni. In the following shot, Rick's arms are not crossed anymore, without him moving them. (00:43)

5. While wandering in the temple, greedy Warden spots a wall filled with blue-gold scarabs and begins to remove them. Warden takes one close to the collar of the figure engraved on the wall, pockets it, and then howls. The scarab he removed is back in place, and Warden gets ready to remove it . . . again. (00:44)

6. To escape from the Mummy, Rick flies on Winston Havelock's plane, with his two partners tied to the wings: Jonathan, dressed in white, on the left wing and Ardeth Bay, black-clothed, on the right wing. For one shot, the two switch positions—and the number on the plane, which reads "B5539," appears to be mirrored. (01:30, 01:32)

7. The crashed plane sinks into the ground. The likelihood of finding quicksand in the desert is next to nil. (01:35)

8. Jonathan gets one of the scarabs underneath his skin. To save him, Rick rips open Jonathan's shirt (a very loud rip is heard) and pierces the poor man's skin with a knife to remove the animal. After a few seconds, Rick, Ardeth Bay, and Jonathan step into a new room: Jonathan has a bandage on his hand, but the shirt looks fine: no rips, no blood stain, nothing. (01:37, 01:38)

9. In trying to stop an army of mummified priests, Ardeth Bay uses a machine gun he borrowed from Havelock's plane. As the heroes back up into a new room, Rick gives Ardeth his shotgun. The machine gun has vanished (yeah, yeah, he could have dropped it. But still . . .). (01:40)

Questions

1. In the library, Evie is in a predicament while balancing on a stepladder. She drops a book, which lands off-screen with a loud "plap!"—but which is out of sight when we see the floor in a wide shot or even from above. Where did the book go? (00:22)

2. While lecturing her workmates, Evie states that, "It's written that if a victim of the Hom-Dai should ever arise, he would bring with him the ten plagues of Egypt" (00:58). Well, Imhotep arises and brings with him the locusts (01:00), the water turned into blood (01:11), the fire from the sky (01:12), darkness (01:15), the flies (01:19), and boils and sores, turning everyone into slaves (01:22). That's six plagues. What happened to the other four?

3. The Mummy "borrows" the eyes of Burns, a treasure hunter who needs glasses to see. Doesn't this affect the Mummy's sight at all? (01:03)

N

NAKED GUN, THE: FROM THE FILES OF POLICE SQUAD! (6)
1988, color, 84 min.

Director: David Zucker

Cast: Leslie Nielsen (Lieutenant Frank Drebin), Priscilla Presley (Jane Spencer), Ricardo Montalban (Vincent Ludwig), George Kennedy (Captain Ed Hocken), O. J. Simpson (Nordberg), Susan Beaublan (Mrs. Nordberg), Nancy Marchand (Mayor), Raye Birk (Papshmir), Jeannette Charles (Queen Elizabeth II), David Katz (Arafat), Charles Gherard (Khomeini), David Lloyd Austin (Gorbachev), Nicholas Worth (Thug No. 1), Ronald G. Joseph (Thug No. 2).

Bumbling cop becomes a hero . . . and yes, it's just a movie.

Bloopers
1. During a dramatic meeting, Lieutenant Drebin (in disguise) stands between Arafat and Gorbachev. Khomeini slams his hands on the table saying, "Gentlemen! This is getting us nowhere!" and Drebin appears behind Khomeini, in the background—but then zaps back between Arafat and Gorbachev. (00:01)
2. When the police car enters the house (after the car wash), it's possible to see the shadow of the camera crane on the door frame of the house in the bottom right corner. (00:04)
3. Nordberg kicks the door on the ship *I Luv U* and his right leg gets stuck in the door—from the outside. From the inside it's the left leg. (00:06)
4. After sending a fisherman into the harbor, Drebin and Ed step out of the car; Ed puts his hat on twice. (00:16)
5. While dining by the fireplace, Drebin shows Jane a picture. He's holding it by the bottom left corner if she is in-frame; or holding it by the top left corner if he is in-frame. (00:38)
6. At Ludwig's Stockyard, Drebin and a thug exchange fire. Just before the thug's gun runs out

of ammo, Drebin holds his gun with his left hand, while the right hand is on his nose. The thug's gun goes click, and Drebin's hands are switched: gun in right, left on nose—and they switch back again in the following close-up. (00:52)

Fun Fact
After Drebin fires one of his cufflinks at Ludwig, Drebin's chest protector suddenly appears to be all wrinkled for no particular reason. (01:17)

DVD Blooper
Jane removes her dress and appears to be naked. However, it's possible to catch a glimpse of the tube top Priscilla was wearing for the frontal shot. (00:40)

NAKED GUN 2½: THE SMELL OF FEAR (3)
1991, color, 85 min.

Director: David Zucker

Cast: Leslie Nielsen (Lieutenant Frank Drebin), Priscilla Presley (Jane Spencer), George Kennedy (Captain Ed Hocken), O. J. Simpson (Nordberg), Robert Goulet (Quentin Hapsburg), Richard Griffiths (Dr. Meinheimer / Earl Hacher), Jacqueline Brookes (Commissioner Brumfield), Anthony James (Hector Savage), Lloyd Bochner (Baggett), Tim O'Connor (Fenswick), Peter Mark Richman (Dunwell), Ed Williams (Ted Olsen).

Bumbling cop becomes a hero again . . . and yes, it's still just a movie.

Bloopers
1. In the Blue Note pub, hanging on the walls are a few "disaster" pictures: the San Francisco Quake, the *Hindenburg*, the *Titanic,* and Michael Dukakis. A few shots later, the *Titanic* and the *Hindenburg* have been replaced for no reason by the Edsel car and by the Hubble Telescope. (00:17, 00:18)
2. When he spots Savage running out of the sex shop, Ed pulls the curtain down with one finger in the main shot but with two in the detail. (00:30)
3. Drebin hands a yearbook page that is folded in half to Hapsburg: the three pictures on the folded half away from the villain are undeniably of three men (all wearing jacket and tie). However, when Hapsburg flips the page open, the picture in the middle is now of a woman. (00:38)

Question
Trying to stop the bomb, Drebin has his jacket literally sucked into the gears. Yet, when the president thanks him, the same jacket is back, nicely ironed. Does he carry a spare with him? (01:16, 01:17)

Fun Fact
When Drebin fires a harpoon to climb to the roof of a warehouse at the harbor, he misses the target the first time and the harpoon

bounces back. It wasn't meant to happen: it's an outtake that was decided to be left in the movie. (00:55)

NAKED GUN 33⅓: THE FINAL INSULT (6)
1994, color, 82 min.

Director: Peter Segal

Cast: Leslie Nielsen (Lieutenant Frank Drebin), Priscilla Presley (Jane Spencer Drebin), George Kennedy (Captain Ed Hocken), O. J. Simpson (Nordberg), Fred Ward (Rocco Dillon), Kathleen Freeman (Muriel Dillon), Anna Nicole Smith (Tanya Peters), Ellen Greene (Louise), Ed Williams (Ted), Raye Birk (Papshmir), Charlotte Zucker (Nurse).

Retired bumbling cop becomes a hero yet once again . . . you know where we're going here.

Bloopers
1. When Drebin gets his number from the nurse at the clinic, the ticket turns 180° in his hands. (00:19)
2. In a phone booth, Jane reads Tanya's address written on a handkerchief: in the detail, her left index finger is over the hankie; in the main shot it's underneath it. (00:42)
3. During Oscar night, Elliot Gould and Mariel Hemingway announce four of the five nominees for Best Supporting

Actress. They are: Mary Lou Retton, Morgan Fairchild, Shannon Doherty, and Florence Henderson. Unfortunately, Oscar nominees are always announced alphabetically. (00:55, 00:56)
4. The police cars arrive at the Oscars, trapping Ed and Nordberg in their car. Ed opens his door twice—once in the main shot, once in the close-up. (01:05)
5. On the stage, it's possible to see Rocco and Drebin fighting for the gun while Muriel holds the cops at gunpoint. Rocco switches the gun from his right hand to his left. The exact same gag is immediately repeated in the next shot. (01:10)
6. Drebin trades Rocco's gun for a bomb in an envelope. During the switch, the flap of the envelope is alternately open and closed, depending on whether Drebin is in the shot or Rocco is. (01:11)

Fun Fact
The siren during the credits changes more than once, most noticeably during the transition between the *Star Wars* segment and the *Jurassic Park* segment. (00:06)

NATIONAL LAMPOON'S ANIMAL HOUSE (11)
1978, color, 109 min.

Director: John Landis

Cast: John Belushi (John "Bluto" Blutarsky), Tim Matheson (Eric

"Otter" Stratton), John Vernon (Dean Vernon Wormer), Verna Bloom (Marion Wormer), Tom Hulce (Larry "Pinto" Kroger), Cesare Danova (Mayor Carmine De Pasto), Peter Riegert (Donald "Boon" Schoenstein), Mary Louise Weller (Mandy Pepperidge), Stephen Furst (Kent "Flounder" Dorfman), Karen Allen (Katy), James Widdoes (Robert Hoover), Sarah Holcomb (Clorette De Pasto), Lisa Baur (Shelly Dubinsky), Kevin Bacon (Chip Diller), Donald Sutherland (Professor Dave Jennings).

Greeks push the envelope with their riotous high jinks.

Bloopers

1. The movie takes place in 1962. The Kingsmen's "Louie, Louie" is heard at the first party—but their version of the song wasn't recorded until 1963. (00:00, 00:05, 00:15)
2. Professor Jennings writes "Satan" on the blackboard, and the word changes shape from one shot to the other. (00:17)
3. Boon and Otter play golf near the training field. Boon passes the golf bag to Otter and grabs a club. But after one shot (where Neidermeyer screams "You're a goddamn disgrace!"), the bag is back on Boon's shoulder—and the club is back in it. (00:20)
4. In order to smoke some pot, Professor Jennings locks his door, sliding a bolt and a chain with his right hand in the detail, but with his left hand in the wide shot. (00:23)
5. As Bluto fills his tray at the school cafeteria, he passes by the burger area, moves on, reaches the dessert area (where he gulps a Jell-o), keeps moving, and concludes his tour by eating ... a burger. (00:32, 00:33)
6. Bluto places an unbelievable amount of food on his tray, including a few bananas. The bananas are placed on the corner closest to the camera—but in the detail, they've slipped to the opposite corner. They'll come back to their original position a couple of seconds later. (00:32)
7. The letters on the railing of the fraternity house are in the wrong order: they should be Delta Tau Chi—but instead they're Delta Chi Tau. (00:45)
8. After being turned down by his girlfriend, Boon stands still and Otter puts his left hand on his shoulder. In the next shot, it's his right hand on Boon's shoulder. (01:00)
9. When they're taken off by a worker, the Greek letters on the railing of the fraternity switch places: they're Delta Tau Chi (and the Tau falls down). But as soon as Boon and Larry reach the place, they're all back up—as Delta Chi Tau! (01:06, 01:07)

10. Otter is making out with Shelley and he's caressing her bare breast. Her bra is hanging off her shoulders. When Otter's friends come back to the car, Shelley dives inside the nearest car: now her bra is back on. (01:16, 01:17)

11. When the Deathmobile rams the podium and everyone flies in the air, Mrs. De Pasto (the wife of the mayor) jumps without her shoes on. The shoes will be back on her feet later on. Did she go through the rubble...? (01:40, 01:43)

Animal House's Ticket to Ride

At the end of the movie, we learn that Babs Jensen (Martha Smith) becomes a tour guide at Universal Studios. The credits for this film (and other John Landis films for Universal) end with the advertisement, "When in Hollywood, visit Universal Studios." And then add, "Ask for Babs." Up until 1989, if you asked for Babs at the ticket booth Universal Studios Hollywood would give you a discount on your ticket.

NEGOTIATOR, THE (2)
1998, color, 141 min.

Director: F. Gary Gray

Cast: Samuel L. Jackson (Lieutenant Danny Roman), Kevin Spacey (Lieutenant Chris Sabian), David Morse (Commander Adam Beck), Ron Rifkin (Commander Grant Frost), John Spencer (Chief Al Travis), J. T. Walsh (Inspector Terence Niebaum), Siobhan Fallon (Maggie), Paul Giamatti (Rudy Timmons), Regina Taylor (Karen Roman), Bruce Beatty (Marcus), Michael Cudlitz (Palermo), Carlos Gómez (Eagle).

Shaft and Kaiser Soze have a long series of swaggering chats.

Bloopers
1. The power is shut down in the building for the first time, and Danny proceeds to make a call on the cordless phone. Without power a cordless phone is useless; the base needs AC to receive. (01:18, 01:21)

2. Danny is on a stretcher waiting to be put in the back of the ambulance. His head is facing the vehicle. Once inside, though, his head is facing the back doors, and they didn't rotate him. Also patients are never loaded in that direction anyway. (02:13, 02:14)

1941 (14)
also Collector's Edition
1979, color, 118 min. / 146 min. (CE)

Director: Steven Spielberg

Cast: Dan Aykroyd (Sergeant Frank Tree), Ned Beatty (Ward Douglas), John Belushi

(Captain Wild Bill Kelso),
Lorraine Gary (Joan Douglas),
Murray Hamilton (Claude
Crumn), Christopher Lee
(Captain Wolfgang Von
Kleinschmidt), Tim Matheson
(Captain Loomis Birkhead),
Toshiro Mifune (Commander
Akiro Mitamura), Warren Oates
(Colonel "Madman" Maddox),
Robert Stack (Major General
Joseph W. Stillwell), Eddie
Deezen (Herbie Kazlminsky),
Lionel Stander (Angelo Scioli).

*After Pearl Harbor, Japan
attacks Hollywood... and
everything destructible in
between.*

Bloopers

1. Commander Mitamura steps
   onto the deck of the Japanese submarine, followed by
   Captain Von Kleinschmidt. A
   shot from above the peri-
   scope shows that Mitamura
   isn't on the deck at all.
   Actually, he's about to step
   onto it again. (00:03, 00:04)
2. During a quarrel between
   Sitarski and Wally, the amount
   of pie frosting on the face of
   the soldier in the diner
   changes while a lady is cleaning him off. (00:08 / 00:09 CE)
3. Wild Bill Kelso smashes a
   Coca-Cola bottle on his windshield. The neck flies away
   but it's back when he drinks
   from the bottle. (00:16 / 00:42
   CE)
4. While in the cockpit with
   Donna, Loomis simulates a

takeoff and yells "We are
rolling!" while unbuttoning
his jacket completely. When
he stops Donna by telling her,
"Don't worry! Don't worry!
You will!" he unbuttons the
top button of his jacket again.
(00:17 / 00:22 CE)

5. Herbie grabs a car of the ferris wheel and swings with it.
   When he lets go, the car
   keeps swinging—but is standing still (and is much lower)
   when Herbie whacks his
   head against it. (00:33, 00:34 /
   00:48 CE)
6. Claude and Herbie take a
   seat on the ferris wheel:
   Claude to the left, Herbie to
   the right. Later on they
   switch positions (and they
   were supposed to be locked
   in) when they fire at Kelso's
   plane. (00:34, 01:22 / 00:49,
   01:47 CE)
7. Herbie fakes a swan dive
   from the ferris wheel. Claude
   asks him to sit. His cigarette
   jumps from his right hand to
   his left. (00:34 / 00:49 CE)
8. Herbie wants to check the
   wind: he wets his left finger,
   raises his left hand up ... but
   in the following shot, he's
   holding up his right hand.
   (00:35 / 00:50 CE)
9. On the Japanese submarine,
   Hollis fakes taking a dump by
   tossing his boots into a toilet. He holds the first boot by
   the heel, drops it in, and the
   detail shows a boot that has
   rotated 180°. (00:38 / 00:52
   CE)

10. While checking the instruments on Colonel Maddox's plane, Loomis is wearing his hat. But when he peeks out the window, asking for a radio, the hat is gone. (00:58 / 01:19, 01:20 CE)

11. Before taking off, Kelso fires his gun for Colonel Maddox. The Colonel screams for joy, Kelso screams back at him—from his sealed cockpit. After a second, Kelso seals his cockpit. (NOTE: this is almost impossible to see on the "pan & scan" VHS.) (01:02, 01:03 / 01:26 CE)

12. The red alert begins to sound among Hollywood's streets. Sergeant Tree says, "This is it!" and takes the gun off his shoulder. In the following shot he takes it off again. (01:09 / 01:33 CE)

13. Scioli motions to Joan with his right hand to move to the side—but in the over-the-shoulder, he's doing it with his left. (01:32 / 01:58 CE)

14. The curtain cord of the window that Joan is looking through is pulled all the way down when she is in the frame but is all the way up when Angelo is. (01:32 / 01:58 CE)

NORTH BY NORTHWEST (7)
1959, color, 136 min.

Director: Alfred Hitchcock

Cast: Cary Grant (Roger O. Thornhill / George Kaplan), Eve Marie Saint (Eve Kendall), James Mason (Phillip Vandamm), Jessie Royce Landis (Clara Thornhill), Leo G. Carroll (The Professor), Josephine Hutchinson (Handsome Woman / Mrs. Townsend), Philip Ober (Lester Townsend), Martin Landau (Leonard), Adam Williams (Valerian), Edward Platt (Victor Larrabee, Thornhill's Attorney), Robert Ellenstein (Licht), Doreen Lang (Maggie, Thornhill's secretary).

1941 Cameos

Just for kicks . . .

CAMEO	ROLE	TIMES
John Landis	Mizerany (driving motorcycle with sidecar)	00:40 / 00:54 CE
David "Squiggy" Lander	Joe (soldier behind Coca-Cola sign)	00:45 / 01:07 CE
Michael "Lenny" McKean	Willy (other soldier behind sign)	00:45 / 01:07 CE

The mother of all the "being-in-the-wrong-place-at-the-wrong-time type movies.

Bloopers

1. Roger and his secretary, Maggie, are in a cab that stops in front of the Plaza Hotel. Through the rear window, it's possible to see a red-hooded cab; yet, when Roger gets out of his car, the cab behind him has a white hood. (00:04)

2. After Mr. Townsend gets stabbed, Roger grabs the knife, the point to the floor. When he flees, the point of the knife is toward the ceiling. (00:38)

3. During the dinner on the train, the bouquet on the table keeps changing size, depending on whether Eve is in the shot or Roger is. (00:46)

4. After Roger puts away his glasses, he toys with his cocktail glass if Eve is in the shot but leaves it alone if he's in the shot. (00:48)

5. When Roger gets out of the bus in the middle of nowhere, the bus' long shadow stretches on the ground to the right of the vehicle. The following shot of Roger shows the shadow pointing in the exact opposite direction. When the first car passes by, its shadow indicates it's almost noon; but then a truck passes by, and its shadow stretches in front of Roger . . . and so on, for the whole sequence. (01:06, 01:07, 01:08)

6. When the car driven by a cop makes a sudden U-turn, Roger leans to his right side—then he looks at the cop close to him for a millisecond, who is sitting straight, and pushes him. Only then, the cop leans to his right. (01:35)

7. In the restaurant at Mount Rushmore, Eve shoots Roger: a kid in the background covers his ears before the gun fires (too many rehearsals?). (01:45)

Fun Fact

HITCHWATCH: Director Alfred Hitchcock can be spotted while trying, with no success, to catch a bus at the beginning of the movie. (00:02)

NOTTING HILL (7)
1999, color, 124 min.

Director: Roger Michell

Cast: Julia Roberts (Anna Scott), Hugh Grant (William Thacker), Richard McCabe (Tony), Rhys Ifans (Spike), James Dreyfus (Martin), Tim McInnerny (Max), Gina McKee (Bella), Emma Chambers (Honey), Hugh Bonneville (Bernie), Phillip Manikum (Harry the Sound Man), Samuel West (Anna's Costar), Lorelei King (Anna's Publicist), Alec Baldwin (Jeff King).

Lonely London bookstore owner hooks up with a famous actress.

Bloopers

1. Two shots of the exterior of William's bookstore are shown: one at the beginning, and the second right before Anna comes back to ask if she should stay in London (at least a year later). In both, the exact same adult (dressed in blue) is squatting down to deal with the exact same child (dressed in beige) in the alley to the left of the store. Coincidence? Yeah right. (00:05, 01:39)

2. When Anna first enters the bookstore, she's browsing in the Turkey section. When William starts talking to her, there are a few book spines to her left titled *Turkey: It's People.* Some book editor needs to take a grammar lesson . . . it should be "*Its.*" (00:06)

3. William spills orange juice on Anna, and some on himself—on the left side of his shirt. When they go to his flat to clean up, the stain on his shirt has grown considerably . . . it now covers the entire left side of the front of his shirt. (00:11, 00:12)

4. When William invites Anna to his flat so that she can clean up, he tells her that the bathroom's on "the top floor." We later discover that it isn't. When Anna is taking a bath and Spike walks in, we see stairs going up from that floor. (00:12, 01:08)

5. William, posing as the *Horse & Hound* journalist, starts to interview Anna. Anna starts to sit on the couch and in the next shot she ends up sitting farther left. (00:26)

6. After bidding goodnight to the most promising of the girls he's been set up with, William comes back into the living room. Bella switches her tea cup from her left to her right hand in order to set it down, and then in the long shot switches it the same way again. (01:03)

7. After hearing Anna's cold-hearted comments to her costar on the set on Hampstead Heath, William gets up and takes his headphones off . . . and the eyeglasses he was wearing have suddenly vanished. (01:38)

0

PHONE PROP-BLEMS

No, we're not talking busy signals and bad reception. Check these out:

A cell phone in *Charlie's Angels*   Blooper No. 12
A 70s phone in *Detroit Rock City*   Blooper No. 1
A phone on a nightstand in *Dogma*   Blooper No. 5
An answering machine in *Office Space*   Blooper No. 1
A phone on a desk in *Pretty Woman*   Blooper No. 5
A message left in *The 6th Day*   Blooper No. 3

OFFICE SPACE (7)
1999, color, 90 min.

Director: Mike Judge

Cast: Ron Livingston (Peter Gibbons), Jennifer Aniston (Joanna), Ajay Naidu (Samir), David Herman (Michael Bolton), Gary Cole (Bill Lumbergh), Stephen Root (Milton Waddams), Richard Riehle (Tom Smykowski), Alexandra Wentworth (Anne), Joe Bays (Dom Portwood), John C. McGinley (Bob Slydell), Paul Willson (Bob Porter), Diedrich Bader (Lawrence).

Boring office life gets spiced up.

Bloopers
1. Peter finally wakes up following his hypnosis and his answering machine has seventeen messages on it. When he fast-forwards to the second message, the display jumps from three to four messages. (00:24)
2. When Peter and Joanna first

have lunch, the levels of their water glasses change throughout the scene without them ever drinking any. On his close-ups they're half-full, on hers they're full. (00:29)

3. Peter meets with Bob and Bob for the first time and as he passes the table, all the chairs on his side are aligned with the table except one that's turned to the side. After he pours himself some water and approaches the table, the turned chair is now aligned. (00:34)

4. When Stan (played by writer/director Mike Judge as "William King") first reprimands Joanna for her lack of flair, he has two bottle-shaped pins on his chest that are flashing alternately. In the next cut, they're flashing in unison, and in the following cut they're alternating again. (00:37)

5. Peter, Michael, and Samir take a fax machine out in a field to beat it to smithereens. They need to pull Michael away because he's going over the edge, and the machine looks demolished. He escapes his friends' grasp to come back and beat it some more, but it's suddenly not as demolished. (00:56)

6. At a party, Peter and friends are shown the mat for the "Jump to Conclusions" game. One of the squares says, "Loose 1 Turn." How does a turn get loose? (01:00)

7. Peter meets Joanna at her new

job. She walks toward him holding her jeans jacket on her arm. Yet when they hug and kiss, she's wearing it. (01:15, 01:16)

ON HER MAJESTY'S SECRET SERVICE (13)
1969, color, 142 min.

Director: Peter Hunt

Cast: George Lazenby (James Bond 007), Diana Rigg (Contessa Teresa "Tracy" DeVicenzo), Telly Savalas (Ernst Stavro Blofeld), Gabriele Ferzetti (Marc-Ange Draco), Ilse Steppat (Irma Bunt), Lois Maxwell (Miss Moneypenny), George Baker (Sir Hilary Bray), Bernard Lee (M), Bernard Horsfall (Campbell), Desmond Llewelyn (Q), Yuri Borionko (Grunther), Virginia North (Olympia).

The sixth outing has the one and only Bond with an Australian accent.

Bloopers
1. To save Tracy from drowning, Bond drives his car on the beach, then stops abruptly. The tires screech. On sand? (00:03)

2. During a fight on the shore, a small anchor on the sand faces right, left, and then right again without anyone touching it. (00:05, 00:06)

3. 007 deals cards at a casino table; the back of the cards

he passes to the man to his right are both white. The man asks for a third (white) card; yet, when he flips the first two cards, one of them now has a red back. (00:11)

4. Also, this same card-playing man is holding a cigar in his right hand, but when he turns the cards the cigar is gone. (00:11)

5. When Countess Tracy tells Bond, "People who want to stay alive play it safe," she places down her left hand. In the following over-the-shoulder shot, her head is resting on her left hand. (00:13)

6. Disguised as Hilary Bray, 007 describes his personal coat of arms as bearing four bezants (gold balls). But earlier when it was shown, there were only three balls. (00:45, 01:01)

7. Sir Hilary Bray and Blofeld say that the Blofeld family has a genetic trait: lack of earlobes. Yet Blofeld does seem to have earlobes. He has no hair and a touch a megalomania . . . but we digress. (00:47, 01:04)

Blind to Bond

In *On Her Majesty's Secret Service*, 007 (pretending to be Sir Bray) meets Blofeld—wearing, as a clever disguise, a Scottish uniform (01:03). Blofeld doesn't recognize him, even though the two have already met during *You Only Live Twice* (01:38).

---

8. Caught unprepared when the cable car departs, Bond winds up hanging on between gears. His grip has the right hand over the left if seen from one side, the left over the right if seen from above. (01:24)

9. Ruby unwraps her Christmas gift, dropping the sheet of paper to the floor. The second detail of the case she's received shows the paper underneath it, on Ruby's lap (as a bonus, also check the position of the case lid. Up, down, up, down . . .). (01:29)

10. 007 enters a phone booth to call London. The door of the booth closes twice. (01:44)

11. During the car chase in the snow circuit, the chaser car hits a red Mini marked with No. 11—the same car that Bond and Tracy pass by a few yards ahead. (01:46)

12. White car No. 6 flips over. The shot of the upside-down driver is flipped (the signs in the background appear to be upside-down, too). (01:47)

13. During the bobsled chase, Blofeld is caught with a Y-shaped tree branch just around his neck. However, he looks quite free in the following long shot. (02:14)

Question

Draco, an Italian businessman, has a calendar on his bookshelf that says, "Setembro." Is this supposed to be Italian? Because if it is, it's dead wrong! ("Settembre" would have been the right spelling.) (00:21)

OUTLAND (4)

1981, color, 109 min.

Director: Peter Hyams

Cast: Sean Connery (Marshal William T. O'Niel), Peter Boyle (Station Manager Mark B. Sheppard), Frances Sternhagen (Dr. Marian Lazarus), James Sikking (Security Sergeant Montone), Kika Markham (Carol O'Neil), Clarke Peters (Security Corporal Ballard), Steven Berkoff (Sagan), John Ratzenberger (Tarlow), Nicholas Barnes (Paul O'Niel), Manning Redwood (Lowell).

Or, Scots in Space!

Bloopers

1. The Marshal's name is O'Niel: it appears on the computer screen and on the tag of his uniform; but when the alleged O'Niel meets Station Manager Sheppard and everyone else, and also when he saves a prostitute from Sagan, his tag says "O'Neil." (00:08, 00:14, 00:29)

2. Marshal O'Niel draws some blood out of Sagan's neck: the blood is transparent. (00:37)

3. To create a diversion, O'Niel tosses a metal panel on the outside of the greenhouse. The panel wobbles and glides and rotates as it falls. Not in space, we're afraid . . . no air, my friend. (01:38)

4. Hanging on for dear life while fighting with Ballard, O'Niel moves his left arm up. At that moment it's possible to catch a glimpse of his bare wrist. In deep space?!?! (01:41)

P

PARENTHOOD (9)
1989, color, 124 min.

Director: Ron Howard

Cast: Steve Martin (Gil Buckman), Mary Steenburgen (Karen Buckman), Dianne Wiest (Helen Buckman), Jason Robards (Frank Buckman), Rick Moranis (Nathan Merrick), Tom Hulce (Larry Buckman), Martha Plimpton (Julie Lampkin), Keanu Reeves (Tod), Harley Jane Kozak (Susan Merrick), Dennis Dugan (David Brodsky), Leaf Phoenix (Garry Lampkin), Eileen Ryan (Marilyn), Max Elliott Slade (Young Gil), Alisan Porter (Taylor).

Ah, quality time with the family!

Bloopers

1. At the baseball stadium, young Gil talks to an Usher: Gil holds a tub of popcorn, but when he says, "Look: you have to understand..." he's holding the program and the ticket for the game. (00:01)

2. When Kevin delights his family with his "Diarrhea" song, Karen is not wearing her seatbelt; then she is. (00:05, 00:06)

3. After the... well, battery-operated device during the blackout, little Taylor asks her mother (who's apparently on the other side of the table) what it was. Karen answers, and suddenly appears behind Taylor. (00:22)

4. Arguing with Julie, Helen stands up, tossing her purse and a bunch of pictures all over the room. When Julie leaves, she picks up the pictures—which are now all together, almost stacked. And the purse has moved almost under the coffee table. (00:28)

5. Before leaving, Julie tells her mother about being so in love with Tod and then she picks up her gray bag... twice. (00:29)

6. Garry talks to his mom about the house being crowded. She places one light brown file in her purse, then she puts it in again. (00:49)

7. While Frank is checking his car

after Larry explains to him why he took it for a ride, a boom mike is reflected in the hood of the car. (01:17)

8. Seated in his dragster, Tod does the sign of the cross with his left hand. (01:44)

9. Running to the smashed dragster, Garry loses his cap. When he's close to Tod, he has the cap back on. (01:45)

Question

In the bedroom, in the time it takes Karen to say, "You know what his teacher asked me?" Gil is able to remove his jeans and hang them in the closet. Is he a quick-change artist? (00:08)

PAYBACK (7)
1999, color, 100 min.

Director: Brian Helgeland

Cast: Mel Gibson (Porter), Gregg Henry (Val Resnick), Maria Bello (Rosie), David Paymer (Arthur Stegman), Bill Duke (Detective Hicks), Deborah Unger (Mrs. Lynn Porter), John Glover (Phil), William Devane (Carter), Lucy Liu (Pearl), Jack Conley (Detective Leary), Kris Kristofferson (Bronson), James Coburn (Fairfax), David Dunard (Doctor).

The good guy is actually a bad guy, but not really bad. Almost good, or good-bad. Oh, crap ... just watch the movie!

Bloopers

1. The doctor who operates on Porter's G.S.W. (gunshot wound) places a scalpel and closed scissors in a glass filled with whiskey. When he brings the glass to the table, the scissors are open. (00:01)

2. Porter wears a gray jacket. He steals a wallet, then stands in front of a mirror, trying to look like the picture on the ID. In the close-up he's wearing a black jacket, in the long shots, a gray one. (00:04)

3. Porter drives his wife's syringe into a wall: his wedding ring is on the needle—but as he walks away, the ring has moved to the middle of the tube. (00:12)

4. When walking to Val, Porter gets run over by a car: he smashes the windshield, but when the thugs get out of the car, the windshield appears to be in one piece. It's smashed again (but a lot less than it was) when Porter is held down on the car's hood. (00:49, 00:50)

5. In the small apartment, Porter says to Rosie, "Nobody knows I'm here." The phone rings and the detail reveals an ashtray in front of it. When Porter emerges from under the bed, the ashtray has moved to the side of the phone. Same thing happens when Bronson is in the same room and the phone rings: the ashtray is in front of the phone, to the left side; when Bronson picks up the microphone, the ashtray has

ME AND MY ROVING SHADOW

Shadows on the ground just don't seem to stay put. Here's a small sampling:

Kurt Russell in *Breakdown*	Blooper No. 4
Brendan Fraser in *The Mummy* (1999)	Blooper No. 1
Cary Grant in *North by Northwest*	Blooper No. 5
The droids in *The Phantom Menace*	Blooper No. 3
Gebe Hackman and Leo Di Caprio in *The Quick and the Dead*	Blooper No. 2
Owen Wilson in *Shanghai Noon*	Blooper No. 2
Catherine Hicks in *Star Trek IV*	Blooper No. 6
The train in *Stand by Me*	Blooper No. 2
Bill Murray's platoon in *Stripes*	Blooper No. 9
Alexander Sidding in *Vertical Limit*	Blooper No. 5

moved to the right. (01:02, 01:03, 01:34)

6. Carter grabs a roll of coins and pushes it along his desk. When he says, "Porter, right. I won't forget it again," the roll has disappeared. It'll be back when Porter grabs an agenda from the desk. (01:08, 01:09, 01:11)

7. Leaving Fairfax's apartment, Porter stops a cab: as he boards, he finds himself face to face with Stegman, and the windows of the car are steamed up. Needless to say, they were crystal clear when the cab stopped. (01:25, 01:26)

Non-Blooper
Porter has a USMC tattoo on his right arm. It appears on his left arm in a picture Val is showing him, only because the picture was taken in a mirror (the woman is holding the flashing camera). (00:10, 00:19)

Question
Bronson shows Porter a briefcase with money in it; Porter is tied to a chair, his boots on. When Bronson gives the order to use a sledgehammer on Porter's feet, he is suddenly barefoot. Who removed his boots and socks? (01:30, 01:31)

PHANTOM MENACE, THE—STAR WARS: EPISODE I (13)
also DVD Version
1999, color, 133 min. / 136 min. (DVD)

Director: George Lucas

Cast: Liam Neeson (Qui-Gon Jinn), Ewan McGregor (Obi-Wan Kenobi), Natalie Portman (Queen Amidala / Padmé Naberrie), Jake Lloyd (Anakin Skywalker), Ian McDiarmid (Senator Cod Palpatine / Darth

Sidious), Pernilla August (Shmi Skywalker), Oliver Ford Davies (Governor Sio Bibble), Hugh Quarshie (Captain Panaka), Ahmed Best (Jar Jar Binks), Anthony Daniels (C-3PO), Kenny Baker (R2-D2), Jenna Green (Amee), Dhruv Chanchani (Kitster), Terence Stamp (Chancellor Finis Valorum).

Schindler introduces a young Darth Vader to the force . . . we guess that all of one's deeds can't be good.

Bloopers

1. After meeting with Jar Jar for the first time, Obi-Wan mentions to him that the sound he's hearing is of "a thousand terrible things heading this way." Obi-Wan's braid of hair jumps from his shoulder to his chest in a back-to-back shot sequence. (00:12)
2. As Jar Jar brings Qui-Gon and Obi-Wan to the underwater city, he's stopped by a guard. When Jar Jar talks to the guard, Obi-Wan's braid switches from the right to the left (only in one shot). (00:14)
3. As Queen Amidala, Governor Sio Bibble, and Captain Panaka are taken away by the droids, everyone casts a very sharp shadow on the ground. Just before Qui-Gon, Obi-Wan and Jar Jar jump down to fight the droids, the shadows are all suddenly gone. (00:22)

4. Padmé cleans R2-D2 when Jar Jar annoys her. When Jar Jar says that he's getting very scared, Padmé's shot is flipped (look at R2's dome and its features). (00:29)
5. When the sandstorm hits Tatooine, Anakin invites Qui-Gon and the others to his home. As they approach the house, Anakin leads the group, Jar Jar is way to his right, the Queen in disguise is behind Anakin, followed by Qui-Gon. But when they enter the house, Jar Jar is suddenly behind Anakin. He shouldn't be there. (00:38)
6. Anakin holds C-3PO's eye in his left hand, places it in the droid's head . . . but in the next shot, he's doing it with his right hand. (00:39)
7. Anakin's mom has an electronic viewer to watch her son's podrace: the visor has two handles on the sides; yet when she looks into it, the handles have disappeared. They're back a minute later. (00:57, 00:59, 01:00 / 00:58, 01:00, 01:01 DVD)
8. When Anakin can't start his vehicle at the beginning of the podrace, Kitster, the kid far in the distance, has one hand in front of his eyes. In the following, matching cut, he has both hands up, having had no time to move them. (00:58 / 00:59 DVD)
9. After Anakin wins, his team celebrates. And R2-D2's dome looks lifted a little more

than usual, for some reason. (01:06 / 01:09 DVD)

10. Before he goes back for Anakin, Qui-Gon talks to Obi-Wan from on top of a camel-like creature. Again, Obi-Wan's braid of hair has moved to the left. (01:08 / 01:11 DVD)

11. Qui-Gon and a free Anakin walk away from the kid's house. His mom stands still. Anakin turns, and in a wide shot his mom is walking toward him, reaching the exact same spot where she was a few seconds earlier. (01:12 / 01:14 DVD)

12. In the wide shot that follows R2-D2 projecting the 3-D map of the city, Amidala's lips don't match with what she says. (01:40 / 01:43 DVD)

13. Zooming out of the Federation battleship, Anakin yells, "Now this is podracing!" The following shot of R2-D2 has been flipped (again, check the features on its dome). (01:59 / 02:03 DVD)

Questions

1. When Qui-Gon introduces himself to Anakin's mom, he says, "I'm Qui-Gon Jinn." Does Padmé mouth the very same line at the same time? Is she a ventriloquist? (00:38)

2. Anakin is showing his vehicle for the podrace, and Amee, the little girl close to Waldo, the Greedo-type alien, says, "You've been working on that thing for years!" She has braces. Does

that mean that in a galaxy far, far away they have lasers and holograms, but they still haven't figured out a better way to straighten teeth? (00:48)

3. Amidala, Panaka, and six soldiers exit a window, launch hooks, and climb up the outside of the royal palace to the throne room. However, when they get into the corridor that leads to the room, there are more than ten of them. Did they procreate on the climb? (01:51, 01:52 / 01:54, 01:55 DVD)

4. When Anakin is mastering the fighter he's flying on, he says, "Let's go left." He moves the control to the left, he goes left. A few seconds later, he says, "I'll try spinning, that's a good trick." He moves the control to the left, the cockpit spins to the right. Who could fly with such unreliable and inconsistent controls? (01:50, 01:51 / 01:54 DVD)

Fun Facts

1. In Watto's junkyard, there's one of the capsules from the movie, *2001: A Space Odyssey* semi-hidden in the background. (00:33)

2. Just so you can tell your friends: during the senate scene, right after Chancellor Valorum sits down, there's a wide shot of part of the arena. In the bottom left part of the screen, there's a group of *E.T.*s. (01:25 / 01:29 DVD)

3. The robot that Jar Jar tips over has an inscription on its back that strongly resembles George Lucas's classic signature number: 1138. (02:00 / 02:03 DVD)

PRETTY WOMAN (11)
also Director's Cut
1990, color, 119 min. / 125 min. (DC)

Director: Garry Marshall

Cast: Richard Gere (Edward Lewis), Julia Roberts (Vivian Ward), Ralph Bellamy (James Morse), Jason Alexander (Philip Stuckey), Laura San Giacomo (Kit De Luca), Hector Elizondo (Bernard "Barney" Thompson, the Hotel Manager), Alex Hyde-White (David Morse), Amy Yasbeck (Elizabeth Stuckey), Elinor Donahue (Bridget), Judith Baldwin (Susan), Hank Azaria (Detective), Allan Kent (Waiter).

Heartwarming hooker-to-princess story.

Bloopers
1. While watching *I Love Lucy* on TV, Vivian gets closer to Edward and removes his tie; she unbuttons his shirt and opens it, but in a close-up, Edward's collar is suspiciously buttoned again. (The pan-and-scan close-up shows Richard Gere wearing a tie again, but in the letterboxed version of the movie, only the collar is closed again.) (00:28 / 00:29 DC)

2. Vivian is having breakfast; she grabs a croissant and nibbles it. A few shots later, she holds a pancake. (00:30, 00:32 / 00:31, 00:33 DC)

> Director Garry Marshall, admitting to many mismatches in *Pretty Woman*, also said that "You must always pick the best performance . . . I don't care if they think I'm a good director or a bad director, as long as my actors are out there and it works!"

3. Edward leaves for work and Vivian is left alone in the hotel, wearing a bathrobe and a towel turban, since she just got out of the bubble bath. Happy as a little kid, she runs to the bed and jumps on it—revealing that the soles of her feet are really dirty. (00:36, 00:37 / 00:37, 00:38 DC)

4. Vivian calls her friend Kit and tells her where she's staying: the Regent Beverly Wilshire. Kit takes note using her lipstick and writes "Reg, Bev, Wil" on a pizza box. The writing changes shape, and the two Coca-Cola cans move in the background, too. (00:38 / 00:39 DC)

5. During a meeting that starts with a few clips of the Port of Long Beach, a phone behind Edward's briefcase moves on the table. This is most noticeable when Philip sits down close to it. (00:45)

6. While having a luxurious dinner with James Morse

and his son David, Vivian struggles with an escargot—which flies away, past a waiter who's standing behind her. The same waiter catches the flying snail without moving from his position. (00:53 / 00:51 DC)

7. During the same dinner, Edward and Vivian are served mint sherbet—which vanishes ("Mr. Morse, you asked for this meeting...") and reappears, is taken away by waiters, but is back on the table when David stands up. (00:53, 00:54 / 00:54, 00:55 DC)

8. Vivian is offended by Edward; she collects her things and flees the hotel room, holding her clothes. He catches up to her at the elevator and apologizes. She holds her clothes over her arm in the wide shot but with her arm over them in the close-up. (01:17 / 01:19 DC)

9. While in the car, Vivian asks Edward if they can stop by the Blue Banana Club, and they do. Inside the car, Edward wasn't wearing a vest; yet as he gets out of the vehicle, there's a vest on him. (01:30, 01:31 DC only)

10. A meeting between Edward and Mr. Morse is held in Edward's office, with a terrific view of Los Angeles. But the flag on the pole doesn't move in the wind (it's a painted backdrop). (01:38 / 01:44 DC)

11. Philip visits Vivian in her penthouse and attacks her. She reacts, and Philip's wristwatch flies away—but it's back in the following shot. (01:43 / 01:49 DC)

Non-Blooper

At the Opera House in San Francisco, the usher does not, in fact, say to Vivian, "The glasses are there, Julia." What he says is, "The glasses are there, enjoy the opera." (01:24 / 01:26 DC)

Fun Fact

Vivian's legs in the poster of the movie don't belong to Julia Roberts—as if there's anyone who doesn't know that by now—but to her body double, Shelley Michell. But Edward's hair in the same poster looks almost black, while in the movie his hair is silver.

PSYCHO (5)

1960, black & white, 109 min.

Director: Alfred Hitchcock

Cast: Anthony Perkins (Norman Bates), Vera Miles (Lila Crane), John Gavin (Sam Loomis), Martin Balsam (Milton Arbogast), John McIntire (Sheriff Chambers), Simon Oakland (Dr. Richmond), Vaughn Taylor (George Lowery), Frank Albertson (Tom Cassidy), Lurene Tuttle (Mrs. Chambers), Patricia Hitchcock (Caroline), John Anderson (California Charlie, Car Salesman), Janet Leigh (Marion Crane).

A classic screwball thriller.

Bloopers

1. As we zoom into the hotel window, between the cuts, the shadow on the blinds becomes longer (even if it's supposed to be in real time). (00:02)
2. Marion gets out of her car at the dealership. She's holding her purse in her hand, but in the following shot it has jumped around her left arm. (00:17)
3. In the Bates Motel, Marion hides the stolen money in a newspaper, then places it flat on her nightstand. In the detail, however, the folded paper appears more plump and round than it is in the master shot. (00:31)
4. Marion hits the floor after being stabbed to death. Her pupils are small (very likely because of the lights on the set). But when you die, there is a phenomenon called midriasis, which causes the opposite effect—dilation of the pupils. (00:48)
5. When Norman cleans the bathroom, he leaves the toilet seat down. Later, when Sam and Lila enter the same bathroom, they find the toilet seat up. (00:53, 01:32)

Non-Blooper
When Marion is murdered under the shower, it is NOT blood on the wall, it's her wet hair that gets stuck to the wall. Hence, Norman does NOT clean the wall because he doesn't HAVE to clean it. (00:47)

Fun Fact
HITCHWATCH: Hitchcock, wearing a Texan hat, stands outside Mr. Lowery's office as Marion walks in. (00:06)

PSYCHO (7)
1998, color, 104 min.

Director: Gus Van Sant

Cast: Vince Vaughn (Norman Bates), Anne Heche (Marion Crane), Julianne Moore (Lila Crane), William H. Macy (Milton Arbogast, Private Eye), Viggo Mortensen (Sam Loomis), Robert Forster (Dr. Simon), Philip Baker Hall (Sheriff Al Chambers), Anne Haney (Mrs. Chambers), Chad Everett (Tom Cassidy), Rance Howard (George Lowery), Rita Wilson (Caroline), James LeGros (Charlie the Car Dealer).

Let's imitate a classic and call it art.

Bloopers

1. The movie opens at 2:43 P.M. After a little hanky-panky, Marion goes back to her office. The clock on her boss' desk reads 2:47. Either his clock is broken, or it's a blooper. (00:03, 00:09)
2. Marion steals $400,000 in $1,000 bills. Then she buys a

car using four of these bills ("She paid me cash"). Unfortunately, you can't use $1,000 bills in merchant transactions. (00:08, 00:19)

3. Before taking her infamous shower, Marian tries to subtract $4,036 from the stolen $400,000. The result? $395,963. Whoops! In character? Maybe. But Anne Heche's fault. (00:43)

4. Marion is killed under the shower. A close-up on her eye shows mydriasis (the pupil starts dilating). Yet in the following shot, the pupil is small as always. (00:45)

5. Before moving the car to hide Marion's body in the trunk, Norman shuts the motel lights off. Yet, when he goes to get the car, it's so bright out that it seems that the lights are back on. (00:49, 00:52)

6. Lila arrives at Sam's workplace to talk to him about Marion. Sam tells the cashier Bob to go and get lunch. Bob has the cash register drawer open. Sam insists that he leave, and the camera cuts back to Bob. The drawer's now closed, even though Bob didn't move. (00:58)

7. Arbogast pulls his car in to the porch of the motel to talk to Norman, and the whole area is well-lit by daylight. Two minutes into the conversation, Norman flips on the motel sign and lights, and before they come on, the daylight seems to be gone. In only two minutes? (01:01, 01:03)

Fun Facts

1. When Marion comes back to the office, a Hitchcock lookalike is seen bawling out a guy next to the front door. The guy is Gus Van Sant. That'll teach him. (00:06)

2. As Marion arrives in Los Angeles before going to the car dealer, in the very first shot of the road ahead in town, on the right side, there's an ad at a bus stop for the movie *Six Days and Seven Nights* . . . starring actress Anne Heche, who's playing Marion. (00:16)

PULP FICTION (17)
1994, color, 154 min.

Director: Quentin Tarantino

Cast: John Travolta (Vincent Vega), Samuel L. Jackson (Jules Winnfield), Bruce Willis (Butch Coolidge), Ving Rhames (Marsellus Wallace), Uma Thurman (Mia Wallace), Harvey Keitel (Winston Wolf), Tim Roth (Pumpkin), Amanda Plummer (Honey Bunny), Eric Stoltz (Lance), Maria de Medeiros (Fabienne), Christopher Walken (Captain Koons), Quentin Tarantino (Jimmie).

Tarantino's seedy L.A. stories snag an Oscar and launch the Travolta revival.

Bloopers

1. Honey Bunny jumps up and yells, ". . . I'll execute every motherf***ing last one of

you!" But in the same sequence at the end of the movie, she yells, "... I'll now execute every one of you motherf***ers!" (00:04, 02:17)

2. Vincent is talking about Europe with Jules in the car. When Vincent says, "It's legal to carry it," you can see, reflected in a window in the background, that the car is actually mounted on a trailer. (00:07)

3. Jules checks his gun and tells Vincent that he has three or four bullets. In Brett's apartment he shoots once at the kid on the couch, once at Brett's shoulder, at least five more times at Brett, and (at the end of the movie) one more time at the Fourth Man. He never reloads once. (00:08, 00:18, 01:53)

4. After killing Brett, Jules's gun barrel slides back—meaning the gun is empty. In "The Bonnie Situation," the same scene is replayed, yet this time the gun barrel doesn't slide back. (00:18, 01:52)

5. At Jackrabbit Slim's, Mia's cigarette jumps from hand to hand both when she orders and when the drinks arrive. (00:37, 00:40)

6. Mia sips her milkshake, and the cherry begins to sink into the glass. But when she slides the drink to Vincent, the cherry is back on top. (00:40)

7. Back at the Wallace's man-

sion, Vincent tells Mia that he has to go to the bathroom. She moves to a tape recorder, and the shadow of Vincent on the wall indicates he's walking away. But in the next cut, he's standing in exactly the same place. (00:50)

8. Mia comes back home wearing Vincent's coat and she plops on the couch, still wearing it. But when she puts a cigarette in her mouth, she's not wearing it. Then, as she produces a lighter, there's the coat again! (00:49, 00:52)

9. Vincent drives in front of Lance's door and crashes the car against a wall. Prick up your eyes: on the grass beyond the "crashed car" are the tracks of the car that actually just drove by, while the crashed car was already set for the shot. (00:56)

10. When Captain Koons first shows Butch his father's watch, it reads either 4:40 or 10:10 (you can't tell which). Then a closer shot shows the watch at 11:45, but the close-up shows it at 12:00 sharp. (01:05, 01:06, 01:07)

11. Butch gets out of the store and checks the keys to Zed's motorcycle. In the sequence of shots, the keys jump from his right hand to his left, then back to his right, then back to his left. (01:49)

12. Before leaving at the end of his adventure, Butch jumps on Zed's chopper and places

his hands on the handlebars
... twice. (01:51)

13. The fourth young man bursts through the door to shoot at Jules and Vincent six times. Look behind Jules before the shots ("Marvin! I'd knock that sh*t off if I was you"); there is already one bullet hole in the wall. (01:52, 01:53)

14. When Jules and Vincent finish shooting the fourth young man who shot at them, we cut back to them to see that there are bullet holes in the wall. And the light on the wall has somehow grown bright all of a sudden. (01:52, 01:53)

15. To check the quality of Jules and Vincent's job in cleaning the car, the Wolf opens the driver's door and looks inside: the detail shows the door closed. (02:08)

16. When Winston tells him to strip, Jules removes his pants. In the next shot, they're still on. (02:09)

17. To help them wash the blood off, Jimmie gives Jules and Vincent each a bar of soap. He grabs them with his left hand but passes them with his right. (02:09)

Questions

1. Vincent tells Jules that he doesn't watch TV. But when he gives his explanation about being missed by the bullets, he says, "D'you ever watch that show, *Cops*? I was watching it, one time ..." Wait! Does he or does he not watch television? (00:09, 01:55)

2. Jules says that he "memorized" a passage from Ezekiel 25:17, but only a couple phrases of what he says is Ezekiel 25:17 ... so where does the rest of it come from? (00:20, 01:51, 02:26)

3. When Vincent is thinking about shooting up, he pictures a case with a glass syringe in it. But when he pictures the actual injection, is it us, or is the syringe plastic? When you're jonesing for smack, can your fantasies have bloopers? (00:30)

Q

QUICK AND THE DEAD, THE (8)
1995, color, 105 min.

Director: Sam Raimi

Cast: Sharon Stone (Ellen), Gene Hackman (John Herod), Russell Crowe (Cort), Leonardo DiCaprio (Kid), Tobin Bell (Dog Kelly), Roberts Blossom (Doc Wallace), Kevin Conway (Eugene Dred), Keith David (Sergeant Cantrell), Lance Henriksen (Ace Hanlon), Pat Hingle (Horace the Bartender), Gary Sinise (Marshall), Mark Boone Junior (Scars).

The fastest gun in town is a she.

Bloopers

1. Ace fans his special, all-aces deck of cards. The first card is an ace of spades, the point toward the ground. But when Ellen walks by him, unimpressed, Ace fans the deck back. The ace of spades' point now is up. (00:07)
2. The duel between the Kid and Herod is scheduled for 1:00 P.M. Yet the shadows on the ground reveal a sun much much lower than what you'd get at 1:00 P.M. (01:20, 01:22)
3. When Ellen comforts Kid in his last moments, she's holding his left hand. Yet in the next shot he's holding her collar with the same hand. (01:25)
4. Ellen has to duel with Cort: as they walk toward each other, there's sun and shadow only from her side and not from his. (01:28)
5. Also, the direction of Cort's shadow on the ground changes when he stops and turns. (01:34)
6. Ellen tosses her father's marshall's star right in front of Herod. But when she shoots Herod he backflips several feet from the point of impact. When Ellen picks the star back up, the star is by Herod's leg — as if he hadn't moved at all. (01:37, 01:40)
7. In the flashback, the Marshall is standing on a stool just a few seconds prior to being hanged. But after he's dead,

the stool has vanished without anyone moving it. (01:38)

8. During the final duel, Herod's shadow is behind him in a wide shot. But after he and Ellen fire their guns, Herod looks down: his shadow is now in front of him. (01:39)

Questions

1. What kind of town is swamped by thunderstorms at night, yet on the very next day is dry as a bone? (00:57, 01:02, 01:06, 01:10, 01:16, 01:19 . . .)

2. Cort decides to have a duel at dawn. Yet look at the shadows on the ground: if that's dawn, where the heck is this town located? (01:30, 01:32)

QUIZ SHOW (4)

1994, color, 133 min.

Director: Robert Redford

Cast: John Turturro (Herbie Stempel), Rob Morrow (Dick Goodwin), Ralph Fiennes (Charles Van Doren), Paul Scofield (Mark Van Doren), David Paymer (Dan Enright), Hank Azaria (Albert Freedman), Christopher McDonald (Jack Barry), Johann Carlo (Toby Stempel), Elizabeth Wilson (Dorothy Van Doren), Allan Rich (Robert Kintner), Mira Sorvino (Sandra Goodwin), George Martin (Chairman).

I'll take "TV Scandals" for $100.

Bloopers

1. The action takes place in 1957 (Herbie states that the Best Picture of 1955, "two years ago," was *Marty*). But at the Embassy theater they're showing Fellini's *La Dolce Vita*, which was made in 1960. (00:26, 00:38)

2. Dick writes Herbie's address on a pad: "106–55," but when he goes to meet with the guy, he knocks at a door marked 2177. (00:45, 00:55)

3. In Van Doren's den, Charles looks at the pictures on the wall: the last three are a photo of two women, a photo of

---

ADDRESS, PLEASE?

. . . we mean the real one.

The street name in *The Brady Bunch Movie*	Question No. 2
A street address in *Dr. No*	Blooper No. 12
An address in *Quiz Show*	Blooper No. 2
A house number in *The Terminator*	Blooper No. 2
A street address in *Terminator 2—SE / ESE*	Blooper No. 39

Charles's father with a friend, and a family picture. But in the master shot, the pictures of the two women and the two men have switched places. (01:16, 01:17)

4. While Dick is projecting old episodes of *Twenty-One,* he catches the "Emily Dickinson incident." He rewinds the film and plays it back—but the amount of film he rewinds is much much less than the portion he re-watches. (01:21)

Quiz Show Cameo

The student who asks Professor Van Doren about *Don Quixote* is an unbilled Ethan Hawke (01:53).

R

RAIDERS OF THE LOST ARK (15)
1981, color, 115 min.

Director: Steven Spielberg

Cast: Harrison Ford (Dr. Henry "Indiana" Jones Jr.), Karen Allen (Marion Ravenwood), Paul Freeman (Rene Belloq), Ronald Lacey (Toht), John Rhys-Davies (Sallah), Alfred Molina (Sapito), Denholm Elliott (Marcus Brody), Wolf Kahler (Dietrich), Anthony Higgins (Gobler), Vic Tablian (Barranca / Monkey Man), Don Fellows (Colonel Musgrove), William Hootkins (Major Eaton), Pat Roach (Giant Sherpa/1st Mechanic).

Adventurous archaeologist snags some religious artifacts before the Nazis do.

Bloopers

1. As Indy flees from the rolling boulder, check the left side of the screen: it is possible to see the pole that was holding the boulder all through the chase. (00:09)

2. Indy slams a large Bible on a table: one of the two clasps that holds the book closed snaps open. After one cut, the clasp is firmly closed, without anyone touching it. (00:15, 00:16)

3. The movie takes place in 1936. But when Indy flies from America to Nepal, you can see Thailand on the map. Siam became Thailand in 1939. (00:23)

4. Marion pulls the medallion out of her shirt and looks at it (and a gust of wind moves the candle flames). During two cuts, the medallion chain swings from Marion's neck to the table. (00:28)

5. At Marion's bar, Indy starts battling the evil guys with a revolver, then he switches for no reason to a semi-automatic pistol. (00:31, 00:32)

6. As Indy runs after the kidnappers in the market, the sweat stain on his shoulders changes shape and size all through the chase. (00:40)

7. The truck carrying Marion in

a basket travels down a narrow street toward some loading docks. Indy fires at the driver of the truck and kills him. The truck then flips on its side in what seems to be a very open square... how did it get there? (00:41)

8. According to the inscription on the medallion, the pole Indy needs to use has to be 6 kadams tall (that's 72 inches), minus 1 kadam to please a divinity. That makes the pole 60 inches tall, which means 5 feet. But when Indy first puts the pole on the ground, it towers over his head by a couple of feet. So, is Indy 3 feet tall? (00:48, 00:53)

9. Indy grabs the pole to which Marion is tied. As she waits to leave, he grabs her by the shoulder, but as we cut back on his close-up, he's still holding the pole. (00:55)

10. Indy ties Marion back up in the tent; her hair is caught in the lace in two different ways (from two different angles). (00:55)

11. As they take a first look into the Well of Souls, Indy is screen left and Sallah is screen right. After Indy drops a flaming torch into the well and mumbles "Snakes," Sallah appears at screen left, as if they've switched positions. (01:00)

12. Indy falls into the snake pit and finds himself face to face with a deadly cobra... and a shiny plate of glass that separates him from the snake. (01:03)

13. As Belloq waves to Indy who's still in the Well of Souls, his hat jumps from his hands to the ground and back again. (01:10)

14. The stone block Indy pushes to get out of the snake pit bounces on the ground (you can see its shadow). (01:15)

15. The huge German mechanic is sliced by the prop of the airplane; his blood splatters on the cockpit—but when Indy sets Marion free, the blood is gone. (01:20)

Questions

1. Indy's gun looks like a six-shooter. Yet, in Marion's bar, he fires more than twenty-five shots without reloading. (00:31)

2. When Indy pushes the stone block to get out of the snake pit, a man is sitting down close to the exit who doesn't move or do anything. Who the hell is this guy? (01:15)

3. As Indy tries to pick up his gun, the plane wheel passes over it. You can see a chain moving from the wheel up to the plane. How many plane wheels are driven by chains? (01:18)

ROBIN HOOD: PRINCE OF THIEVES (14)

1991, color, 143 min.

Director: Kevin Reynolds

Cast: Kevin Costner (Robin of Locksley), Morgan Freeman (Azeem Edin Bashir Al Bakir), Mary Elizabeth Mastrantonio (Marian), Christian Slater (Will Scarlett), Alan Rickman (George, the Sheriff of Nottingham), Geraldine McEwan (Mortianna), Michael McShane (Friar Tuck), Brian Blessed (Lord Locksley), Michael Wincott (Guy of Gisborne), Nick Brimble (Little John), Liam Halligan (Peter Dubois).

Kevin Costner robs from the rich and gives to the poor... but can't manage to acquire a proper accent.

Bloopers
1. The movie takes place during the years A.D. 1194–1195. Many "Proclamation" posters (one is affixed to a door, another one will be ripped off a shack) seem suspiciously the same, as if they were printed via Gutenberg's method, which the German inventor will create in 1455. True, printing was invented by the Chinese in the second Century A.D.—but not the kind used in the movie. (00:02, 01:03)
2. As soon as they escape from the prison, and Robin gets the ring from Peter, Azeem turns because "they're coming!" His turn is in reverse play: the cloth around his face moves before he does. (00:06)

3. Lord Locksley writes a letter and is heard reading it. He says, "Were you present at his capture near Jerusalem? Do you know the name of the potentate who holds him?" The paper says, "Were you present at... near Acre? Do you know the potentate who holds him?" Hmm... (00:08, 00:09)
4. On the beach in England, Robin stretches his right hand to be helped by Azeem. However, the Moor grabs Robin's left hand in the next shot. (00:12)
5. Robin swears over his father's tomb ("I swear by my own blood."), and in doing so he squeezes his hand so hard that blood drips between his fingers. But only in the detail. In the master shot, his hand is perfectly clean. (00:24)
6. Azeem assembles and uses a rudimentary telescope (or something very similar). Despite the fact that ancient Egyptians were already familiar with glass and presumably lenses, the first known appearance of a telescope was 1608 by the Dutchman Hans Lippershey, and it was later improved upon by Galileo. Just a bit early here, folks. (00:33, 01:05, 01:34)
7. The horse bits are made of stainless steel, which was not yet invented. (00:34, 01:07)
8. During the battle on the river

with Little John, Robin gets hit in the face and his nose starts bleeding profusely. But as he's hit one more time ("Swimming time again, old chum!"), his face has no blood on it. (00:42, 00:43)

9. The Sheriff of Nottingham uses the word "twit," even if it was coined in the sixteenth century. (00:55, 02:04)

10. A "Proclamation" poster is attached by one of the sheriff's soldiers to a pole. Robin runs an arrow through the poster and Little John rips it off the pole. But in the following master shot where the soldiers drop the goodies, the poster is back on the pole. (01:02)

11. Again, good ol' Azeem uses gunpowder for the final assault on Nottingham. Gunpowder was invented in China during the tenth century but was brought to Europe by Marco Polo during his travels. Marco Polo wasn't born until 1254. Also, it seems that the English scientist Sir Roger Bacon wrote a formula to produce an explosive black powder. But that was in 1242. (01:52)

12. When he sees Will in the crowd, the Sheriff of Nottingham says, "a turncoat." That phrase originated in the middle of the sixteenth century. (01:59)

13. Robin and Azeem are launched by a catapult; an astonished Will proclaims, "F*** me, he cleared it!" Needless to say,

the F-word wasn't very common at that time; not because it's a curse word, but because it didn't come around until the late seventeenth century. (02:06)

14. Robin bursts into the room where the sheriff and Lady Marian are getting married. Robin shatters the window, leaving a lot of shards hanging by the frame—but one second later, the window is clear: no glass anywhere. (02:10)

Questions

1. After Robin tells Guy to "get off my land," it's possible to see Azeem in the background going up the wall and then down, to join Robin. Is he lost or something? (00:18)

2. Robin disguises himself as a stinky old man in order to enter the castle of Nottingham and rescue a few of his merry friends. He wears a dark gray hood over a brownish cloak and carries a long cane. A few minutes later, he joins Little John and his wife—but this time he's wearing a dark purple robe in one piece and carrying two canes. Is one old man disguise not enough? (01:55, 01:58)

ROBOCOP (15)
Director's Cut
1987, color, 103 min.

Director: Paul Verhoeven

Cast: Peter Weller (Alex J. Murphy / RoboCop), Nancy

Allen (Anne Lewis), Dan O'Herlihy (The Old Man, Head OCP), Ronny Cox (Dick Jones), Kurtwood Smith (Clarence J. Boddicker), Miguel Ferrer (Robert "Bob" Morton), Robert DoQui (Sergeant Reed), Ray Wise (Leon C. Nash), Felton Perry (Johnson), Paul McCrane (Emil M. Antonowsky), Stephen Berrer (Roosevelt), Sage Parker (Tyler).

Cop is shot, then turned into a robot.

Bloopers

1. Murphy is called by Sergeant Reed after he states, "Police officers don't strike!" In the background, the cop close to the bare-chested one (with a white towel on his shoulders) vanishes between cuts. (00:05)

2. Bob Morton and two colleagues take an elevator to go to a meeting. As they step out of the car, a voice says, "95th floor; have a nice day." After the meeting, they take the same elevator down: a sign on the wall says they're on floor 120. (00:06, 00:13)

3. After the first close-up of ED 209's firing gun, it's possible to catch a glimpse of a "blood bag" under the jacket of Kinney, as he gets hit by the bullets. (00:11)

4. During the voice/stress test, Tyler says "Now, playback." Roosevelt adds, "Bring it up 50 percent." RoboCop plays it back, but after "Now, play-back." and "Bring it up 50 percent," Tyler adds "Gimme a full frame." She never said that. (00:31)

5. When RoboCop is sitting down for the first tests, a shot reveals that his feet have a toe. During the fight with ED 209, RoboCop flies through a door: his feet now are roundish, with no toe. The toe will be back very soon. (00:31, 01:11)

6. The holes on the training target used by Lewis are different from the front and the back. (00:32)

7. When Grocery Pop kneels down to open the safe, there are four Lite beer cans on top of it. In the next shot, there are seven. (00:35)

8. RoboCop enters a building and grabs former City Councilman Miller, then throws him down to the sidewalk. A few cameramen follow the fall. But when the scene is replayed on Jesse Perkins's news bulletin, you can see the legs of the stuntman bouncing back from his landing mattress. (00:40)

9. You can catch a quick glimpse of the camera reflected on a back wall of Morton's house when Clarence breaks in and yells to the two guests, "Bit**es leave!" (00:59)

10. When RoboCop kills almost everyone in Clarence's drug warehouse, two guys (side by side, one wearing a jeans jacket, the other a beige

jacket) are killed: the one in the jeans jacket has a cable that runs to the ground (probably an explosive device for special effects). (01:05)

11. When Clarence is thrown through the windows by RoboCop, the panes (particularly the second one) shatter a little before Clarence actually hits them. (01:06)

12. Further proof that RoboCop's playback is not very effective: Clarence yells, "Don't you get it, you co**sucker! I work for Dick Jones! Dick Jones!" But when RoboCop replays the taping, Clarence says, "Don't you get it? I work for Dick Jones! Dick Jones!" and his position is different. (01:06, 01:09)

13. Another faulty playback: RoboCop tapes Dick Jones saying, "I had to kill Bob Morton because he made a mistake. Now it's time to erase that mistake." When RoboCop plays this taping, Jones's tone of voice is completely different (also, when taping the line, RoboCop was about to be deactivated, yet the final product is excellent). (01:11, 01:35)

14. A few seconds before Lewis rams Clarence's car, it's possible to see the crew on a dolly reflected in Clarence's car door. (01:29)

15. Clarence's car loses its right rear hubcap. A few seconds later, the hubcap is back in place. (01:30)

Questions

1. RoboCop unscrews his helmet and removes it. Till the last moment, he's also wearing the neck and chin band. As he takes off the helmet, the band is gone, too. Was it part of the helmet? (01:21)

2. After being stabbed by Murphy, Clarence stumbles and falls into the water. Behind the flipped car . . . is that a man wearing a gray baseball hat? (01:32)

Fun Fact

Clarence decides his men have tried the new weapons enough; while Leon yells, "All right, cut the horsesh**," Clarence slams the rear door of his car. The rearview mirror detaches and falls. (01:25)

ROCK, THE (17)

1996, color, 135 min.

Director: Michael Bay

Cast: Sean Connery (John Patrick Mason), Nicolas Cage (Dr. Stanley Goodspeed), Ed Harris (General Francis X Hummel), John Spencer (FBI Director Womack), David Morse (Major Tom Baxter), William Forsythe (Ernest Paxton), Michael Biehn (Commander Anderson), Vanessa Marcil (Carla Pestalozzi), John C. McGinley (Marine Captain Hendrix), Gregory Sporleder (Captain Frye), Tony Todd (Captain Darrow), Danny Nucci (Lieutenant Shephard).

The FBI gets the only man to ever escape Alcatraz to help them take "The Rock" back from terrorists. And the escapee practically destroys San Francisco in the process.

Bloopers

1. Mason is imprisoned in 1962 because he stole the FBI's microfilm files for British intelligence and never returned them. In the end, when Goodspeed gets ahold of the same microfilms, he asks his wife if she wants to know who really killed JFK. But Kennedy was shot in 1963. Huh? (00:30, 01:17, 02:10)

2. The hole Mason makes in the jail's one-way mirror changes shape. (00:37)

3. During the chase in San Francisco, the Humvee hits a water truck. The windshield breaks, but in the following shots it's intact. (00:45)

4. Mason slams the Humvee into a parking enforcement vehicle, skidding to a stop. In the following shot, the Humvee is still on the move. (00:45)

5. A tourist cable car is moving on tracks. Just before it's hit by the Humvee, it appears to be moving on rubber tires, then on tracks again, and finally, as it smashes against a parked car, on tires one more time. (00:47, 00:48)

6. The windshield of Good-speed's yellow Ferrari breaks as the car flies through a window. Yet in the shot that follows, it appears to be intact. (00:46)

7. Goodspeed smashes several parking meters with the Ferrari; again, the windshield is broken by the impact—but as the car veers in the middle of the road, we see an intact windshield. (00:48)

8. Goodspeed points to a target on a satellite picture with his right hand, using a black pen that he hadn't been holding. As they walk away, now he has a silver pointer stick... in his left hand. (00:55)

9. While flying toward Alcatraz, Lieutenant Shephard puts on a headset, but in the following shot it's gone. (01:01)

10. Mason pulls the first lever using a rope and opens the wrong cell door. When he pulls the correct lever, the one he pulled first has reset all by itself (even if the corresponding cell door is still open). (01:42)

11. When Hummel and Frye are arguing in a room, Goodspeed peeks through an open slot in the wall, then invites Mason to do the same. But when Mason gets to the slot, he has to open it. (01:54)

12. General Hummel gets shot and falls backward on a dark gray mat. But when Mason drags him away, the mat is gone. (01:55, 01:56)

13. One ball of VX rolls away;

Goodspeed dives to catch it: he stretches his right arm, catches the ball with his left hand, and then he has it in his right hand. (01:59)

14. The number of planes flying toward Alcatraz keeps changing: first, five; then six; as they approach the Golden Gate, four; and when they fly underneath it, five again. (02:01, 02:03, 02:04)

15. It seems that the syringe Goodspeed uses to save himself vanishes as he stands up and waves the flares. (02:03, 02:05)

16. In the morning, Goodspeed sees the sun rise beyond the Golden Gate . . . unfortunately that's west of Alcatraz, and the sun rises in the east. (02:04, 02:09)

17. As the bomb hits Alcatraz— after the shot from above, the cables that hold Goodspeed (which allow him to be blasted away) can be seen (3 frames only). (02:05)

Questions

1. When Goodspeed and Isherwood begin the examination on the wooden crate labeled "Aid to Bosnia," Goodspeed says for the record that they start at 0900 hours. Yet in their office, some time before, a tiny clock behind Isherwood said 9:25. What time is it, exactly? (00:08, 00:09)

2. It is said that Alcatraz was closed in 1963 as a prison facility. When Goodspeed asks Mason how he made it through prison without even talking to other inmates, among the things Mason says is that he dreamt of meeting his daughter. But his daughter was born after 1972, so . . . ? (00:14, 01:18, 01:41)

3. As the group thinks they're "sitting ducks," Mason explains how he escaped: he memorized the timing of the boiler fire blasts, so he could roll in between them. So he does it backward, and subsequently he opens the door to the soldiers. Then why didn't he simply open the door when he escaped the first time, instead of endangering his life with the fire? (01:05)

4. After Goodspeed tells Womack that Mason is dead, Mason tells him that it's been a long time since he's said "thank you" to somebody. But he said "thank you" only the day before to Goodspeed for handling Mason's recapture in front of his daughter discreetly (00:53). Maybe for Mason "a long time" means "24 hours?" (02:08)

ROCKY HORROR PICTURE SHOW, THE (23)
1975, color, 100 min.

Director: Jim Sharman

Cast: Tim Curry (Dr. Frank-N-Furter), Susan Sarandon (Janet Weiss), Barry Bostwick (Brad Majors), Richard O'Brien (Riff

Raff), Patricia Quinn (Magenta), Nell Campbell (Columbia), Jonathan Adams (Dr. Everett V. Scott), Peter Hinwood (Rocky Horror), Meat Loaf (Eddie), Charles Gray (Criminologist / Narrator).

Tim Curry's sweet alien transvestite scientist causes a little playful mayhem.

Bloopers

1. After the photo at the marriage, the father of the groom goes up the church steps twice. (00:05)
2. Brad draws a heart on the church door. The heart changes shape between two takes. (00:08)
3. When Brad gives his ring to Janet, the purse is behind her feet, lying on one side. After a few seconds, the purse, still lying on one side, has jumped in front of Janet's feet. (00:08)
4. While Brad and Janet's car drives in the rain, the windshield wipers' movement doesn't match between wide shots and close-ups. (00:12)
5. During the song "There's a Light," Janet's sweater seems to change color, from whitish to light blue, and back to whitish. (00:15)
6. As Brad and Janet enter "The Time Warp" room, it's possible to see a long red carpet crossing the room from wall to wall. But when Riff Raff and Magenta dance,

moving through the room, the carpet seems to have disappeared, and only a portion of it is visible, to the end of the steps. It'll come back later in all its splendor (and length). (00:20, 00:21)

7. When the congregation sings, "...that really drives you insane!" A fat man to the left is passing a tray with hors d'ouvres—but in the following shot he's holding the tray again. (00:20)
8. Columbia sits on the jukebox, a golden top hat on her head. As the crowd sings, "You bring your knees in tight," the hat is visible on the floor, far away from Columbia. After the dance, Columbia is wearing her hat again. (00:21, 00:22)
9. At the end of "The Time Warp," when everyone collapses to the floor, in the background Janet begins her line—but you can't hear her. You can *see* her because she nudges Brad, the same action she repeats a few seconds later. (00:23)
10. Dr. Frank-N-Furter walks along the red carpet (singing "Sweet Transvestite") and he passes by Magenta, Riff Raff, and Columbia. As he walks back, he passes by Riff Raff, Magenta, and Columbia. Did the three trade places? (00:24, 00:25)
11. When Janet sees Frank for the first time, she raises her left hand—but in her close-

up she's raising her right. (00:24)

12. When Magenta helps undress Brad, she removes his vest, revealing an already-unbuttoned shirt. After a cut, she's unbuttoning the now-buttoned shirt. (00:28)

13. Going up in the elevator, Brad and Janet see—among other things—a cable that looks suspiciously like one used for movie lighting. (00:29)

14. While delivering his speech before giving life to Rocky, Dr. Frank-N-Furter puts his pink gloves on: the left one is alternately folded around his hand or straight along his arm. (00:33)

15. Riff Raff turns a wheel clockwise in order to lower the goo-dispenser for the animation of Rocky. As Rocky grabs the dispenser he's lifted up, thanks to Riff Raff who's turning the wheel . . . clockwise. A few instants later, he's turning it counterclockwise. (00:34, 00:36)

16. The gym horse that Frank gives to Rocky goes away ("When in just seven days, oh baby, I can make you a man"). It's pulled by the hands of a crew member. (00:41)

17. The saxophone Eddie plays has no ligature, no reed, and therefore it couldn't produce any sound (it's actually a "stunt sax," used in music videos and such). (00:43)

18. Blood can be seen on the floor before Dr. Frank-N-Furter kills Eddie with a pickax. (00:45)

19. When Dr. Frank-N-Furter pulls the lever to drag Dr. Scott into the lab, in the long shot he begins to lift up his left leg, but in the detail he's lifting up the right. (01:01)

20. When the electro-magnet pulls Dr. Scott and his wheelchair, it's possible to see not only the track and the cable pulling the chair, but also part of a carpet flipping up as the cable pulls the chair by. (01:01)

21. Riff Raff starts serving one slice of meat to Brad in a close-up, then in the long shot he has to do it again (during the "Happy Birthday" song). (01:05)

22. Dr. Frank-N-Furter gets out of the pool for the last part of the floor show. The tattoo on his right arm (a heart with "boss" on top of it) looks washed out and restored in various shots. (01:23, 01:25)

23. Dr. Scott is carried out of the castle by Brad and Janet. But after the house/spaceship takes off, his wheelchair suddenly appears next to him. (01:34)

Questions

1. The criminologist says the events took place "that late November evening." But when Brad and Janet are listening to the car radio, they hear Nixon's resignation speech.

Nixon resigned in August 1974. Was it a rerun? (00:11, 00:12)

2. It seems that Brad hits or kicks Janet when saying "Just exactly what are you implying?" Watch her expression . . . did he goose her? (01:06)

Fun Facts

1. Being the first to be "de-Medusa-ed," Columbia sings her solo. As she sings, "rose tints my world," her breast pops out of her corset. She doesn't stop dancing and fixes it on the run. (01:17)

2. During the final song, right after Riff Raff sings "We return to Transylvania," Janet steps on Brad's foot with one of her high heels (check out Brad's face). (01:25)

ROMANCING THE STONE (7)
1984, color, 105 min.

Director: Robert Zemeckis

Cast: Michael Douglas (Jack T. Colton), Kathleen Turner (Joan Wilder), Danny DeVito (Ralph), Zack Norman (Ira), Alfonso Arau (Juan), Manuel Ojeda (Señor Zolo), Holland Taylor (Gloria Horne), Mary Ellen Trainor (Elaine), Eve Smith (Mrs. Irwin).

Adventure, romance, passion . . . but look at those snappers!!

Bloopers

1. Joan is looking for some paper tissue when she finds her "Don't Forget—Buy Tissue!" note attached to a mirror. The note moves from the left of the mirror to the center of it before she takes it to blow her nose in. (00:04)

2. Joan says good-bye to her publisher and they kiss in the snow: the scene is observed by Señor Zolo. But from the inside of his car, the windshield wipers move faster than they do on his close-up. (00:18)

3. When Zolo wants Ralph's car, he shows his ID through the windshield: Zolo holds it in two different ways, depending on whether the shot is from the inside or the outside of Ralph's vehicle. (00:27)

ROCK "SOLID"

"Hard as a rock?" Well, we beg to differ.

A rollerblader's splash in *Big Daddy*	Blooper No. 1
A stone block in *Raiders of the Lost Ark*	Blooper No. 14
Michael Douglas's landing in *Romancing the Stone*	Blooper No. 5
A thug's crash in *Under Siege 2*	Blooper No. 2

4. After the wild ride along the mud, Jack's hair changes after every single shot in the large puddle. (00:33)

5. Jack follows Joan's example and swings on a vine, hits a rock ... and bounces back off it (rubber stones in the forest?). (00:40)

6. While in the plane wreckage, Jack examines Joan's map and he mumbles "Tenedor del Diablo ... The Devil's fork!" The detail shows a map that is completely open; his close-up shows a map with its right side folded back. (00:53)

7. At a restaurant, Jack wants to give Joan a little gift: he produces an elaborate necklace. But when she picks it up, the necklace has become a simple chain with a small heart ("El Corazón?") attached to it. (01:09)

Questions

1. While arguing on the phone with his cousin Ralph, Ira yells, "Of all the things you can say to me right now, 'I've lost her, Ralph' is gonna get the most teeth broken in your mouth!" Shouldn't he have said "I've lost her, Ira," since, if he's quoting Ralph, "I've lost her ..." would have been directed *at* Ira? Or are we hearing things? (01:05)

2. Jack and Joan are kissing on board their boat *Angelina*, which takes off, pulled by a truck, down a Manhattan avenue. The truck passes a street ... but wait! Isn't the light red? (01:42)

RONIN (11)
1998, color, 121 min.

Director: John Frankenheimer

Cast: Robert De Niro (Sam), Jean Reno (Vincent), Natascha McElhone (Dierdre), Stellan Skarsgård (Gregor), Sean Bean (Spence), Skipp Sudduth (Larry), Michel Lonsdale (Jean-Pierre), Jan Triska (Dapper Gent), Jonathan Pryce (Seamus), Ron Perkins (The Man with the Newspaper), Féodor Atkine (Mikhi), Katarina Witt (Natacha Kirilova), Lionel Vitrant (The "Target").

Nothing is as it seems in this mysterious, low-key crime yarn ... which is chock full o' killer car chases.

Bloopers

1. Before they turn onto the dirt road in the Nice car chase, the Audi is trailing the Citroën by only a few feet. But just as the Citroën swerves onto the dirt road to avoid the truck, the Audi is nowhere to be seen behind it. (00:47)

2. During this chase, the model of the Citroën carrying the case changes. Notice the logo on the grill of the car just before it swerves onto the dirt road to avoid the truck, then later in Nice (yet the license plate remains the same). (00:47)

3. On the dirt road, the Audi's

headlights are both broken. By the time they get to Nice, they're both intact. (00:47)

4. As the Citroën speeds through Nice, its license plate is coming off. When it swerves into a street stand, the plate is back in place. (00:48)

5. When the Citroën swerves into the stand, it's immediately followed by the Mercedes, which should have been behind the Audi (which should have been behind the Citroën). Then the Mercedes speeds by the crashed car as if in pursuit of something else. Huh? (00:48)

6. Sam tends to Larry's leg wound by pouring alcohol on it. He then puts the bottle down on the bed. In the next shot, he puts it down again! (00:53)

7. Gregor jumps down a flight of stairs in the arena in Arles, while fleeing from Sam. He tumbles down the stairs, and his wire-rimmed glasses fly off his head. One second later, he's off running again, with the glasses securely back on his head. Just a bit too quick of a recovery. (01:06)

8. In Arles, Dierdre arrives back at the car and gets in the passenger side to find Larry with his throat slit in the driver's seat. Seamus, sitting in the backseat, tells her to "Drive!" Sam and Vincent are a dozen yards behind her in pursuit. Several seconds later, the car is speeding away with

Dierdre driving, and Larry's body is on the pavement. Is she super fast and strong, or . . . oh, never mind. (01:08)

9. During the Paris car chase, Dierdre has her driver-side window wide open, yet her hair is rarely affected by the breeze that would be generated by traveling at speeds of 60 mph plus. At a few points, her hair flops around just a little bit (01:28), but nothing close to how much it really would. (01:26, 01:28)

10. After Dierdre, Seamus, and Gregor emerge from the second tunnel while going against traffic, even though they've been traveling on a two-lane road, now they're on a three-lane road. Merge lane? Perhaps. But when Sam and Vincent come out following them, it's clear they're on a two-lane road in a few shots; several other shots until the end of the chase alternate between a two-lane and a three-lane road. (01:32, 01:33)

11. Right before the end of the chase, Seamus shoots off Sam's side-view mirror. It's back in the next shot. (01:33)

Question

Gregor shoots a dapper gent in his car—point blank in the face—and blood splatters on the passenger window. If the bullet exited the head at such a velocity, shouldn't it have shattered or at least cracked the window as well? (00:57)

S

SCREAM (21)
also Director's Cut
1996, color, 111 min. / 111 min.
(DC)

Director: Wes Craven

Cast: David Arquette (Deputy Dwight "Dewey" Riley), Neve Campbell (Sidney Prescott), Courtney Cox (Gale Weathers), Matthew Lillard (Stuart Macher), Rose McGowan (Tatum Riley), Skeet Ulrich (Billy Loomis), Jamie Kennedy (Randy Meeks), W. Earl Brown (Kenny, the Cameraman), Joseph Whipp (Sheriff Burke), Liev Schreiber (Cotton Weary), Drew Barrymore (Casey Becker), Roger L. Jackson (Phone Voice), Lawrence Hecht (Neil Prescott).

Start of the tongue-in-cheek horror sensation.

Bloopers

1. Casey peels off the popcorn cover, ripping it in half, and she sets it on the kitchen counter, the ripped half standing up. When she comes back to the kitchen, the cover is laying flat, in one piece. (00:01, 00:03)

2. Billy puts his left hand in the window frame, but he lands with his right on Sidney. (00:13)

3. When Sidney is scared by Billy, her dad knocks and opens the door, which gets stuck on the closet door. Sidney says to her dad, "Can you knock?" Well, he *did* knock. (00:13)

4. Sidney is talking on a cordless phone while walking out of her house. Before she says, "It's like déjà vu all over again," a boom mike shadow is briefly visible on the handrail of the stairs. (00:22)

5. When Sidney gets a call from Tatum, her left sleeve is up to her wrist. A shot from above reveals the same sleeve at the elbow, and as she picks up the phone when the killer calls, the sleeve has moved again to her wrist. (00:24, 00:25)

6. When Sidney gets the call, it's 7:15 and dark outside. When the stores close for the curfew at 9:00, it's bright as day. (00:24, 00:57)

7. The door of the handicapped stall in the bathroom is closed, but open when Sidney steps into it. (00:45)

8. Dewey is approached by Gale outside Sidney's school. He removes his sunglasses and places them in his shirt collar—the lenses are facing toward his right. When he turns to listen to the P.A., the glasses have rotated 180° and now the lenses are facing toward his left. When he steps up the stairs, the glasses have rotated 180° more. (00:48, 00:49)

9. Principal Himbry opens his closet and parts the clothes hanging on the rack. Yet when he closes the door, the clothes are perfectly distributed across the rack. (00:52)

10. The cigarette Sheriff Burke is smoking gets longer and shorter all through the sequence. (00:59)

11. When Gale hides the camera, she places it under the TV set. The image she gets later is from a much higher position. (01:04, 01:08)

12. Tatum goes to get the beers but gets locked inside. However, the killer seems to have no problem opening the door a little later. (01:05, 01:07)

13. When Tatum throws beer at the killer, he's drenched. As he hits the floor, he's dry. (01:06)

14. Everybody seems to be leaving because of the curfew, but later on everyone is on the couch, watching *Halloween*. (01:07, 01:12)

15. Randy sees Sidney and Billy going upstairs; he says, "I'm gonna check on them," and heads for the stairs. However, we find him on the couch, watching a movie. (01:08, 01:13)

16. Randy explains the three rules, and a white phone is seen close to the TV; Dewey enters the house and a white phone is still seen close to the TV; Sidney smashes the TV on top of Stu, but where is the white phone? (01:13, 01:25, 01:40)

17. The "rules" speech starts and it's immediately followed by a replay of the speech (seen through Gale's monitor). The lines and rhythm are different. (01:13)

18. When Gale leaves the van with Dewey, she says to him, "Be right back," but she mouths, "Keep watching." (01:14)

19. Gale stops her van while in reverse: the cameraman's body falls in front of the vehicle. The laws of physics say that this is impossible. (01:26)

20. Gale tries to shoot Billy, but the gun doesn't fire. He knocks her out and mutters something about the safety

being on. Later on, she uses the gun and says that she remembered the safety this time. How did Gale know what Billy said if she was unconscious? (01:37, 01:42)

21. Being one of the survivors of the night in the slaughterhouse, Gale makes a piece for the news when the sun is rising. Fine. The sun is rising exactly where it was setting two nights before, in the west. (01:43, 00:24)

DVD Blooper

While being tortured by the killer on the phone, Casey is asked to "Name the killer in *Halloween*." She answers "Michael . . . Michael Myers." The DVD subtitles as well as the Closed Captioning say "Michael . . . Michael, Michael!" (00:06)

Fun Fact

Billy has a mustache and a beard on the poster but he's clean-shaven in the movie.

The Loomis Connection

In *Scream* (1996), Billy's last name is Loomis, which was also the last name of Donald Pleasance's character in *Halloween* (1978). *Scream* writer Kevin Williamson said that *Halloween* is his favorite movie. Also, the name of Pleasance's character, Sam Loomis, is an affectionate homage to one of *Halloween* director John Carpenter's favorites, *Psycho* (1960). Sam Loomis was the name of Marion Crane's lover in the Hitchcock classic.

SCREAM 2 (11)

1997, color, 120 min.

Director: Wes Craven

Cast: David Arquette (Dwight "Dewey" Riley), Neve Campbell (Sidney Prescott), Courtney Cox (Gale Weathers), Sarah Michelle Gellar (Casey "CiCi" Cooper), Jamie Kennedy (Randy Meeks), Elise Neal (Hallie), Laurie Metcalf (Reporter Debbie Salt), Jerry O'Connell (Derek), Timothy Olyphant (Mickey), Jada Pinkett (Maureen Evans), Liev Schreiber (Cotton Weary), Lewis Arquette (Chief Louis Hartley), Duane Martin (Joel, the Cameraman), Rebecca Gayheart (Sorority Sister Lois), Portia de Rossi (Sorority Sister Murphy).

Sydney goes to college . . . and gets stalked again.

Bloopers

1. During the showing of *Stab*, Maureen orders a medium popcorn and a small Pepsi at concessions, but when she comes back, she definitely has a HUGE Pepsi. (00:05)

2. When Maureen stumbles across the theater aisle and gets grabbed by the killer again, he places his right arm around her neck and stabs her with his left hand. In the following shot, the killer's arms are both behind Maureen, the knife in his right hand. (00:10)

3. Sidney is left by Dewey and she's standing in a gazebo. From a side shot, her head appears to be very close to a pole of the gazebo. From the wide shot, she's much further away from it—and then she gets closer. (00:24)

4. The killer grabs CiCi and throws her over a second floor balcony at the sorority house. At the very end of the first shot of the fall, a man's head pops up beyond the edge of the balcony. (00:35)

5. After the third murder, Chief Hartley writes on a blackboard "Maureen Evans, Phil Stevens, Cici—" and as the shot cuts away, the names are clearly written in a different way. (00:43)

6. Gale underlines two names on the blackboard; the lines change shape and length between cuts. (00:43)

7. Dewey places his hand on a pay phone, grabbing its edge. From behind, his hand is far from the edge. (01:14)

8. Dewey bangs on a soundproof window with his fist from his side of the glass and with his open hand from Gale's side of the glass. (01:21)

9. When Dewey gets stabbed against the soundproof glass, more blood shows on it when Gale is in the shot than when the killer is. (01:22)

10. Sidney leaves Derek and gets in the car from the rear door on the left side of the car. Hallie sits close to her, on the right. Later, when the car stops at a light, Sidney has switched with Hallie—now she's on the right side of the car. (01:24, 01:25)

11. Mickey shoots Derek using a hammerless gun—but the sound heard is of a gun's hammer being cocked. (01:36)

Questions

1. Since when would a pro camera man (with a pro camera) be recording his footage on VHS tapes? (00:18, 01:16)

2. Sidney gets a frightening message while working on a library computer. She is told to check it by pushing "Alt-Tab," but the sound that is heard is of five keys being pressed. Does she stutter when she types? (01:06)

Fun Fact

In film class, one of the guys quotes *Aliens:* "Get away from her, you bitch!" Randy corrects him by saying that the line is, "Stay away from her, you bitch!" Nope. The first guy was right. (00:16)

SCREAM 3 (9)
2000, color, 116 min.

Director: Wes Craven

Cast: David Arquette (Dwight "Dewey" Riley), Neve Campbell (Sidney Prescott), Courtney Cox Arquette (Gale Weathers), Patrick Dempsey (Detective Mark Kincaid), Scott

Foley (Roman Bridger), Lance Henriksen (John Milton), Matt Keeslar (Tom Prinze), Jenny McCarthy (Sarah Darling), Emily Mortimer (Angelina Tyler), Parker Posey (Jennifer Jolie), Deon Richmond (Tyson Fox), Patrick Warburton (Steve Stone), Liev Schreiber (Cotton Weary), Heather Matarazzo (Martha Weeks), Carrie Fisher (Bianca Burnadette).

Sydney moves to the country ... and gets stalked again; so she heads to Hollywood ... and gets stalked yet again.

Bloopers

1. When Roman shows Dewey the beheaded award he found in his office, the award rotates 180° from the shot of Roman to the shot of Dewey. (00:34)
2. Jennifer runs into the house by the fax machine: there's no paper in the holder, yet a page comes through. And when the second page is received, there's a lot of paper in the holder. (00:44)
3. Detective Kinkaid retrieves a third picture of Sidney's mother; on the back is written "I killed her." The wall of the office has copies of the previously found pictures, along with the "I killed her" message. The word "COPY" is printed on every image. Still, the "I killed her" writing doesn't match the original's. (00:48, 01:12)
4. When Sidney opens the door over the reproduction of her old bedroom on the set, the left nightstand (the one with a blue phone on it) has its long side against the wall. But when the killer falls onto the bed, the same nightstand has rotated 90°, as its shorter side is now against the wall. (01:05)
5. Looking for a ringing cell phone, Gale and Dewey open a closet and find a voice modulator. Gale picks it up, revealing blood on her right hand. But as she brings it close to her mouth, the blood is gone. (01:19)
6. Detective Kincaid places a green post-it on his bulletin board, right above the "I killed her" copy. After chatting with Sidney, he stands up ("I think what you saw is real"). The green post-it has moved to the left, away from the copy. Later on, when Sidney is on the phone with the killer, she goes into an empty office: when she walks back out in front of the board, the post-it has moved back above the copy. (01:12, 01:14, 01:29)
7. Sidney receives a call on her cell phone when she's at the police station. The phone has a Nokia logo displayed quite prominently on the bottom. But in the following shots in that office, the Nokia logo is gone. It'll come back as Sidney moves into a rear office. (01:28)
8. Sidney fires a few rounds at

the masked killer, who falls in the corridor of Milton's villa. When Gale notices that the killer is gone, the detail shows that the door to the patio is partly open. When Detective Kincaid steps into the same area, the door is firmly closed (and will be smashed by the killer a few seconds later). (01:33)

9. Dewey unties Gale from her chair: she lifts her left arm, revealing a rope around her wrist, but in the next shot the rope is gone. (01:38)

Questions

1. When Cotton's girlfriend Christine locks herself in the den, the white ceiling has a skylight. When Cotton later lies on the floor of the same room, he looks up at the killer: the ceiling now has wooden beams. Is the killer also a makeshift architect? (00:05, 00:09)

2. In the Hollywood hills, five people are about to panic because the killer has just struck. The lights go off in the whole house and everyone runs outside—but a phone rings: it's the fax machine, and the killer is sending pages of a new script. But the power is off; so, is the fax on some special battery? And while we're at it, do the pool lights run on separate power, too? (00:44, 00:45)

3. Randy makes a cameo appearance while he's leaving his legacy on VHS tape. While talking, he's bothered by someone who's banging on his door. He springs out of his chair to go to the door—but the tape shows

Scream Series Cameos		
Oh, what the heck . . .		
SCREAM	ROLE	TIMES
Linda Blair	Reporter at school	00:39
Director Wes Craven	Janitor (wearing "Freddy" getup)	00:52
SCREAM 2	ROLE	TIMES
Writer Kevin Williamson	Cotton's interviewer	00:13
Tori Spelling	As Herself	00:50
SCREAM 3	ROLE	TIMES
Roger Corman	Studio executive leaning against the rail	00:13
Jason Mewes and Kevin Smith	Studio tour guests "recognizing" Gale	00:45

a cut after he gets up. So, if he edited his legacy tape, couldn't he cut out the banging on the door too? (00:53)

SHANGHAI NOON (8)
2000, color, 110 min.

Director: Tom Dey

Cast: Jackie Chan (Chon Wang), Owen Wilson (Roy O'Bannon), Lucy Liu (Princess Pei Pei), Brandon Merrill (Indian Wife), Roger Yuan (Lo Fang), Xander Berkeley (Van Cleef), Rong Guang Yu (Imperial Guard), Cui Ya Hi (Imperian Guard), Eric Chi Cheng Chen (Imperial Guard), Jason Connery (Andrews).

East meets West and uses fists rather than guns.

Bloopers
1. Roy is buried in the sand, a vulture chewing on his left ear. When he screams, a wide shot shows the vulture quite far away from the ear—but the following shot catches the vulture nibbling again. (00:18)
2. When Chon reaches Roy (still buried), the shadows go to the right. But as Roy pleads, "Oh, come on. Water!" the shadows go to the left. (00:18)
3. Chon orders the horse to sit down and the animal obeys. And the smoke in the background goes *back into* the chimney. (00:33)
4. Roy's card-replacer device goes back in his sleeve, but it's right back out in the following shot. (00:36)
5. In the bathtubs, Roy loses the first match of the drinking game. Chon pours him a drink from an almost empty bottle, but when he slams it back on the table, the bottle is almost completely full. (01:05)
6. Sentenced to death, Roy and Chon have nooses placed around their necks. The knots of the nooses lay on their right breasts, but in the wide shot, the knots hang behind their backs. (01:13)
7. Chon decides to proceed alone, leaving Roy behind. When Chon says, "You said I wasn't your friend," his hat is in his hands. In the over-the-shoulder shot, the hat has jumped around his neck and now hangs on his back. (01:16)
8. When Princess Pei Pei places the Imperial decree on the candles in the church, the whole roll catches fire—but in the following shots, only one small part is on fire. (01:26)

6TH DAY, THE (6)
2000, color, 123 min.

Director: Roger Spottiswoode

Cast: Arnold Schwarzenegger (Adam Gibson), Michael Rapaport (Hank Morgan), Tony Goldwyn (Michael Drucker), Michael Rooker (Robert Marshall), Sarah Wynter (Talia Elsworth), Wendy Crewson (Natalie Gibson), Rodney Rowland (Wiley), Terry Crews

(Vincent), Ken Pogue (Speaker Day), Colin Cunningham (Tripp), Robert Duvall (Dr. Griffin Weir), Wanda Cannon (Katherine Weir).

How many clones could a woodcloner clone if a woodcloner could clone clones?

Bloopers

1. The introduction says, "Soon after [06/26/2000], anti-cloning protests take place in Rome." Trust us: in Rome, there is no chance in hell that you'll find a cop with "Police" written on his uniform, nor a sign saying, "No Stops—Tow Away" on the meters. (00:01)
2. While driving to the airport, Adam tells Hank that "Your primary relation is with a piece of software." It's possible to see the reflection of some equipment and a crew member on the window. (00:07)
3. In a taxicab, Adam leaves a message for Hank. The message ends with "Uhm, look, I'm heading home now. If you get this message..." When Hank checks his messages, Adam's message concludes with "I'm heading home, OK?" (00:21, 00:44)
4. Adam enters the Nu Organ building, smuggling a gun inside a cooler. He takes the lid off, drops it to the floor, freezes when a woman walks by (the lid is back in place), then grabs the gun. (01:06)
5. Landing his chopper on Mr. Drucker's private heliport, Adam

shows his charter contract (a copy of a previous one). They green-light his landing—even if the form is not filled out at all. (01:25)
6. On the floor, Drucker bleeds from his mouth and it runs down his neck. But when his clone looks at himself in the mirror, Drucker's blood is gone. It happens again when the clone lands on Drucker: a stream of blood runs down the man's right cheek. But it's gone a few moments later when Drucker says, "Go after him." (01:46, 01:48, 01:49)

Question

As soon as he's awakened, Drucker's clone takes Drucker's clothes. What about his glasses? Or do the clones see better than the originals? (01:46)

SLEEPER (7)

1973, color, 87 min.

Director: Woody Allen

Cast: Woody Allen (Miles Monroe), Diane Keaton (Luna Schlosser), John Beck (Erno Windt), Mary Gregory (Dr. Melik), Don Keefer (Dr. Tryon), John McLiam (Dr. Agon), Bartlett Robinson (Dr. Orva), Chris Forbes (Rainer Krebs), Marya Small (Dr. Nero), Peter Hobbs (Dr. Dean), Susan Miller (Ellen Pogrebin).

A funny man is frozen for two hundred years and wakes up in a completely different world.

Bloopers

1. Fleeing from the police, Miles steals a flying pack but gets stuck in a tree, spinning clockwise. When he jumps down, he keeps spinning. Counterclockwise. (00:21, 00:22)

2. When Miles hides in the Domesticon van, he activates a bunch of butler-robots via remote. The robot on the left (only his left hand is visible) moves before the others, starting immediately when Miles flicks the switch. All the others start moving a second later. They're also out of sync in stopping: Miles flicks the switch one more time and only half of the robots freeze. The other half need half a second more. (00:23)

3. Hunting for food, Miles grabs a very large banana and one stick of celery. After the "being pecked to death" remark, the banana turns 180° in his hands while he's running. (00:41)

4. 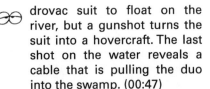Miles and Luna stop by the river, and Miles takes off using a hydrovac suit, which allows him to float in the air. But while he's in the air you can see the cables that pull the suit up (especially after the cop says, "Take her in! We'll have her reprogrammed!"). (00:45)

5. Luna knocks a cop out using a log, which she drops on the arm of a second cop, who's lying unconscious. When Miles and Luna get closer to the river, the log has moved nearer to the first cop. (00:46)

6. Miles and Luna use the hy- drovac suit to float on the river, but a gunshot turns the suit into a hovercraft. The last shot on the water reveals a cable that is pulling the duo into the swamp. (00:47)

7. Erno and Luna reenact a family scene to deprogram Miles. When Erno says, "Let's eat," he drops the script—but in the following shot he's holding it in his left hand. (01:05)

SLEEPY HOLLOW (7)
1999, color, 105 min.

Director: Tim Burton

Cast: Johnny Depp (Constable Ichabod Crane), Christina Ricci (Katrina Van Tassel), Miranda Richardson (Lady Van Tassel), Michael Gambon (Baltus Van Tassel), Casper Van Dien (Brom Van Brunt), Jeffrey Jones (Reverend Steenwick), Christopher Lee (Burgomaster), Richard Griffiths (Magistrate Samuel Philipse), Ian McDiarmid (Doctor Thomas Lancaster), Michael Gough (Notary James Hardenbrook), Mark Pickering (Young Masbath), Martin Landau (Peter Van Garrett).

A headless horseman terrorizes a small town, and everyone loses their heads. Sorry, we just couldn't resist.

Bloopers

1. Peter Van Garrett looks out of the left side of the coach he's

traveling in and sees a frightening scarecrow. But the scarecrow's shot appears to be moving as if it were taken from the *right* side of the coach. (00:02)

2. Ichabod sets his red bird free. He grabs the animal with a clean hand—but a few minutes later, when he stares at his hand in the coach, it appears to be thoroughly covered with little scars. (00:07, 00:08)

3. It is said about the Hessian Horseman that "he had filed his teeth down to sharp points." However, when his skull is shown, the teeth look absolutely normal. (00:16, 01:24)

4. While Ichabod is checking a headless victim, Magistrate Philipse squeezes his talisman ("The devil's fire!"). In the close-ups, the magistrate is holding it close to his breast—in the detail, close to his belt. (00:24)

5. They examine the corpse of the widow Winship: as the body is placed on the operating table, Ichabod produces one instrument from his bag—but as he puts it down, three or four are already on the table (which was totally clear when they placed the corpse on it). Also, the grip of Ichabod's hand changes between the master shot and the detail. (00:28)

6. Ichabod flips the bird-in-the-cage toy he's carrying with him. The detail from his point of view shows the bird in the correct position (head up, feet down), but it should have been upside down, according to the master shot. (01:21)

7. While learning the truth from her stepmother, Katrina is lying on one side: her half-heart pendant is in the middle of her chest in the close-ups but in the long shots it's hidden by her dress. The necklace also seems to grow longer in the long shots. (01:24, 01:25)

Question
The story takes place in New York, 1799. However, Constable Crane states in the Municipal Watchhouse that "the millennium is almost upon us." Does "almost upon us" mean to him "a little more than 200 years?" (00:03, 00:04)

SMOKEY AND THE BANDIT (14)
1977, color, 96 min.

Director: Hal Needham

Cast: Burt Reynolds (Bo "Bandit" Darville), Sally Field (Carrie), Jerry Reed (Cledus "Snowman" Snow), Mike Henry (Junior Justice), Paul Williams (Little Enos), Pat McCormick (Big Enos), Alfie Wise (Patrolman, Traffic Jam), George Reynolds (Branford), Macon McCalmna (Mr. B), Jackie Gleason (Sheriff Buford T. Justice of Portague County).

The first (and best) comedy "on wheels" about bootlegging beer, cops, Texarcana— loads of fun.

Bloopers

1. When in Texarcana, the Bandit uses a forklift to move some boxes of Coors beer. Cledus is sent flying through the cases—which are clearly empty when he hits them. (00:17)
2. The Bandit fishtails on the road the first time he sees Carrie . . . and leaves extensive skidmarks on the asphalt. They're all gone when Cledus's truck passes by a few moments later. (00:18, 00:19)
3. The Bandit's car's odometer reads 1108.8 the first time Carrie notices how fast they're going. And, despite a pretty long chase, a few discussions and the first run-in with Sheriff Justice, it has only advanced to 1108.9 ("Well, let's see what he's got under the hood."). (00:21, 00:30)
4. Sheriff Buford T. Justice gets out of his car and removes the safety belt around his gun. But when he kicks one of the kids who are working around the wedding car ("That's an attention-getter."), the gun and holster are gone. They'll come right back, exactly where they were before. (00:21, 00:22)
5. Still in Texas (or perhaps Arkansas), the Bandit places his CB by Carrie to let Cledus hear what she's saying. When Carrie says, "I think he was from Texas or something," they pass by a sign for State Highway 54. The sign is a Georgia sign, not a Texas or an Arkansas sign. (00:24)
6. The Bandit is fleeing from the first officer in Arkansas, and while Bandit's rounding a curve, something reddish dangles in front of his windshield. But there's nothing in the following wide shot that even resembles it—might it have been part of the camera? (00:28)
7. Scared by the Bandit's wild driving, Carrie begins to climb into the back seat. But when Bandit goes off the road, passing Cledus's truck on the right and smashing a few mailboxes, Carrie appears to be sitting in the passenger seat. (00:31)
8. Sheriff Justice's car is smashed against Cledus's truck, and it also gets smashed when he knocks one of the police cars from the Mulberry Bridge. It's later back in pristine condition, apparently without ever stopping by a body shop. (00:32, 00:37, 00:44)
9. The Bandit aims toward the Mulberry Bridge, without knowing that it has been dismantled. He hits the brakes and the car skids to the right—but the detail shows a car skidding to the left. (00:37)
10. When the sheriff's car passes underneath a truck and gets "decapitated," the sheriff peeks out of the wreckage:

he (actually, his stunt double) is wearing protective goggles. (00:45)

11. Sheriff Justice is in pursuit with his "roofless" car; his son Junior, without a hat, is holding the sheriff's hat. But later on, when they're stalled by a funeral, they both have their hats on. And only then does Sheriff Justice bark at Junior, "Hold my hat!" and Junior's hat flies away. Hmm . . . (00:46, 00:48)

12. Carrie drives Bandit's car through a football field and to get out she smashes a wooden wall: the CB antenna gets knocked off and falls in the middle of the road—but it's back in place a few minutes later. (00:49, 00:50)

13. The Bandit drives away from a gas station where Sheriff Buford T. Justice had also stopped. The sheriff sees the Bandit driving away, and his son Junior seems to be looking in the distance. However, in the following matching cut Junior is fast asleep. (00:52)

14. Sheriff Buford T. Justice stops by a tow truck and gets out of his car, leaving the door open. A truck is approaching, and the "Banzai" driver sees the car and aims at it. But in the wide shot after the driver's close-up, the door appears to be closed. It'll be open in the following shot, when it gets ripped off. (00:59)

Question

Carrie takes a glimpse at the speedometer and screams, "Are we really going 110?" The speedometer reads 110 *kilometers* per hour (therefore only 70 miles per hour). Doesn't she know that in America speed is measured in miles per hour? (00:21)

Fun Facts

1. The first time we see the Bandit, laying in the hammock (00:05), he's wearing a blue ring on his left hand: well, it keeps jumping from his middle finger to his ring finger and back all through the picture: the ring is on the ring finger when Bandit goes to visit Cledus, (00:07); it's back on the middle finger when Bandit buys a sandwich for the Sheriff (00:41); it's back on the ring finger when he gives Cledus a sandwich (00:50); then it's on the middle finger when Bandit and Carrie are in the woods (01:02) . . .

2. During a romantic interlude in the woods, when Carrie asks Bandit, "Do you think we have anything in common?" you can see that Burt Reynolds is wearing a girdle. (01:04)

SOUTH PARK: BIGGER, LONGER & UNCUT (11)

1999, color, 80 min.

Director: Trey Parker

Cast: Trey Parker (Stan Marsh / Eric Cartman / Mr. Garrison /

Mr. Hat / Officer Barbrady / various others), Matt Stone (Kyle Broslofski / Kenny McCormick / Saddam Hussein / Jimbo Kearn), Mary Kay Bergman (Mrs. Cartman / Sheila Broslofski / Female Body Part / Nurse / Mole's Mother / Little Girls), George Clooney (Dr. Gouache), Franchesca Clifford / Anthony Cross-Thomas / Jesse Howell (Ike Broslofski), Minnie Driver (Brooke Shields), Dave Foley (The Baldwins), Isaac Hayes (Jerome "Chef" McElroy), Eric Idle (Dr. Vosknocker), Brent Spiner (Conan O'Brien), Toddy Walters (Winona Ryder), Stewart Copeland (American Soldier No. 1), Howard McGillin (Gregory—Singing), Mike Judge (Kenny McCormick).

Cutout animated kids cause international stir then sway Satan to stay away ... all while swearing their asses off.

Bloopers

1. Mrs. Broslofsky opens the door to her house and tells Kyle to take Ike with him. The door has hinges to the left, and a knob to the right. When we cut to Mrs. Broslofsky inside the house, the door now has the knob to the right— but there should have been hinges there. (00:02, 00:03)

2. Cartman is eating Cheesy Poofs with his bare hands, but right after he sees the

newspaper clipping of the Terrance & Phillip movie, he yells, "Yes! Yes!" and gloves appear on his hands. (00:03)

3. At school, Stan has a T & P sweater with blue sleeves and an image of the Canadian duo farting fire at each other. Later on, when Stan is holding up the line at the cafeteria, the image on his sweater now looks exactly like Kyle's (a close-up of T & P), but when the kids reach Chef, Stan's sweater is back like it was before. (00:09, 00:11, 00:12)

4. When the kids meet Chef for the first time, his apron says "Chef" ("Hello, there, children!"), but it says "CHEF" in the following shot ("Hey Chef!!"). (00:11)

5. The midget in a bikini on the news refers to a pop chart with a few words ("T & P Uncle F***er," "Other Singles"). When we cut to the studio, the midget is still on the air, in a small square to the right of the screen, but his chart now has no words on it. (00:13)

6. At the very end of his song, "Kyle's Mom's a B**ch," Cartman is caught red-handed by Kyle's mom. She has her hands on her hips during Cartman's close-up, and to her sides in the master shot. (00:32)

7. During the song "La Resistance," after a shot of Stan and Kyle, Gregory and the kids sing, "For though you

die, La Resistance lives on!" Nine kids join Gregory to sing "You may get stabbed in the head with a dagger or a sword..." In the next angle, there are only seven kids. The next shot shows nine kids again. (00:50)

8. When the kids reach the U.S.O. Show, Cartman has a yellow backpack on. After being scared by Kenny's ghost, Cartman runs to Stan and Kyle to tell them what he found. Here, the backpack is gone. But when the trio reaches the hole where the Mole is getting mauled by the dogs, Cartman has his backpack on again. (00:56, 01:03, 01:04)

9. During the show, Terrance and Phillip are strapped to two electric chairs: Terrance (red sweater) to the left, Phillip (blue sweater) to the right. When the Mole peeks out from his hole on stage, Terrance and Phillip have switched positions: Phillip is to the left, Terrance to the right. They return to their original positions when Big Gay Al introduces the execution. (00:57, 01:03, 01:05)

10. Terrance and Phillip's executioner (a.k.a. Anonymous, a.k.a. Mr. Garrison) pulls the switch down to electrocute the two actors. When Cartman goes to stop the electrocution, he flips the switch down—again. But he should have been flipping it up. (01:06)

11. Mrs. Broslofsky shoots Phil-lip in the head and the chest: the bullet hits exactly in the middle of the *P* on the sweater—yet, the blood comes out of a hole that is to the side of the *P*. (01:11)

Non-Blooper
Cartman has a V-chip implanted, so he cannot curse. He does NOT sing the two lines from the song "What Would Brian Boitano Do?": "I'm sure he'd kick an ass or two" and "'cause Brian Boitano doesn't take sh** from anyone!" Only Stan and Kyle sing those two lines. Cartman joins them on "from anyone." (00:36, 00:37)

DVD Blooper
In Trailer 1, among the actors listed as stars of the feature is "Sadaam Hussein." But his name is spelled "Saddam" (corrected for the motion picture).

Question
Cartman dismisses Terrance & Phillip's movie by saying that "the animation's all crappy," thus implying that the movie is a cartoon. Later on, Kyle's mom explains that Terrance & Phillip are "two very untalented actors from Canada," and the duo appears on *The Conan O'Brien Show.* Huh? (00:04, 00:11, 00:23)

SPEED (25)
1994, color, 116 min.

Director: Jan de Bont

Cast: Keanu Reeves (Officer Jack Traven), Dennis Hopper (Howard Payne), Sandra

Bullock (Annie Porter), Joe Morton (Captain Herb "Mac" McMahon), Jeff Daniels (Detective Officer Harold "Harry" Temple), Alan Ruck (Stephens), Glenn Plummer (Jaguar Owner), Richard Lineback (Norwood), Beth Grant (Helen), Hawthorne James (Sam), Carlos Carrasco (Ortiz), David Kriegel (Terry).

Oh, no! There's a bomb on a bus! And Sandra Bullock is driving! And Dennis Hopper is sober! Luckily, Keanu doesn't have to act in order to save the day.

Bloopers

1. One of the "elevator women" is helped by two men. After she's out, one of the two men turns to the last woman, but he's alone. The other man has vanished. (00:16)

2. Before Jack and Harry get to Howard's elevator, the car is at floor 20. But just as Howard keys in 46 as his next destination, the red indicator reads 28. (00:19, 00:20)

3. Howard presses floor 46 because it's the top floor and Jack will have to get into the elevator or be crushed. When the others are watching the monitor a label says that 52 is the top floor for that elevator. (00:20, 00:21)

4. Howard makes the police chief think he's on the third floor on the freight elevator,

but the console indicating floor changes clicks one too many times. We see "7, click, 6, click, 5, click, 4, click," the camera switches to the police chief and we hear another 2 clicks. Back to the numbers: "4, click." Shouldn't it be on floor 2? (00:21)

5. During the hostage situation, Jack shoots Harry's left leg, but later on Harry has a bandage around his right leg and he limps with the right leg. The limp switches to the left leg in the bar scene that follows. (00:22, 00:23, 00:26)

6. Before the bus blows up, Jack places his coffee on the roof, *behind* the bar of the luggage rack. Then the bus blows up and Jack runs away. When he returns, the cup has moved *in front of* the bar. (00:27, 00:30)

7. Jack is holding his keys and is about to open his car. The bus blows up, Jack runs away, answers the phone, comes back . . . and opens the car door without his keys. Evidently, the door has unlocked itself. (00:27, 00:30)

8. After the first bus is blown up, you can see a red van pulling the burning bus with a cable. (00:27)

9. When the first bus has blown up, you see the flames reflected on the pay phones. But they are located much too far away and at the wrong angle from the explo-

sion for the reflection to be seen. (00:28)

10. Jack checks his Casio wristwatch, but it's showing the alarm time (AL 8:05). (00:30)

11. The glass door that Jack smashes on the second bus repairs itself. (00:34)

12. When Jack runs on the freeway to stop the bus, as soon as he reaches the door, a guy with a baseball hat is reflected in the bus door window. Who is he? (00:34)

13. When Jack floors the gas pedal of the Jaguar and we cut from behind the car, the rearview mirror is gone, without anybody touching it. It'll come back the next time the car is seen. (00:35)

14. As the Jaguar owner slips and loses the note that says, "Bomb on bus," he knocks off the rearview mirror of his Jaguar. On Jack's following close-up, the mirror is back in place. (00:37)

15. The Jaguar is about to hit the water-filled impact buffers on the freeway, and we see the windshield get wet before impact. (00:40)

16. When the bus exits the freeway, it rams into a series of cars on the off-ramp. Look carefully, a camera is mounted right behind the bus' front left wheel. (00:46)

17. An overhead view of the bus with the cop cars all around it shows the front of the bus dipping down from braking so it doesn't hit the back of the police car. So much for maintaining 50 mph. (00:52)

18. When Helen tries to get off, Jack turns quickly and grabs her left shoulder. After a cut to Howard, Jack is farther back and has not yet reached Helen's shoulder when the bomb under the step explodes. (00:59)

19. Before Jack unhandcuffs Ortiz from the railing, in the same pan a bald crew member wearing headphones can be seen ducking behind the railing panel. (01:04)

20. Before the bus jumps the freeway gap, the film is cranked to make the bus appear to be going faster. The policemen in the truck move in fast-forward as well. (01:05)

21. After Jack gets out of the bus at the airport, the "Good Vibrations" sign on the left side of the bus vanishes in one shot and then comes back before the final explosion. (01:08, 01:11, 01:29)

22. Howard snaps his fingers, even though he is missing his thumb! (01:09)

23. When the bus is aiming toward the plane at the airport, there is a shot straight ahead of the bus; on the left side of the screen, it's possible to see the cable pulling the bus. (01:30)

24. Jack introduces Joe's character to Annie as "Lieutenant McMahon." In the closing credits, Joe's character is listed as "Captain McMahon." (01:32, 01:51)

25. When the camera pulls back in the final shot on Hollywood Boulevard, camera tracks are seen on the sidewalk to the left. (01:50)

Question
As we see the gap in the freeway from a distance, there is a shadow from the "missing section" on the ground. Was it the bridge painted away? Maybe, maybe not... (01:05)

SPEED 2: CRUISE CONTROL (5)
1997, color, 121 min.

Director: Jan de Bont

Cast: Sandra Bullock (Annie Porter), Jason Patrick (Officer Alex Shaw), Willem Dafoe (John Geiger), Temuera Morrison (Juliano), Brian McCardie (Merced), Christine Firkins (Drew), Michael G. Hagerty (Harvey), Colleen Camp (Debbie), Lois Chiles (Celeste), Francis Guinan (Rupert).

As you may know, "speed" is a relative term...

Bloopers
1. Alex's entrance with the motorcycle seems to be lacking in one detail: his earpiece, which appears in the following close-up. (00:00)
2. Annie goes to the cabin bathroom to put a sarong over her swimsuit. When Alex looks for his ring, she's already wearing the sarong, but in the following shot, she's putting it on again. (00:11)
3. Geiger activates a countdown to engine shutdown. When the timer indicates 05:06 (and counting), Geiger removes his captain's shirt. As he looks at the computer again, it says 05:05—but at least 5 seconds have gone by. (00:33)

SMOKING IS DANGEROUS

Both for your health and your acting. Here are merely a few testimonials:

Humphrey Bogart in *Casablanca*	Blooper No. 8
Ben Affleck in *Chasing Amy*	Blooper No. 7
Lin Shaye in *Detroit Rock City*	Blooper No. 4
Sean Connery in *Dr. No*	Blooper No. 3
Ellen Burstyn in *The Exorcist*	Blooper No. 6
Bernard Lee in *From Russia with Love*	Blooper No. 6
Nancy Stephens in *Halloween*	Blooper No. 2
River Phoenix in *Stand by Me*	Blooper No. 1
Kevin Bacon and Neve Campbell in *Wild Things*	Blooper No. 6

4. The *Seabourn Legend* cruise ship steers at the last minute to avoid a disasterous collision with an oil tanker. As the two ships separate, they are almost parallel; yet from Geiger's boat, while Annie cheers, the ships are in completely different positions. (01:34)

5. When a motorboat jumps from the water and crashes into a store, its propeller isn't spinning while it's in midair. (01:39)

STAND BY ME (9)
1986, color, 91 min.

Director: Rob Reiner

Cast: Wil Wheaton (Gordon "Gordie" Lachance), River Phoenix (Chris Chambers), Corey Feldman (Teddy Duchamp), Jerry O'Connell (Vern Tessio), Kiefer Sutherland (Ace Merrill), Casey Siemaszko (Billy Tessio), Gary Riley (Charlie Hogan), Bradley Gregg (Eyeball Chambers), Jason Oliver (Vince Dejardins), Marshall Bell (Mr. Lachance), Frances Lee McCain (Mrs. Lachance), Richard Dreyfuss (The Writer), Andy Lindberg (David "Lardass" Hogan).

The best coming-of-age adventure ever lived by four kids and one corpse.

Bloopers

1. While playing cards in the treehouse, Chris smokes a cigarette and keeps the pack rolled up in his right sleeve. When he says, "29!" and slams his hand on the table, the pack is gone. When Chris says, "Come on, man, deal!" the pack is back. It'll go away one more time when the kids let Vern in, and it'll come back a few seconds later. (00:02, 00:03)

2. Teddy wants to dodge a train, but Chris pulls him off the tracks in the nick of time. The train passes by, and its shadow "covers" the four kids. In the opposite shot, the train shadow appears to be on the other side of the track, and the kids are in sunlight. (00:17)

3. After Teddy is saved by Chris from the train, the group resume their walk: the battery of Verne's radio mike flops on his left ankle. (00:18)

> Director Rob Reiner said that they always had problems with Jerry, who "was always getting into scraps during the film."

4. In the junkyard, the four kids are sitting in the shade. Teddy's trademark dogtag isn't visible. Yet when they decide to toss coins to decide who's going to buy food, the dogtag has popped out from under his shirt. (00:22, 00:23)

5. During Gordie's story, "Lardass" eats as many blueberry pies as he can. When he says, "Done!" the amount of blue-

berries and crumbs on his face changes (it'll happen later too, when he stands up to gurgle). (00:47, 00:48)

6. After a collective decision, the four kids walk and plunge into a swamp: Chris's and Gordie's heads stay clearly above the water, but after two shots they're shown emerging from underwater. (01:04)

7. Still in the swamp, after Vern says, "I told you we should've stuck to the tracks," Teddy's hair changes after every shot, and the strap of his bag moves on his shoulder. (01:04)

8. When Teddy attacks Vern, Chris yells, "Act your age!" Teddy answers, "This is my age!" He's not wearing glasses. But in the following close-up, there they are, right on his nose. (01:04)

9. While arguing in the water, Chris, Vern, and Teddy fight— but Gordie moves toward the other shore. His first steps in the foreground reveal that his hair is completely dry . . . even if he'd emerged from under-water less than 30 seconds earlier. (01:04)

Question

The writer ends his story with "Jesus, does anyone?" Then he stands up and turns the computer off without saving it! Did he lose the whole story? (01:24)

STAR TREK—THE MOTION PICTURE (6)

also Special Longer Version and Director's Edition 1979, color, 132 min. / 144 min. (SLV) / 136 min. (DE)

Director: Robert Wise

Cast: William Shatner (Admiral / Captain James Tiberius Kirk), Leonard Nimoy (Commander Spock), DeForest Kelley (Commander Leonard "Bones" McCoy, M.D.), James Doohan (Commander Montgomery "Scotty" Scott), George Takei (Lieutenant Commander Hikaru Sulu), Walter Koenig (Lieutenant Pavel Chekov), Nichelle Nichols (Lieutenant Commander Nyota Uhura), Majel Barrett (Dr. Christine Chapel), Persis Khambatta (Lieutenant Ilia), Stephen Collins (Captain / Commander Willard Decker), Grace Lee Whitney (Chief Petty Officer Janice Rand).

The first adventure after ten years. Oh, but please: speed up the tour around the Enterprise!!

[**Note:** subtract 1 min. 40 sec. from the listed times if you choose to start after the overture / 3 min., 1 sec. if you have the Director's Edition.]

Bloopers

1. When the communication from the Klingon starship is played back, the ship vanishes but the background still remains on

the screen. But if the communication was sent from a Klingon camera on board their ship, shouldn't the camera have gone along with the ship? (00:28 / 00:29 DE)

2. In their first meeting with Kirk, Spock and McCoy wear gray uniforms in the long shot and azure uniforms for the close-ups and when they're sitting and talking. (00:52 / 00:54 SLV / 00:53 DE)

3. The USS *Enterprise* is visited by a "plasma-energy combination" probe that emits a high-pitched tone. The crew members cover their ears, including Captain Kirk, who brings both hands to his ears, then removes his left—but in the over-the-shoulder shot, he has both hands in front of his face. After a close-up, he sits down in the same chair he was already sitting in. (01:12 / 01:18 SLV / 01:13 DE)

4. As Kirk leaves the *Enterprise* to go after Spock, a portion of the matte is missing, leaving the scaffolding that surrounds the set exposed. (01:39 SLV only)

5. When Kirk, Spock, Bones, Decker, and Ilia exit the *Enterprise*, their shadows go in front of them, from a light on the ship. But in the following shot, their shadows go behind them, from VGER's lights (which were already on). (01:51, 01:52 / 02:04 SLV / fixed in DE)

6. Spock's cloak has a red strip

on the left shoulder and McCoy's has a gray strip. But when they're back on the *Enterprise*, and Kirk orders Mr. Sulu to go to "warp one," their strip colors have switched. (02:05, 02:06 / 02:18, 02:19 SLV / 02:09, 02:11 DE)

Questions

1. A computer intercepts and translates a Klingon message. The computer begins stating, "Intruder unidentified" but before this, "Unfamiliar weaponry" is displayed on the screen, which is ignored by the computer. Why? (00:06 / not visible in SLV / fixed in DE)

2. When Kirk reaches the "official level" of the space station, port 5 is empty. A few seconds later, he and Scotty board a shuttle from port 5. So, if this shuttle is so quick, how come the tour around the *Enterprise* lasts so damned long? (00:13, 00:14 / fixed in DE)

STAR TREK II—THE WRATH OF KHAN (8)

1982, color, 113 min.

Director: Nicholas Meyer

Cast: William Shatner (Admiral James T. Kirk), Leonard Nimoy (Captain Spock), DeForest Kelley (Commander Leonard "Bones" McCoy, M.D.), James Doohan (Commander Montgomery "Scotty" Scott), Walter Koenig (Commander Pavel Chekov), George Takei

(Commander Hikaru Sulu), Nichelle Nichols (Commander Nyota Uhura), Bibi Besch (Dr. Carol Marcus), Merritt Butrick (Dr. David Marcus), Paul Winfield (Captain Terrell), Kirstie Alley (Lieutenant Saavik), Ricardo Montalban (Khan Noonien Singh), Judson Earney Scott (Joachim).

Khan!! What is the meaning of this attack? Simply the best.

Bloopers

1. Khan stares at Chekov and positively states, "I never forget a face." Khan refers to the first time he had to deal with Captain Kirk, in the TV episode "Space Seed" (1967). But in that particular episode from the first season, Chekov wasn't part of the crew of the *Enterprise*. Yet. He would join the following season. Maybe Khan watches reruns. (00:18)

2. Khan places two "pets" in a small bowl, then grabs the bowl with both hands—but as he turns, he's holding the bowl only with one hand. (00:23)

3. Kirk is on the elevator with McCoy and is called on an intercom, which he presses with his index finger to answer. In the matching cut, he's pressing it with his thumb. (00:35)

4. Preston, a young trainee, dies because of wounds sustained from an explosion. Before passing away, he grabs Kirk's jacket and asks, "Is the word given, Admiral?" He stains Kirk's jacket flap with a handful of blood . . . which changes shape, size, and position in the following scenes. (00:56, 00:57, 00:58)

5. They're waiting for the crew to fix the *Enterprise*, when David Marcus says, "We can't just sit here." Kirk puts on his reading glasses, checks his watch, and after a couple seconds his glasses are no longer on. (01:12)

6. Kirk and Saavik are beamed onto the *Enterprise* while still carrying on a discussion. Someone helps Kirk put on his jacket; he puts his left arm in the sleeve, but in the following cut he has his right arm in the sleeve instead. (01:17)

7. Khan reaches for a mortally wounded soldier, Joachim, who says "Yours . . . is a superior—" and then passes away—with his eyes open. As Khan hugs him, Joachim closes his eyes. (01:25)

8. After running to the engine room to see the dying Spock, Kirk's jacket flap is closed, then open, half open, and wide open. Oopsie-daisy! (01:36)

Fun Fact

Kirk, Spock, and McCoy are watching the Project Genesis proposal, which features the simulation of the "Genesis Effect." We zoom over the surface of the simulated planet, heading straight for some mountains, when all of the sudden a canyon appears out of nowhere in the middle of the mountains to show the creation of water. (00:44)

COMPUTER MELTDOWNS

You can hit CTRL+ALT+DEL all you want. You just can't delete these bloopers.

A computer camera in *American Pie*   Blooper No. 8
Arnold Schwarzenegger in *Eraser*   Blooper No. 10
Jeff Goldblum's laptop in *Independence Day*   Blooper No. 13
Samuel L. Jackson's commands in *Jurassic Park*   Blooper No. 24
The main computer in *Star Trek III*   Blooper No. 4
Joshua in *Wargames*   Blooper No. 9

STAR TREK III—THE SEARCH FOR SPOCK (3)

1984, color, 105 min.

Director: Leonard Nimoy

Cast: William Shatner (Admiral James Tiberius Kirk), DeForest Kelley (Commander Leonard "Bones" McCoy, M.D.), James Doohan (Commander Montgomery "Scotty" Scott), George Takei (Commander Hikaru Sulu), Walter Koenig (Commander Pavel Chekov), Nichelle Nichols (Commander Nyota Uhura), Mark Lenard (Ambassador Sarek), Christopher Lloyd (Kruge), Leonard Nimoy (Captain Spock / Elevator Voice—as "Frank Force"), Merritt Butrick (Dr. David Marcus), Judith Anderson (T'Lar), Teresa E. Victor (Enterprise Computer).

The crew of the Enterprise *is after a Vulcan . . .*

Bloopers

1. In Kirk's apartment a wall is decorated with six old pistols: the top four are facing one another, the other two are turned in opposite directions. But when Kirk tells Sarek how much his son meant to him, one of the two pistols in the middle has rotated 180°. (00:23, 00:24)

2. In a bar, Kirk and Admiral Morrow discuss the *Enterprise*. A few moments later, two drinks suddenly appear in front of them. (00:31, 00:32)

3. After Kirk, Chekov, and Scotty activate the destruction sequence on the *Enterprise*, the computer begins the 1-minute countdown. It lasts 1 minute and 40 seconds. So much for sophisticated computers. (01:13)

Question

The computer diligently displays every step of the destruction sequence. The final command Kirk gives is, "Zero, zero, zero . . . Destruct. Zero." Yet the computer only displays, "0 0 0" and begins the countdown. What happened to the final two commands? (01:12, 01:13)

Fun Fact

Just for good measure, a repeat demonstration of the "Genesis Effect" from the previous movie is included, with the canyon appearing out of nowhere just like before. (00:18)

STAR TREK IV — THE VOYAGE HOME (11)

1986, color, 119 min.

Director: Leonard Nimoy

Cast: William Shatner (Admiral / Captain James T. Kirk), Leonard Nimoy (Captain Spock), DeForest Kelley (Commander Leonard "Bones" McCoy, M.D.), James Doohan (Captain Montgomery "Scotty" Scott), George Takei (Commander Hikaru Sulu), Walter Koenig (Commander Pavel Chekov), Nichelle Nichols (Commander Nyota Uhura), Mark Lenard (Sarek), Jane Wyatt (Amanda), Majel Barrett (Commander Christine Chapel), Robert Ellenstein (Federation Council President), Catherine Hicks (Dr. Gillian Taylor), Scott DeVenney (Bob Briggs), Kirk Thatcher (Punk on Bus).

A Greenpeace-like mission for the Enterprise.

Bloopers

1. Kirk goes into an antique store to sell his "eighteenth-century" glasses he received as a gift from McCoy. However, the transparent plastic thing at the end of the temples looks suspiciously twentieth century. (00:40)

2. Kirk and Spock are on a bus, sitting in front of a punk with a very loud radio. The reflection in the window behind Spock doesn't match with the punk—especially after he's "out of order." No one else is sitting close to the punk, facing Spock. (00:43)

3. When Bob talks to Gillian ("Heard there was some excitement"), a red garden hose is unraveled all across a wet surface behind him. After one cut, the hose is much more straight. (00:52)

4. While Scotty is typing furiously at the Plexicorp factory computer, the noise heard on the second shot of his hands doesn't match with the movement of his fingers on the keys. (01:01)

5. During a dinner in an Italian restaurant, a candle in a vase in the middle of the table appears longer when Kirk is in the shot, and shorter when Gillian is. (01:03)

6. When Gillian runs in the middle of the "empty" park and hits the cloaked spacecraft, she pounds on it, yelling for Kirk. The shadow she casts changes from the shot from the ground to the shot from Scotty's point of view. (01:19)

7. Kirk traps a few doctors in a room and melts the lock using one of his gadgets. He holds the device with his left

hand in the master shot, with his right in the detail, and then it's back in his left hand again. (01:25)

8. When the whales, George and Gracie, swim in the open sea, the wave condition and color of the water changes between the shots of the whales and the the shots of the whaling ship. (01:31)

9. When the Klingon's starship appears above the whaling ship, a wide shot reveals the boat's in shadow (caused by the starship). But none of the shots of the fishermen reveal any shadow at all. (01:33)

10. The hatch is blown open to let the crew get out of the Klingon craft. But looking out through the opening, it's possible to see something that looks like a metal structure—yet the hatch is on the top of the craft, so nothing should be seen but the outside. (01:40)

11. Kirk and his crew see the whales jumping in the open sea . . . and then swimming toward the Golden Gate, which was nowhere to be seen when the mammals were jumping out of the water. (01:46, 01:47)

Questions

1. The Federation Council president states that Admiral Kirk "has been charged with nine violations of Starfleet regulations." Then at the end, when Kirk and his crew are facing the president, he states the charges: "Conspiracy, assault on Federation officers, theft of Federation property . . . sabotage . . . willful destruction of Federation property . . . and finally disobeying direct orders of the Starfleet commander." This is only six. Were three dropped, and nobody told us? (00:06, 01:48)

2. It's a good thing that the Klingon starship which Kirk and his crew borrowed had a computer that catalogued information on Earth mammals of the past, don't you think? (00:24)

3. During a very distorted broadcast, a technician wipes a monitor with a rug—then, in the following shot, he wipes the same monitor again. Why? (00:28)

4. The cloaked starship lands in a park, flattening a trash can and pushing down an area of grass. So how come every single blade of grass is still standing up straight, and not flattened as they should be? (00:38)

Fun Fact

Trying to locate Chekov after beaming up Uhura, Scotty yells, "Please signal again!" and spits like you wouldn't believe. (01:14)

STAR TREK V—THE FINAL FRONTIER (9)
1989, color, 107 min.

Director: William Shatner

Cast: William Shatner (Captain James Tiberius Kirk), Leonard Nimoy (Captain Spock), DeForest Kelley (Commander Leonard "Bones" McCoy, M.D.), James Doohan (Captain Montgomery "Scotty" Scott), Walter Koenig (Commander Pavel Chekov), Nichelle Nichols (Commander Nyota Uhura), George Takei (Commander Hikaru Sulu), David Warner (St. John Talbot), Laurence Luckinbill (Sybok), Charles Cooper (General Korrd), Cynthia Gouw (Caithlin Dar), Todd Bryant (Captain Klaa).

Oh! The horror!!

Bloopers

1. Kirk climbs a mountain at Yosemite National Park: he's wearing a blue jacket and blue climbing shoes. Later on, he slips and falls from the mountain; the blue jacket and shoes become black during the fall and are back to blue when Spock stops him. Also, Spock's blue-and-green jacket becomes black-and-green during "the chase." (00:06, 00:10)

2. Doctor McCoy stands in front of a mountain in Yosemite. He uses binoculars to check on Kirk. The image McCoy sees through the binoculars doesn't match with his position in front of the mountain. (00:08)

3. While around the campfire, Spock is given a bowl of McCoy's beans. Spock holds the bowl in his right hand and

a spoon in his left. To sit more comfortably, he passes the spoon to his right hand ("In that case I have little choice but to sample your beans"). As he sits, the spoon is back in his left hand. (00:18)

4. Bones comments on the Vulcan's metabolism and produces a bottle of Tennessee whiskey that is half empty. But when he explains to Spock that "Row, row, row your boat" is just a song, the bottle is filled to the top. (00:19, 00:22)

5. After their crash-landing on the *Enterprise*, Kirk and Sybok fight in the hangar. Sybok causes Kirk to fly all over the place. But . . . are those a couple of cables by Kirk's waist, in the close-up when he slams against the shuttle? (00:51)

6. In order to go faster up a shaft, Kirk jumps on Spock's turbo boots, and McCoy joins him. A shot from Spock's point of view, though, reveals Kirk's and McCoy's feet dangling in the air. There's no way Spock could have held them up solely with the power of his arms. (01:02, 01:03)

7. When Kirk yells, "Spock, the booster rockets!" it's possible to catch a glimpse of the harness that helps Spock fly, connected to the wall behind him. (01:03)

8. Spock, Kirk, and McCoy fly up the shaft past these floors, in order: 35, 52, 64, 52, 77, 78, and 78 again. (01:03)

9. When Kirk is facing "God," a Klingon starship emerges from behind a mountain. Kirk turns and raises his arms with enthusiasm—but in the following close-up, his arms are along his sides. (01:36)

Question
On the *Enterprise*, Uhura receives a red alert communication. She advises Sulu and Chekov, who are walking in the daylight, and then she goes to pick up Kirk, Spock, and McCoy. But they are rescued during the nighttime. Not such an urgent red alert, then . . . ? (00:16, 00:17, 00:25)

STAR WARS (60)
also Special Edition
1977, color, 121 min. / 125 min. (SE)

Director: George Lucas

Cast: Mark Hamill (Luke Skywalker), Harrison Ford (Han Solo), Carrie Fisher (Princess Leia Organa), Peter Cushing (Grand Moff Wilhuff Tarkin), Alec Guinness (Ben "Obi-Wan" Kenobi), Anthony Daniels (C-3PO), Kenny Baker (R2-D2), Peter Mayhew (Chewbacca), David Prowse (Darth Vader), Phil Brown (Uncle Owen Lars), Shelagh Fraser (Aunt Beru Lars), Denis Lawson (Wedge Antilles—Red Two), Graham Ashley (Gold Five), Drewe Hemley (Red Leader).

"A long time ago in a galaxy far, far away . . ."

Bloopers
1. When Darth Vader lifts up the captain of the consular starship, in the background one of the stormtroopers has his gun on his waist in the long shot, then on his chest in the close-up. (00:05)
2. Just before being sucked into the Jawa transport, Artoo

NOT-SO-SPECIAL EFFECTS

Now you see it, now . . . well, you actually see it.

Tony Curtis in *The Great Race*	Blooper No. 2
Herbie in *Herbie Rides Again*	Blooper No. 5
A velociraptor in *Jurassic Park*	Blooper No. 43
Keanu Reeve's backflip in *The Matrix*	Blooper No. 25
The bus in *Speed*	Blooper No. 23
An alien in *Star Wars*	Blooper No. 17

has a restraining bolt placed on its front. The Jawa gets closer and places the bolt in the middle of a rectangular area on the little robot. After one shot, the bolt is in the top part of the area. When Artoo is inside the vehicle, the bolt has returned to the middle of the area. (00:13, 00:14)

3. Inside the Jawa transport, Artoo looks around; in the last frame, it is possible to see Kenny Baker's face through the robot's eye. (00:14)

4. Luke is called by his aunt and he runs and looks down into the family's residence. From the desert level, we see only one bush, but from inside the residence, three extra bushes have popped out of nowhere. (00:17)

5. When Uncle Owen inspects the robots, he calls "Lu-uke!" At this point it is possible to see a cable running from C-3PO's head to the base of its neck, but it vanishes for the rest of the movie. (00:17 / 00:18 SE)

6. When Luke walks toward his house with C-3PO and the red robot—the one that explodes—there's a close-up of Artoo. Behind Artoo, it is possible to see the very same droid that has just blown up near Luke. (00:18, 00:19)

7. The first time the hologram is seen, Leia's message is out of sync with the line she says in various shots. (00:20, 00:21 / 00:21 SE)

8. The partial message from Leia is playing. In the background, there's a coiled hose. After a few moments, when C-3PO explains about the restraining bolt, the background flips and the hose zaps to the left. (00:20, 00:22 / 00:21, 00:22 SE)

9. Right after being called by Aunt Beru, Luke talks to the droids. Artoo's head changes position during the cuts. (00:22 / 00:23 SE)

10. When Luke goes to dine, he leaves the two robots alone. C-3PO has a cloth in his hands, but the cloth vanishes and comes back in the last four shots of the scene. (00:22 / 00:23 SE)

11. Aunt Beru pours a bluish liquid into Luke's glass. He steps in, sits down, and pours the same liquid into the same glass, having not consumed any of the liquid his Aunt poured. (00:23 / 00:23, 00:24 SE)

12. During dinner, Luke sips a drink holding the glass with his left hand—and then it's in his right hand. (00:24)

13. Luke and C-3PO run after Artoo, even though C-3PO couldn't have possibly kept up; then the sky grows darker in their close-up (fixed in the *Special Edition*). (00:26)

14. In Obi-Wan's house, Luke fixes C-3PO's arm. The robot asks permission to "close

down for a while," and does so. But when Obi-Wan checks the message from Princess Leia, C-3PO is everything but deactivated, and Luke is working on its arm—again. Later on, the robot is once again in the off position. (00:32, 00:34 / 00:33, 00:35 SE)

15. While Luke is fixing C-3PO's arm, one brown curtain vanishes from the arch where it's hanging. (00:33)

16. Obi-Wan finds the message from the princess, and Artoo projects it on a table. On the table are two saltshaker–type things and a bowl / oil dispenser, but halfway through the message the bowl is gone. It'll return at the end of the message. (00:34 / 00:35 SE)

17. In the cantina, one little alien bangs his hands on the counter; as he turns his head, you can see through his eyes (the mask was longer than the actor's head). (00:43 / 00:45 SE)

18. Luke spots two blue aliens talking to each other. The first one has "alien hands," the second one wears two ordinary human-shaped white gloves. (00:44 / 00:46 SE)

19. As two stormtroopers question the bartender, a small alien drinks from a glass . . . through his chin! (00:48 / 00:49 SE)

20. When Han fires at Greedo, just before the alien ex-plodes it's possible to see (for one single frame) a terrible stand-in for Greedo. (00:49 / 00:50 SE)

21. After the cantina episode, while Luke and Ben are heading to docking bay 94, an alien walks by who looks exactly like Greedo (the same one that Han has just killed). He may be an alien of the same race—but wearing the same clothes? (00:51 / 00:52 SE)

22. We see the *Millennium Falcon* for the very first time, notice that the round dish on the upper deck is missing. (00:51 / 00:54 SE)

23. When Luke and Ben go downstairs, check out Artoo to the far left: it clearly has some problems with the steps, and it moves left and right as if it were bouncing, but making no progress. After a few seconds, its round dome appears from the bottom of the screen, inexplicably still bouncing. (00:51 / 00:54 SE)

24. As the stormtroopers enter the docking bay and fire at Han Solo, he returns the fire using his gun. One of the troopers, who was standing underneath a wall that explodes, trips and falls to his knees and then on his face . . . and again and again, in the following two shots. (00:52 / 00:55 SE)

25. From the outside, the *Millennium Falcon*'s cockpit

(one large window, four windows around it, and even more windows around that) doesn't match with the cockpit view as seen from the inside (there are only three windows). (00:52, 00:53 / 00:55, 00:56 SE)

26. Right after the *Millennium Falcon* takes off, there is a close-up on Han. Behind him, it is possible to see a man in a green shirt, walking away from the cockpit. Who the heck is he? (It was Obi-Wan, leaving the cockpit—actually this is a close-up of Han lifted from the tail-end of the following scene while he's prepping the ship to jump into hyperspace.) (00:52 / 00:55 SE)

27. As Han sits down after telling Chewie to "Stay sharp. Two more [star destroyers] coming in," he grabs the dashboard—which tilts and lifts up. (00:53 / 00:56 SE)

28. Up until the moment of the jump into hyperspace, Han is wearing gloves. As he pulls the lever to actually jump, his gloves have disappeared. (00:53 / 00:56 SE)

29. When Han and Chewbacca welcome Obi-Wan and Luke into the cockpit, Chewie is not wearing his trademark belt. But he is when they jump into hyperspace. (00:53 / 00:56 SE)

30. Governor Tarkin is upset to find out that Princess Leia lied to him. Darth Vader says,
"I told you she would never consciously betray the Rebellion." But then Vader keeps gesturing for a couple of seconds (a little dubbing problem). (01:00 / 01:03 SE)

31. When the *Millennium Falcon* enters the Death Star, it flies through a large door surrounded by a white light. But the light is broken by the silhouette of the stand for the model of the starship. (01:03 / 01:05 SE)

32. Once our heroes are inside the Death Star command center, while Artoo plugs in to interpret the computer Obi-Wan says, "I don't think you boys can help." A circular scanner behind him has a red part rotating counterclockwise. Between shots, the part jumps ahead by at least 180°. (01:07 / 01:09 SE)

33. Han and Luke, disguised as stormtroopers, escort Chewbacca to an elevator. A black droid walks by them, a soldier with a gray uniform passes by as well, moving away. In the following cut, the black droid is still there, but the soldier's now wearing a black jacket. (01:10 / 01:12 SE)

34. When Luke calls C-3PO via comlink, the droid walks by a rack with three blasters on it. When the stormtroopers burst into the same room—a little later on—the rack is holding four blasters. (01:15, 01:20 / 01:17, 01:22 SE)

35. While firing at the storm-troopers, Han's gun (a modified Sterling 9-mm submachine gun) still ejects spent cases. But it's supposed to be a laser gun!! (01:15 / 01:18 SE)

36. Trapped in the cell corridor, Leia says, "This is some rescue!" A lock of her hair falls on her forehead; after Han's close-up, her hair is back up. (01:16 / 01:18 SE)

37. When entering the trash compactor, Chewbacca places his foot in the hole twice. (01:16 / 01:18 SE)

38. After the roar of the Dianoga (the trash compactor creature), Luke turns and mouths "Listen! What was that?" but we don't hear anything. (01:17 / 01:19 SE)

39. When the Dianoga grabs Luke's leg, it coils around up to Luke's crotch. But when he's pulled underwater, the tentacle is gone. (01:18 / 01:20 SE)

40. As Han lifts a pole to stop the moving walls of the trash compactor, Leia's hands are at her side—but in the following shot she's holding the pole. (01:19 / 01:21 SE)

41. As a bunch of stormtroopers enter the room where the two robots are hiding, the soldier to the far right hits his head on the sliding door frame. (01:20 / 01:22 SE)

42. The stormtroopers leave the room, but one of them stays to guard the door, which is low enough to make him duck if he had to get out. But as C-3PO steps out of his hideout and approaches the door, it is high enough to let the droid step out without any problem. (01:20 / 01:22 SE)

43. Chewbacca is pushing one of the walls of the trash compactor; then he walks away. In a wide shot, he's still pushing and walks away. In the following shot, he's still pushing. (01:21 / 01:23 SE)

44. As the quartet of heroes have stepped into safety, the trash compactor behind them looks dark. But after the roar of the Dianoga, a pile of bright orange trash appears to the left of the screen. (01:23 / 01:25 SE)

45. After Han blasts the Dianoga, Leia says "From now on, you do what I tell you." In this sequence, Luke's holding his blaster in his left hand, close to his head. In the following cut, the blaster is down and Luke's hand has jumped to his head. (01:23 / 01:26 SE)

46. Leia kisses Luke for luck, and remains with her head close to his, her arms around his neck. As they swing across the chasm, Leia's hands are holding Luke's waist and her head is much lower, lying on his chest. (01:27 / 01:29 SE)

47. During the light saber duel, frequently Darth Vader's image is flipped—you can see that the buttons on his chest jump from the left to

the right (for instance, when he says, "You should not have come back"). (01:28 / 01:30 SE)

48. Just prior to their escape from the Death Star, Han and Chewbacca run toward the *Millennium Falcon* and squeeze themselves against a wall. See Luke and Leia's shadows on the wall, waiting for their cue? (01:29 / 01:31 SE)

49. After Darth Vader kills Obi-Wan, Leia runs inside the *Millennium Falcon* . . . twice. And so does Artoo. (01:30 / 01:32 SE)

50. The blast door slides closed after Obi-Wan's death; in this shot, Darth Vader's light saber is white, not red. (01:30 / 01:32 SE)

51. The *Millennium Falcon* flees the Death Star, and is chased by four TIE fighters. Leia announces, "Here they come," and we see the small spaceships approaching. After a close-up of one of the pilots, there's his point of view through the windshield. Checking on the white glow coming from the *Falcon's* engine, it's possible to see the black vertical bar (the support of the model) breaking the glow. (01:32 / 01:34 SE)

52. As the group of heroes reach the Yavin base, Han's holster has jumped to the left (even though he carries it on his right leg all through the picture). (01:36 / 01:38 SE)

53. During the X-wing attack, the microphones of the rebels jump from the right to the left and vice versa (for instance, when Luke wipes his nose). (01:43, 01:44 / 01:45, 01:47 SE)

54. While flying in deep space, Artoo's dome is black, not blue (a little blue screen problem). (01:43 / 01:45 SE)

55. During the battle on the Death Star, Luke has a TIE fighter on his tail. Calling for help, Luke finds it in Wedge, who says, "I'm on him, Luke. Hold on!" But Luke is impatient, and says, "Blast it! Biggs, where are you?" Biggs?? Not to mention that after the TIE fighter is destroyed, Luke says, "Thanks, Wedge." So what the hell happened to Biggs? (01:46 / 01:48 SE)

56. During the final battle, Gold Five calls out, "Gold Five to Red Leader." The answer to that call comes from Red Leader who says, "I copy, Gold Leader." (01:48 / 01:50 SE)

57. As Wedge leaves the Death Star, Darth Vader says, "Let him go. Stay on the leader." There's a window behind Vader, and the background is running in an odd direction. That window never shows up at any other time during the battle, nor is it visible from the outside of the ship. (01:52 / 01:54 SE)

58. After Artoo is hit by Vader's laser, the bump on C-3PO's forehead jumps from the left

to the right (only in one shot, though). (01:53 / 01:56 SE)

59. As Luke jumps off his X-wing and runs to hug Leia, he yells "Carrie!" He must have thought he was already at the cast party. (01:54 / 01:57 SE)

60. During the final credits, Wedge Antilles appears to be played by Dennis Lawson. His name is actually Denis, with one *n*. His name will be correctly spelled in the other two chapters of the saga. (02:00 / 02:03 SE)

Non-Bloopers

1. When the troopers are looking for rebels, Princess Leia peeks from behind a pillar. We look back at the troopers, and there's a strange white apparition in the bottom part of the screen, between two pillars. Actually, it's the reflection of the first stormtrooper's arm. (00:06)

2. After the assault on the prison, Han talks into a microphone, and at a certain point he says "How are you?" Then he turns his head away because he's laughing. But he keeps going. It's *almost* a blooper. (01:13 / 01:15 SE)

Questions

1. Luke stares at the suns of his planet. The detail of the two suns shows them closer together (and a mountain has even appeared in front of the lower one). Huh? (00:25)

2. After a dissolve, our heroes walk toward docking bay 94. Artoo (to the left) is slowing down. The pan follows Luke, Obi-Wan, and C-3PO, and all of the sudden Artoo arrives from one side. Does the robot also have a special speed-propulsion system? (00:51 / 00:54 SE)

3. As the Death Star is approaching the rebel base of Yavin, a monitor shows the graphic of the movement and a voice announces that the base will be in range in 30 minutes. But the countdown on the screen doesn't match the announcement (it says 32 seconds the first time) and, in fact, never does. So just how do they measure time on the Death Star? (01:35 / 01:41 SE)

4. In the Yavin base, all the pilots have bright white helmets with blue logos exactly like Luke's (except his are red). However, in space, you never see the pilots wearing these helmets. Was that group left on Yavin? (01:39, 01:42 / 01:41, 01:45 SE)

Fun Facts

1. After Princess Leia gives her message to Artoo, the robot stretches its third foot and rolls toward C-3PO. The scene is cut, because Artoo would have hit (and actually did, if you ever have the chance to see the complete take) one of the pillars in the corridor. (00:05)

2. The first time Luke sees Leia's message, he is startled so violently that C-3PO jumps too,

and then trips from the step he is standing on. The robot regains his balance, and the scene was cut and printed. (00:21)

STAR WARS: EPISODE I (SEE "PHANTOM MENACE, THE — STAR WARS: EPISODE I")

STRIKING DISTANCE (10)
101, color, 101 min.

Director: Rowdy Herrington

Cast: Bruce Willis (Thomas Hardy), Sarah Jessica Parker (Jo Christman / Detective Emily Harper), Dennis Farina (Nick Detillo), Tom Sizemore (Danny Detillo), Brion James (Detective Eddie Eiler), Robert Pastorelli (Detective Jimmy Detillo), Timothy Busfield (Sacco), John Mahoney (Vincent Thomas Hardy), Andre Braugher (District Attorney), Tom Atkins (Uncle Fred Hardy), Gareth Williams (Chick Chicanis), Sigrid Arienne (Nurse Paula Puglisi).

Former cop can't let go of an old case, even if he's now a river patrolman.

Bloopers
1. Tom and Vince get in a car and talk about the "Little Red Riding Hood" killer before the car chase. The first time they are in a shot together, the rearview mirror of the car is missing, then it's there, then it's crooked, then straight, and then crooked again when Vince asks, "What happened to that nurse ... ?" (00:04, 00:05, 00:06)
2. During the chase, the "evil car" hits a van and loses its front bumper — which is back in place after a few seconds. (00:08)
3. The evil car stops abruptly at a roadblock and one of its left hubcaps comes off and rolls away, clanging against one of the police cars. When the evil car backs up and takes a plunge into a lower parking area, both left hubcaps are in place. (00:09, 00:10)
4. During the second part of the chase, the evil car and all of the police vehicles enter a bumpy road and begin jumping up and down. The first police car behind the evil car loses its flashing lights — but a close-up of the "evil driver" shows the police car with its lights back in place. (00:10, 00:11)
5. Jimmy commits suicide by jumping from a bridge into the river. A devastated Thomas crawls to the handrail of the bridge, leaving his crutch on the ground. When he's looking down into the river, though, he has the crutch underneath his left arm. (00:18)
6. A nurse crosses a parking space and she's about to put the key in the lock of her car, but she finds it sealed. Her

purse has slipped off her shoulder and she's fighting to put it back on, but when she says "Goddammit!" the strap is visible on her shoulder—even though in the following shot she's still working on it. (00:39)

7. Thomas enters a bar to look for Chicanis and he approaches a short guy with black hair and a mustache who's playing pool. In the following shot, the guy has become a fat, taller guy with a blue hat. (00:44)

8. When Chicanis shows up there's a short pursuit, and Thomas stops the suspect. Thomas cocks his gun, placing the barrel against Chicanis's right cheek. When Jo tells Thomas to drop his gun, the barrel has moved to the left side of Chicanis's throat—but it'll be back on the right cheek when Thomas removes it. (00:44)

9. Thomas marks on a map of the river the positions of the first two bodies he recovered. A black marker, in the meanwhile, rotates 180° between the detail and the master shot. (00:56)

10. Jimmy forces Thomas to drink some liquor and he places the bottle against the poor man's mouth. The label of the bottle changes its position between the close-ups and the master shot. (01:24)

Question

At a police party, Thomas meets Jo, who's wearing an elegant red dress with spaghetti-thin straps. Yet, when the two get ready to make love later that same night, Thomas removes the dress and Jo has on a white bra with very prominent straps. Where did it come from? (00:57, 01:02)

SOUNDS LIKE A BLOOPER

If seeing is believing, then hearing is . . . well, just listen to these:

Jim Carrey's door in *Ace Ventura: Pet Detective*	Blooper No. 3
Thomas Jane in *Deep Blue Sea*	Blooper No. 3
A hearse's door in *Diamonds Are Forever*	Blooper No. 1
A Coca-Cola can in *Die Hard*	Blooper No. 17
A villain in *Dr. No*	Blooper No. 17
Orestes Matacena's gun in *The Mask*	Blooper No. 7
Dennis Hopper in *Speed*	Blooper No. 22
The band leader in *Stripes*	Blooper No. 8

STRIPES (9)
1981, color, 105 min.

Director: Ivan Reitman

Cast: Bill Murray (John Winger), Harold Ramis (Russell Ziskey), Warren Oates (Sergeant Hulka), P. J. Soles (Stella Hansen), Sean Young (Louise Cooper), John Candy (Dewey "Ox" Oxberger), John Larroquette (Captain Stillman), John Voldstad (Tyler, Captain Stillman's Aide), John Diehl (Howard J. "Cruiser" Turkstra), Lance LeGault (Colonel Glass), Roberta Leighton (Anita), Fran Ryan (Dowager in Cab).

Is the Army really ready for soldiers like this?

Bloopers

1. John leaves the cab to chase two passengers who haven't paid. His car window is rolled halfway down. When he comes back to the cab, the window is rolled all the way up; then, when he invites a lady in, it's down again. (00:01, 00:02)

2. The cab John drives looks brand new. However, after the gag with the camera, an outside shot reveals a dent on the rear left panel. The dent is gone later when John stops the cab on the bridge. (00:01, 00:04, 00:06)

3. While on the bridge, John's cab is followed by a brownish van (seen through the rear windshield). When John stops

the cab, not only has the van vanished, but several cars have appeared. (00:05, 00:06)

4. John gets home to find out that Anita is leaving him. She is very irritated, and puts her left boot on, then grabs the right. She then proceeds to put the left boot on, and then the right. (00:10)

5. John impresses Russell by doing five push-ups in a row. Russell tosses him three dollar bills. After two shots, there are five dollar bills. (00:14)

6. John and Russell fight when John tries to sneak out of the camp. John's duffel bag lies on the ground close to his legs from one side, under his head from the other, and then far away from him as the jeep arrives. At the same time, his cap falls off his head, then is back on again. (00:47)

7. John "volunteers" Ox for a mud-wrestling match. He shows $413 while standing, a towel draped over his left shoulder. In the following wide shot, the towel is still on his left shoulder, but the other end of it has moved onto his right shoulder. (00:54)

8. During the graduation ceremony, the band stops playing. Only then does John's company enter the field ("Boom . . . boom . . . boom . . . boom . . ."). In a wide shot, it's possible to see the band leader still conducting the music. (01:10, 01:11)

9. When the company reaches the ceremony and performs

for the audience, look at the shadows on the ground: they're there, then they aren't, then they're back, gone, back, gone . . . in almost every cut. (01:11)

Question
When the heroes come back home, every one of them is put on a magazine cover. Ziskey makes the cover of *GUTS*, with a picture of him firing a gun during the mission in Czechoslovakia on the EM-50. Who took this picture? (01:41)

SUPERMAN—THE MOVIE (10)
also Director's Cut
1978, color, 143 min. / 151 min. (DC)

Director: Richard Donner

Cast: Marlon Brando (Jor-El), Gene Hackman (Lex Luthor), Christopher Reeve (Clark Kent / Superman), Ned Beatty (Otis), Jackie Cooper (Perry White), Glenn Ford (Jonathan Kent), Trevor Howard (First Elder), Margot Kidder (Lois Lane), Jack O'Halloran (Non), Valerie Perrine (Eve Teschmacher), Maria Schell (Vond-Ah), Terence Stamp (General Zod).

The man of steel comes to town in his first exciting adventure.

Bloopers
1. Saying, "I've never been otherwise," Jor-El places his hands on the Second El-

der's chest. In the over-the-shoulder shot, Jor-El's hands are over the Elder's shoulders, then on his chest again. (00:12)
2. Jor-El places his son in the capsule to save him. In doing so, Jor-El's sleeve runs a little too far up his arm, and we can see the actor's wristwatch (later on, when Jor-El gets the green crystal, the sleeves reveal a bare wrist). (00:16, 00:17 / 00:17, 00:19 DC)
3. Young Clark Kent is left alone in the football field. The sky behind him is blue and clear. When he kicks the ball, though, clouds have suddenly appeared. (00:27 / 00:29 DC)
4. When he's running along with the train, Clark is on the street in the close-ups, and on the grass in the long shots. (00:28)
5. After he jumps in front of the train, a shot shows Clark running in the distance through the train cars' windows. You can also see the cameraman reflected. (00:28 / 00:30 DC)
6. When Clark asks Mr. White to send half of his salary to his mom, he holds a note with her address. The position of his hand changes after every shot. (00:51 / 00:53 DC)
7. Clark gets Lois trapped inside the revolving door at the *Daily Planet*. The cameraman's reflection shows in the very same door. (00:52 / 00:55 DC)

8. Going to Lex Luthor's secret place, Otis passes by a train. It has a lit "5048" on the left side, and "50" on the right (the lights behind "48" are out). Otis then moves to track 22, where a train is approaching. The number of this train is the same (5048 on the left, 50 on the right). Then Harry the undercover cop is pushed by Luthor under a passing train, numbered 5048 . . . oh, you get the picture. (00:57, 00:58, 00:59 / 00:59, 01:00, 01:01 DC)

9. Flying above the clouds, after the bird passes by, Superman becomes somewhat transparent (a couple of stars shine through). (01:31 / 01:36 DC)

10. Desperate because Lois has died, the man of steel screams "No!" very loud, and lets us see that he has fillings in his teeth. How this "man of steel" got the cavities, and then how they drilled his teeth, we'll never know . . . (02:10 / 02:18 DC)

Questions

1. While traveling to Earth, Jor-El talks to his son in the space capsule. The first thing he says is related to Einstein's Theory of Relativity. But if Jor-El has been dead for thousands of years . . . ? (00:21 / 00:23 DC)

2. Jor-El tells his eighteen-year-old son that he's been dead for many thousands of our years. Yet Luthor mentions that in an interview, Superman said that Krypton exploded in 1948. Huh? (00:44, 01:35 / 00:46, 01:40 DC)

3. In the shot where Superman and Lois are flying over Metropolis and they both appear from the top of the screen . . . does the traffic in the street below go backward? (01:27 / 01:32 DC)

SUPERMAN II (10)
1980, color, 127 min.

Director: Richard Lester

Cast: Gene Hackman (Lex Luthor), Christopher Reeve (Superman / Clark Kent), Ned Beatty (Otis), Jackie Cooper (Perry White), Sarah Douglas (Ursa), Margot Kidder (Lois Lane), Jack O'Halloran (Non), Valerie Perrine (Eve Teschmacher), Susannah York (Lara), Clifton James (Sheriff), E. G. Marshall (The President), Marc McClure (Jimmy Olsen), Terence Stamp (General Zod).

The man of steel comes to town in his second exciting adventure.

Bloopers

1. A flashback shows little Superman being placed in the capsule by his mother, but, curiously enough, not his father (Marlon Brando's contract for the first movie didn't include a sequel). (00:03

2. When Clark enters Lois's office, there's a pair of roller skates hanging from the door. The skates point in the same direction at first, but when Clark enters, they are facing each other, then the same direction, and so on. (00:20)

3. While on the hot air balloon, Lex points north with his left hand and in the next cut with his right. (00:37)

4. At Niagara Falls, Lois tells Clark that she's convinced he's Superman. Lois sets her purse and camera down on a bench and sits on the handrail behind it. After she jumps in the water, Clark runs to the handrail—where Lois's purse is now resting. (00:46, 00:47)

5. After the sheriff sees the three villians for the first time standing in the middle of the road, he places his hat on the dashboard . . . twice. (00:55)

6. Using a white ray coming out of his finger, Zod lifts one man way above a pole. The closer shot of the man shows him at the same height as the pole. (01:01)

7. When Superman tells Lois that as Clark he makes a fool of himself, Lois has a glass in her hand, but in the over-the-shoulder shot the glass is on the table. (01:08)

8. Lex Luthor's cigar jumps from his left hand to his right when he sits in the oval office ("My needs are small."). (01:28)

9. After the three villains chase Superman out of the *Daily Planet*, a few bystanders are in front of a road construction zone, with a "No Entry" sign in front of it. Right after Zod gets the prefab wall ready to toss at Superman, a few bystanders look up at him: it's the same shot as before, only flipped. Check the sign now: it says "yrtnE oN." (01:33, 01:34)

10. Superman delivers a new flag to the White House: look at the fountains in front of the building: they are "frozen in time." (02:02)

Questions

1. It's the same old question: Why, in Paris, France, do the police talk to each other in English? (00:15)

2. In his Fortress of Solitude, Superman tricks Non with a fake image of himself then tells Lois, "We used to play this game at school. Never was very good at it." However, Superman was placed in the space pod by his father when he was an infant, and Non was already an adult. So, where exactly did Superman play this game before? (01:49)

Fun Fact

When Superman lifts a screaming Zod with one arm, we can see a spot of perspiration in his right armpit. (01:53)

Director Richard Donner's Cameos

MOVIE	ROLE	TIMES
The Goonies	Cop with sunglasses on the ATV	01:41
Superman—The Movie (DC)	"That'll be the day" onlooker	01:22
Superman II	Man with pipe walking by Don's Diner	01:18

SUPERMAN III (8)
1983, color, 125 min.

Director: Richard Lester

Cast: Christopher Reeve (Superman / Clark Kent), Richard Pryor (Gus Gorman), Jackie Cooper (Perry White), Marc McClure (Jimmy Olsen), Annette O'Toole (Lana Lang), Annie Ross (Vera Webster), Pamela Stephenson (Lorelei Ambrosia), Robert Vaughn (Ross Webster), Margot Kidder (Lois Lane), Gavan O'Herlihy (Brad), Nancy Roberts (Unemployment Clerk), Graham Stark (Blind Man), John Bluthal (Pisa Vendor).

The man of steel tries to leave town after his third, not-so-exciting adventure.

Bloopers

1. The man of steel flies high and low, and sometimes he's helped by a couple of cables. For instance, when he first lands at the chemical plant site, when he takes off from the same location, before he stops the machine that's about to kill Lana's son, or when he lands at the junkyard. (00:16, 00:42, 01:26)

2. In Pisa, a kiosk vendor sings "Quando la tu' mamma t'ha fatto," which is a typical song ... only from Naples, not Pisa. He also curses Superman using his thumb on his teeth, which is an insult completely unknown on the Old Continent. (01:09, 01:10)

3. On the oil tanker British Reliance they receive a communication. The officer who rips it from the printer uses his right hand, but in the following shot he has it in his left. (01:16)

4. Superman is drunk in the bar of the St. Louis Hotel. From the outside view, he grabs a bowl of peanuts with his right hand and turns it upside-down. Back inside, though, he flips it one more time, using both hands. (01:24)

5. During the fight in the junkyard, Superman knocks Clark unconscious and places him on a conveyor belt. He pro-

ceeds to remove his glasses, folding them at the temples. After he pushes the button of the machine, he folds them again. (01:31, 01:32)

6. Superman regains strength after a collision with a large missile in a canyon. As he takes off from the rock he smashed into, the rock's surface wobbles. (01:42)

7. The position of Gus's hand when he holds the "vital screw" of his supercomputer changes when Webster approaches him. (01:45)

8. Back in Pisa, the vendor (who apparently knows only one Italian song) cleans a model of the new Pisa tower. He holds it from the base, but in the following shot, he's holding it from the middle. (02:00)

Questions

1. A lot of smoke is seen coming from a chemical plant fire. Clark Kent sneaks into a police car to change, and reflected in the car's windshield are two huge explosions with giant balls of fire . . . but we don't hear a sound. Is the car highly soundproofed? (00:15)

2. At the 1965 class reunion, Clark has a picture from his high school days up on the wall. But during his high school days (see *Superman— The Movie)* he didn't look like that at all! Who's the impostor? (00:23)

SUPERMAN IV: THE QUEST FOR PEACE (6)

1987, color, 90 min.

Director: Sidney J. Furie

Cast: Christopher Reeve (Superman / Clark Kent), Gene Hackman (Lex Luthor), Jackie Cooper (Perry White), Marc McClure (Jimmy Olsen), Jon Cryer (Lenny), Sam Wanamaker (David Warfield), Mark Pillow (Nuclear Man), Mariel Hemingway (Lacy Warfield), Margot Kidder (Lois Lane), Damien McLawhorn (Jeremy), William Hootkins (Harry Howler), Jim Broadbent (Jean Pierre Dubois).

. . . and so the excitement fades.

Bloopers

1. Superman's cape flutters in the wind . . . when Superman flies in space?!! (00:04, 00:34, 00:58)

2. To stop a subway train, Superman flies in front of many passengers who are standing at the station. None of them seem to even notice Superman flying right in front of their noses. (00:13)

3. In the office of the *Daily Planet,* Clark walks by Lacy's office. She tries a sexy pose on her desk, and when she stands up to try a new one, Clark walks by her office again—in the same direction. (00:20)

4. Clark jumps off the balcony with Lois and comes back up

as Superman, still wearing Clark's glasses. The right frame of the glasses vanishes briefly as he tilts his head. (00:27)

5. Soldier Goram answers the phone, places it back on the cradle, and communicates to Lex Luthor that there's a weather problem. Lex tells him to proceed with the launch. The soldier close to Goram is talking on the phone, but when Lex pushes the button, the phone has zapped back onto the cradle. (00:40, 00:41)

6. The missile Lex has fired travels toward the camera: in the bottom part of the screen you can catch a glimpse of the stand that the model of the missile was placed on. (00:41)

👀 **Question**

Lacy is brought into space by Nuclear Man (she even catches an image of the Earth way in the distance), yet she doesn't seem to have any trouble breathing. Is she from another planet, too? (01:20)

T

TALENTED MR. RIPLEY, THE (11)
1999, color, 139 min.

Director: Anthony Minghella

Cast: Matt Damon (Tom Ripley), Gwyneth Paltrow (Marge Sherwood), Jude Law (Dickie Greenleaf), Cate Blanchett (Meredith Logue), Philip Seymour Hoffman (Freddie Miles), Jack Davenport (Peter Smith-Kingsley), James Rebhorn (Herbert Greenleaf), Sergio Rubini (Inspector Roverini), Philip Baker Hall (Alvin MacCarron), Celia Weston (Aunt Joan), Fiorello (Fausto).

A lonely wanna-be gets murderous.

Bloopers

1. When Ripley returns the borrowed Princeton jacket to its legitimate owner, he approaches the car window twice (once in the long shot, and again in the close-up). (00:03)
2. Ripley checks out Dickie and Marge while they're on the beach. The point of view of the binoculars changes from being at sea level, to being above it (when Ripley sees the boat *Bird*), then back to sea level again. (00:11)
3. After the visit to the jazz club, Dickie's typing a letter to his dad while simultaneously speaking it out loud. He says, "I bumped into an old friend from Princeton—a fellow called Tom Ripley. He says he's going to haunt me until I agree to go back to New York with him." But on the page, there's a phrase typed between "Tom Ripley" and "He says" that ends with " . . . here for a few weeks." Also "come back" is typed instead of "go back." (00:22)
4. The morning following the jazz club, Tom wakes up at Dickie's with his hair mussed up. Throughout the scene, Tom's hair switches among different versions of mussed up. (00:22, 00:23)
5. Dickie and Marge take Tom

sailing. In the close shots, the sun is shining brightly; in the long shots it's overcast. (00:25)

6. Dickie and Ripley are riding a motorcycle when Dickie complains that Ripley is breaking his ribs. As Ripley replies, "What?" you can see the shadow of the crew in the background. (00:28)

7. Dickie is in the bathtub, playing chess with Tom. Dickie's right rook pawn is at square three, his right bishop pawn is at square two, and his right knight's at home, with its pawn at square four. As he starts his next move, his rook pawn is now back at square two, his knight's pawn is back at square two, and the knight is now in front of the queen. In chess, however, you can only move one piece per turn, and pawns can't move backward. (00:31)

8. In Rome, Ripley sees Freddie arriving with his red car. As Freddie stops the car, its shadow stretches out in front. When he jumps out of it, the shadow goes to one side of the car. (00:34)

9. After telling Tom about Dickie's note, Marge walks out toward the veranda, passing by a stack of LPs in an alcove on the left. The frontmost LP has a picture of a silhouetted man's face. This is the cover of Miles Davis's 1986 album "Tutu." The movie, however, is set in the 1950s. (01:02, 01:03)

10. MacCarran talks to Tom on the balcony in Venice. When Tom says, "I hope she never knows," his bangs are perfect; in the very next cut, his hair is mussed up. (02:02)

11. Tom bids Marge, Mr. Greenleaf, and Detective MacCarron goodbye in Venice. Marge feebly attacks Tom and the others pull her back. Tom starts to fix his hair, but his hands are at his sides in the next shot. (02:04)

Questions

1. When the ship is leaving New York, the strip of water on the bottom of the screen has been "duplicated." Check out the waves, and tell us . . . why? (00:07)

2. Marge comes out of the water and walks on the boat to Ripley. On the deck there's already a set of footprints and a larger wet area that's exactly where Marge is going to stop. Perhaps the ancient remains of a previous take? (00:39)

10 (8)
1979, color, 118 min.

Director: Blake Edwards

Cast: Dudley Moore (George Webber), Julie Andrews (Samantha Taylor), Bo Derek (Jennifer Miles), Robert Webber (Hugh), Dee Wallace-Stone (Mary Lewis), Sam J. Jones (David Hanley), Brian Dennehy (Donald), Max Showalter

(Reverend), Rad Daly (Josh), Nedra Volz (Mrs. Kissel), James Noble (Dr. Miles), Virginia Kiser (Ethel Miles).

Middle-age crises and funny sexual fantasies set to the rhythm of sensual music.

Bloopers

1. Hugh stands up to go to the piano where George is playing: he holds his cup by the brim, but in the following matching shot, he's holding it by the handle. (00:06)
2. As George backs up his Rolls Royce at Hugh's house, the crew is reflected on the car's side. (00:08)
3. When George turns right to enter the highway, not only is it possible to see the shadow of the chopper used for the aerial shot, but the direction of the shadows on the ground change suddenly when we move "up into the sky." (00:08)
4. George stops at a traffic light and the car with Jennifer in it stops next to him. The rearview mirror of George's Rolls is gone (00:10). But it was there earlier (00:08) and will come back quite soon.
5. Once home, George uses his telescope to spy on his neighbor. He can't find him at first, so he pans to the left (at least from his point of view); yet the telescope never moves. (00:17, 00:18)
6. Dr. Miles tells George that he's

"Got six cavities." The dentist's hands move from both sides of George's head to his right side. (00:39)
7. From his neighbor's home, George looks at his house via telescope. From George's house, Sam spies on the neighbor's home. The two "meet in the middle," yet they don't look straight into the scope's lens as they should. According to the way they are shot, they shouldn't have been able to see each other. (00:50)
8. During the vacation in Acapulco, David falls asleep on a surfboard; his hair is dry in the first shot, then wet in the second—but he's still asleep. (01:18)

10 THINGS I HATE ABOUT YOU (6)

1999, color, 97 min.

Director: Gil Junger

Cast: Julia Stiles (Katarina "Kat" Stratford), Heath Ledger (Patrick Verona), Joseph Gordon-Levitt (Cameron James), Larisa Oleynik (Bianca Stratford), Larry Miller (Walter Stratford), Andrew Keegan (Joey Donner), David Krumholtz (Michael Eckman), Susan May Pratt (Mandella), Daryl Chill Mitchell (Mr. Morgan), Allison Janney (Ms. Perky), David Eisure (Mr. Chapin), Gabrielle Union (Chastity).

Boy meets girl, girl has a sister who's from beyond Venus, boy has to find a date for the Venusian . . .

Bloopers

1. At the school parking lot, Michael stops by Kat's car. He's riding his motorcycle with his goggles up on his helmet. But when he stops by Cameron, the goggles have moved onto his eyes (without him touching them). (00:11)

2. While on the motorcycle, Michael seems to have the goggle strap over his helmet (which, by the way, is reflecting the lights of the crew). Michael swerves to miss an oncoming car and falls down the hill. When he stands up, the goggle strap has somehow moved underneath his helmet. (00:11, 00:12)

3. During frog dissection lab, Patrick produces his knife in the background (while Michael is talking) and produces the knife again on his close-up. (00:18)

4. Using a black felt pen, Joey draws a penis on Michael's face. The drawing is more marked when Michael talks to Cameron on his way out of the cafeteria. (00:20, 00:21)

5. Kat grabs a guitar in a store and begins to play. As the camera pans around her, it's possible to catch more than a glimpse of the steadicam operator's hand, reflected in a window. (01:00)

6. When Patrick and Kat are playing paint ball, the spots of colored paint don't match from one cut to the next—particularly after a fake truce, Kat hides behind a structure made with straw balls, and her uniform looks much much cleaner than it was a shot earlier. (01:08, 01:09)

SHOTS OF THE LIVING DEAD

Playing the possum is harder than you think.

Daniel Stern in *Blue Thunder*	Blooper No. 8
Andreas Wisniewski in *Die Hard*	Blooper No. 9
James Cromwell in *Eraser*	Blooper No. 4
Judson Earney Scott in *Star Trek II*	Blooper No. 7
A cop in *The Terminator*	Blooper No. 7
One of the mobsters in *The Untouchables*	Blooper No. 2

TERMINATOR, THE (9)
1984, color, 108 min.

Director: James Cameron

Cast: Arnold Schwarzenegger (The Terminator T-800), Michael Biehn (Kyle Reese), Linda Hamilton (Sarah Connor), Paul Winfield (Lieutenant Traxler), Lance Henriksen (Detective Vukovich), Rich Rossovich (Matt), Bess Motta (Ginger), Earl Boen (Dr. Silberman), Ed Dogans (Cop in Alley), Marianne Muellerleile (Wrong Sarah), Bruce M. Kerner (Desk Sergeant), Philip Gordon Anthony T. Trujillo (Mexican Boy).

Arnold goes robot and finds his calling as an evil cyborg.

Bloopers
1. Kyle arrives in 1984 and, after being chased, asks a cop what day it is; the puzzled cop answers, "12 . . . May . . . Thursday." May 12, 1984 was a Saturday. (00:08)
2. The Terminator looks for Sarah Connor's address in a phone book. There are three Sarah Connors, and their street numbers are 1823, 2816, 309. The first Sarah the terminator visits lives at 14239. (00:15)
3. Sarah and Ginger listen to their phone messages while Sarah holds Pugsley, her pet iguana. The position of the animal changes noticeably from the wide shot to the close-up. (00:23)
4. Ginger's message on the answering machine goes, "Hi there! [pause] Ha ha ha, fooled you, you're talking to a machine . . ." When the Terminator is in the apartment and Sarah calls to warn Ginger, the message goes, "Hi there! Ha ha ha, fooled you . . ." No pause this time. Oops! (00:25, 00:32)
5. While patrolling a garage in a "borrowed" police car, the Terminator stops the vehicle, which allows us to read what's written on its door: "To care and to protect." During the following car chase, Kyle fires a gunshot and hits the Terminator, who flinches while driving. Now the door of the car says "Dedicated . . ." When Sarah realizes the Terminator has escaped from the smashed car, the whole door is visible: "Dedicated to serve." (00:47, 00:49, 00:50)
6. After the "I'll be back" line, the Terminator destroys a police station; the officer sitting at the desk is lit up by the headlights of the Terminator's approaching truck—but as the vehicle bursts into the room, its headlights are off. (00:59)
7. The Terminator enters the police station firing guns. As he fires his machine gun into the open door on the left at the end of the hall, the dead victim on the floor in the foreground flinches at both of his shots. (01:00)
8. Sarah calls her mom and gives her the phone number of the

Tiki Motel—(408) 555-1439. The Terminator, who was impersonating Sarah's mom, dials back, but dials 555-1639 instead. And somehow gets the Tiki Motel. (01:16)

9. The picture of Sarah that the Mexican boy snaps with his Polaroid becomes a regular picture with a uniform border (Polaroid stills have a larger border at the bottom). (01:41)

Questions

1. To reach Sarah Connor and protect her, Kyle flips a phone book open and checks the names, which he finds on the book's right page. The Terminator does the same, in another phone book—and he finds the three names on the book's left page. Sarah checks too, and she finds the names on the right page again. Different phone book publishers, or simply a blooper? (00:11, 00:15, 00:27)

2. The Terminator pays a non-courtesy visit to Ginger. After the first gunshot, Ginger stumbles on a table and falls to the floor: the noise that accompanies her fall is suspiciously similar to a phone crashing down. Yet, when Sarah calls in, the phone in the apartment rings just fine . . . huh? (00:31)

3. To fix his damaged eye, the Terminator grabs a scalpel. As he brings the scalpel up to his eye from the right angle, is the blade now missing? (00:54)

TERMINATOR 2: JUDGMENT DAY (51)
also Special Edition and Extended Special Edition
1991, color, 137 min. / 152 min. (SE) / 155 min. (ESE)

Director: James Cameron

Cast: Arnold Schwarzenegger (The Terminator T-800), Linda Hamilton (Sarah Connor),

---

T2 Special Edition DVD Tip

1. On the DVD menu, go to the Special Edition Menu.
2. Slowly punch in 82997 (Judgment Day, get it?).
3. As each digit is punched, a sequence of yellow words appears: "The Future Is Not Set." (This is already cool in and of itself, but wait: there's more!)
4. This will allow access to the Extended Special Edition, which has two more sequences than the Special Edition, including the original ending.

(NOTE: if your remote doesn't allow you to punch in 82997, just select Title 3 for the same result.)

Edward Furlong (John Connor), Robert Patrick (T-1000), Earl Boen (Dr. Silberman), Joe Morton (Miles Bennett Dyson), S. Epatha Merkerson (Tarissa Dyson), Castulo Guerra (Enrique Salceda), Danny Cooksey (Tim), Jenette Goldstein (Janelle Voight), Xander Berkeley (Todd Voight), Robert Winley (Cigar Biker), Michael Biehn (Kyle Reese).

Arnold reprises his evil robot role . . . only this time as a good robot.

Bloopers

1. In the truckstop, the truck to the right has a yellowish sticker on its rear door (probably a "Caution" sticker). After the T-800's energy sphere appears, the yellow sticker is gone. (00:05, 00:06)
2. As T-800 steps to the bar, he scans the bikes and the car parked outside. His analysis of the car says "Plymouth Sedan"—but the car is a Ford. (00:06)
3. The Cigar Biker is thrown on the stove by T-800. But the smoke that's allegedly produced by his hands and clothes on the burning surface is actually coming from a couple of tubes on the side of the stove. One even stops smoking a few moments after the biker has jumped down. (00:08)
4. When T-800 gets stabbed in the bar, the blade bends. (00:08)

5. Just before stealing a pair of sunglasses, T-800 releases his grip from a shotgun, twice. (00:09)
6. John, talking with Tim about his mom, puts on the right strap of his backpack, then puts on the left, then puts on the left one once again. (00:17 / 00:18 SE and ESE)
7. During the fight that starts in a mall, T-1000 fires many bullets into T-800's back, piercing his leather jacket. Yet when T-1000 tosses T-800 through an arcade window, the holes in the jacket are gone. (00:27, 00:28 / 00:32 SE and ESE)
8. In the service corridor, T-800 slams T-1000 against a wall, then against a second wall. But this second wall already has a hole in it. (00:28 / 00:32 SE and ESE)
9. If you really, really, really, really, really carefully pause the movie at the right moment, you can see the camera on the right side of the truck, after it rams two cars while it's chasing John. (00:30 / 00:34 SE and ESE)
10. T-1000 drives a semi off a bridge and into a man-made riverbed; when it lands, the wheels of the truck are irreparably bent—but the truck drives in the riverbed faster than a speeding bullet. (00:30 / 00:35 SE and ESE)
11. The windshields of the truck pop out upon impact, too— but they're back on when T-1000 pushes them out of

his way. (00:30, 00:32 / 00:35, 00:36 SE and ESE)

12. A wave of sparks comes from the truck—before it hits the wall. (00:31 / 00:36 SE and ESE)

13. John's motorcycle is run over by the truck T-1000 is driving: the bike turns 180° underneath the wheels of the truck. (00:32 / 00:37 SE and ESE)

14. After the truck explodes, a flaming tire rolls toward the T-800, who cocks his gun but doesn't shoot. Later on, when he stops at John's request, the T-800 removes an empty shell from the gun. (00:33, 00:34 / 00:38, 00:39 SE and ESE)

15. When John asks T-800 if he has a quarter, T-800 smashes the pay phone. The bottom of it is already set to be crushed. (00:36 / 00:41 SE and ESE)

16. Todd drinks milk straight from the carton, holding it with his right hand. After he's killed, it's his lifeless left hand that drops from the carton. (00:37, 00:38 / 00:43 SE / 00:42, 00:43 ESE)

17. When T-1000 (disguised as Janelle, John's stepmother) kills John's stepfather Todd, he does it with his left arm as a blade. When T-1000 melts at the end and reprises all his disguises, the woman's right arm is the one with the blade. (00:38, 02:06 / 00:43, 02:22 SE / 00:43, 02:23 ESE)

18. When the T-1000 removes the blade with which he's stabbed Todd, Todd falls to the floor: the mechanism that pulled the blade from his head is briefly visible. (00:38 / 00:43 SE and ESE)

19. John tells the T-800 to put the gun down. The T-800 obeys, placing the gun to the right of his right leg. When John picks it up, he finds it between the T-800's legs. (00:43 / 00:48 SE / 00:50 ESE)

20. When John hands the gun to the T-800, it's cocked; when the T-800 grabs it, it's not; then when he puts it into his pants, it's cocked again. (00:43, 00:44 / 00:49 SE / 00:50, 00:51 ESE)

21. Lewis, the night guard, says he has a "full house" on his coffee cup: he actually has two jacks, two aces and, on the bottom of the cup, what looks to be a queen. Huh? (00:48 / 00:53 SE / 00:54, 00:55 ESE)

22. When he gets shish-kabobbed through the eye by the T-1000, Lewis drops his cup on the floor. Two jacks are on the cup on the far left (diamonds and hearts), two aces on the right (clubs and hearts), and a queen on the bottom. After it's dropped, a jack and the ace of diamonds are on the left and the bottom no longer has a queen. (00:48 / 00:54 SE / 00:55 ESE)

T2 Twin Pairings

Lewis the guard gets killed at the coffee machine by the T-1000 who's impersonating him—but it's not exactly a special effect. Lewis and the T-1000 are played by Don and Dan Stanton, a couple of twin-brother actors who also appeared in *Gremlins 2: The New Batch* and *Good Morning Vietnam*.

The same situation happened with Linda Hamilton (Sarah Connor) and her twin near the end of the movie. Leslie Hamilton Gearren, Linda's twin sister, filled in as her double while the T-1000 was impersonating her.

23. Sarah hits a guard with a wood broomstick; it bends. (00:49 / 00:55 SE / 00:56 ESE)
24. Sarah runs barefoot in the hospital, but the noise that is heard suspiciously sounds like running shoes. (00:50 / 00:55 SE / 00:57 ESE)
25. Sarah says that the human body is made up of 215 bones. Wrong: there are 206. (00:51 / 00:56 SE / 00:58 ESE)
26. T-800 smashes a window at the hospital reception area; later, when he crashes the gate of the hospital with a car, the same window is intact. (00:52, 00:59 / 00:57, 01:05 SE / 00:59, 01:06 ESE)
27. A guard punches T-800 in the face: his sunglasses slant to the left, but in the following shot they're slanting to the right. Also, T-800 is hit in the right side of the face, yet it's the left lens that gets broken. (00:55 / 01:01 SE / 01:02 ESE)
28. T-1000 passes by Dr. Silberman twice while running. (00:56 / 01:02 SE / 01:03 ESE)
29. Uncannily enough, T-1000 fires twenty-six times without reloading his gun. (00:56 / 01:02 SE / 01:03 ESE)
30. While running to the elevator, T-1000 tosses his empty gun to the floor. But when he chases the police car driving in reverse, the gun is back in his holster. (00:56, 00:58 / 01:02, 01:04 SE / 01:03, 01:05 ESE)
31. T-800 fires straight at the head of the T-1000, which splits open. Just before the explosion, it's possible to see that the T-1000's head is already split. (00:57 / 01:02 SE / 01:03 ESE)
32. Sarah forces a cop out of his car by firing at the windshield, cracking it. When T-800 shuts off the lights and drives in "Image Enhance" mode, the crack in the windshield is gone. (00:58, 01:01 / 01:03, 01:06 SE / 01:05, 01:08 ESE)
33. T-800 steals a car to go to Mexico, and to do so he smashes the driver's side window—the same window that can be seen rolled down a few minutes later. (01:04, 01:06 / 01:13, 01:16 SE / 01:14, 01:17 ESE)
34. When Sarah gets in the stolen car, she opens the rear

door, showing, in the window, the reflection of the crew. (01:05 / 01:13 SE / 01:15 ESE)

35. Sarah uses a knife to carve "No Fate" into a table. The tip of the blade curves toward Sarah in the detail and away from her in the wide shot. (01:15 / 01:29 SE / 01:31 ESE)

36. The magazines on Dyson's coffee table alternate between being in two piles and being displayed in an orderly fashion. (01:22 / 01:37 SE / 01:39 ESE)

37. In Dyson's house, John hugs his mom: his wristwatch reads 10:30 in one shot, 11:55 in the next. (01:24 / 01:39 SE / 01:40 ESE)

38. T-800 has a belt with some twelve grenades on it. He fires four of them, but when he walks toward the SWAT team, almost all of the grenades are gone from the belt. (01:31, 01:42 / 01:46, 01:58 SE / 01:48, 02:00 ESE)

39. T-1000 enters Dyson's home. Through his radio, he hears a dispatcher saying that there's a "211 in progress, 2144 Kramer Street." When several patrol cars race to the Cyberdyne building, one cop asks for an address confirmation. The dispatcher says, "2111 Kramer." (01:48, 01:49 SE / 01:50, 01:51 ESE only)

40. T-1000 enters the building with the police bike he stole. But when he climbs the stairs with the same bike, it

is clearly a motocross bike painted like a police bike. Pay attention to the tires. (01:43, 01:44 / 01:58, 01:59 SE / 01:59, 02:01 ESE)

41. When T-800 drives the SWAT van into the building lobby, the impact makes the left rearview mirror fall to one side. As the gang escapes, the mirror is back in place. (01:44, 01:45 / 02:00 SE / 02:01, 02:02 ESE)

42. On his bike, T-1000 blasts out through a window, aiming at a chopper. During the jump, the windshield of his motorcycle detaches. But it's back in place when the motorcycle hits the ground. (01:45 / 02:01 SE / 02:02 ESE)

43. T-1000 smashes the helicopter's windshield and enters the cockpit. When he flies away to chase the van T-800 is driving, the hole is gone. (01:45, 01:46 / 02:01 / 02:02, 02:03 ESE)

44. T-1000 tells the chopper pilot to "get out." The poor guy does so, and the door slams shut. In the next cut, T-1000 stretches and closes the same door one more time. (01:45 / 02:01 SE / 02:03 ESE)

45. The glass of the locked rear door of the van gets shattered by machine gun bullets, but it comes back in one piece as the van hits another car. (01:47 / 02:03 SE / 02:04 ESE)

46. When the nitrogen truck flips on its side and skids on the

ground, you can see a few metal cables pulling it. (01:52 / 02:08 SE / 02:09 ESE)

47. Sarah grabs a shotgun in the steel mill with eight bullets on it. She fires the first one, loses the second, puts the third in the barrel, later on places all the others in the gun, and at the end she fires one shot at her duplicate, and six more at the T-1000. Count 'em: 1 + 1 + 1 + 6 = 9. Oops. (01:59, 02:04 / 02:14, 02:21 SE / 02:17, 02:22 ESE)

48. After being hit with an enormous I-beam, T-800 collapses to the floor and crawls toward his gun. The stump (where his left arm was) moves as well, thanks to a wire visible in the bottom right corner of the screen. (02:01 / 02:18 SE / 02:19 ESE)

49. Sarah fires six times at the T-1000, and after each shot, the cyborg jumps backward a little bit. When she runs out of ammo, he restores his holes. But there are only five holes, not six. (02:04 / 02:21 SE / 02:22 ESE)

50. When Sarah has to lower the T-800 into the molten metal, she pushes the button that would raise the T-800 up. (02:10 / 02:26 SE / 02:28 ESE)

51. "Grandma" Connor says that August 29, 1997 came and went, and that on that day Michael Jackson turned 40. A-hem. Mr. Jackson turned 40 on August 29, 1998. (02:29 ESE only)

Questions

1. At Cyberdyne Systems, Dr. Dyson enters what seems to be a clean room (everyone is wearing full-body suits and masks) as if he were casually stepping out onto the verandah for a smoke. Is he naturally more sterile than the others? (00:21 / 00:26 SE and ESE)

2. The police car, running in reverse, jumps through the security barricade. Is that the head of a stunt driver that appears in the middle of the rear windshield? (00:59 / 01:04 SE / 01:06 ESE)

3. When T-1000 melts and replays all his disguises, he doesn't do his Sarah Connor impression, which he did a few minutes earlier. What, did he forget? (02:04, 02:05 / 02:20, 02:22 SE / 02:22, 02:24 ESE)

Fun Facts

1. Michael Biehn reprised his role as Kyle in a Sarah dream sequence. He was cut out of the theatrical release, but his part lives on in the director's cut. (00:19 SE and ESE only)

2. Inside the mall, T-800 hides his gun in a box of roses. Guess what rock group made a song for the soundtrack . . . ? (00:26 / 00:31 SE and ESE)

3. After the chopper flies underneath an overpass, there's a shot of the T-1000, who's reloading his gun and flying the chopper: he has three hands. Same on the shot in profile

after he's flown over an overpass: he has two left hands. But a T-1000 can do this, of course. (01:47 / 02:03 SE / 02:04, 02:05 ESE)

THEY LIVE (4)
1988, color, 94 min.

Director: John Carpenter

Cast: Roddy Piper (Nada), Keith David (Frank), Meg Foster (Holly), George "Buck" Flower (Drifter), Peter Jason (Gilbert), Raymond St. Jacques (Street Preacher), Jason Robards III (Family Man), John F. Goff (Well-Dressed Customer), Norm Wilson (Vendor).

A conspiracy to rob earth of its natural resources and turn us into helpless consumers . . . orchestrated by aliens, of course.

Bloopers
1. Nada is discovering the secret powers of the sunglasses and can't help but stare at a well-dressed customer at a newsstand. The customer notices this and is so distracted that he takes the change from the vendor . . . twice (once as a ghoul, once as a human being). (00:34)
2. Holly gives Nada a lift. During the conversation in the car, the door lock on the passenger's side goes up and down many times. (00:44)
3. Nada asks Frank to put the

sunglasses on. Frank says no and the two begin to fight. Frank takes off his backpack and kicks it into the middle of the alley. After a few seconds, the backpack has moved close to a dumpster, without anybody touching it. (00:55, 00:56)
4. When Frank refuses one more time to wear the glasses, he turns to leave. Nada removes his glasses, and Frank turns again and leaves. (00:55)

Sean Finally Struts the Strut

Because *Thunderball* was the first Bond movie shot in Cinemascope, the gun barrel opening sequence had to be reshot. And Sean Connery performed it for the first time. In the first three 007 movies, the Bond walking in the gun barrel was actually stuntman Bob Simmons (1933-1988).

THUNDERBALL (29)
1965, color, 130 min.

Director: Terence Young

Cast: Sean Connery (James Bond 007), Claudine Auger (Domino Derval), Adolfo Celi (Emilio Largo), Luciana Paluzzi (Fiona Volpe), Rick Van Nutter (Felix Leiter), Martine Beswick (Paula Caplan), Bernard Lee (M), Guy Doleman (Count Lippe), Paul Stassino (Angelo Palazzi / Major Françoise Derval), Rose Alba (Colonel Boitier in female disguise),

Maryse Guy Mitsouko (Mademoiselle LaPorte), Molly Peters (Patricia Fearing), Loix Maxwell (Miss Moneypenny), Desmond Llewelyn (Q), Earl Cameron (Pinder).

The fourth Bond finds 007 swimming with sharks — literally.

Bloopers

1. 007 fights with a widow (who turns out to be Colonel Boitier). To stop her, Bond drops a cupboard on the lady, who loses her hat and veil. As 007 flips the cupboard over, the hat and veil are back in place. (00:02)
2. During the same fight, Bond sends the "woman" over a coffee table by the fireplace, where a nice fire is going. As Boitier stands up and attacks Bond with the poker, the fire seems to be all but extinct. (00:03)
3. Bond uses the Bell Jet Pack to escape from Boitier's château and he lands by the Aston Martin, creating a huge cloud of dust. When he opens the trunk to put the jet pack away, the dust is almost entirely gone. But as they raise the bulletproof shield, there's enough dust on the trunk to choke a buffalo. (00:04)
4. A "bandaged man" (Angelo) opens the door of a hotel room while Bond is hiding behind it. Bond's right hand slips inside his jacket, ready to draw the gun — but in the long shot Bond's hand is still along his side. Then it's back inside his jacket. (00:13)
5. Once he's dead, Major Derval gets bandaged: his eyes are closed. When Bond unwraps him, the Major's eyes are wide open. (00:21, 00:25)
6. The real Derval gets bandaged: the first two wraps of the bandage go over his forehead. Later, when 007 unbandages the cadaver, the first two wraps he removes are from the forehead — but they should have been the last two, since he was going backwards. (00:21, 00:25)
7. One night, Bond goes for "a little exercise" in the Shrublands health clinic: he wears a long sleeve black shirt — but he rolls his sleeves all the way up. Yet, when he discovers the body of Major Derval and begins to unwrap it, his sleeves are down (only in one shot). (00:23, 00:25)
8. When Bond discovers Major Derval's cadaver, he unwraps the major's face — but in the wide shot, there's more bandage on the face than there was in the close-up. (00:25)
9. While in the conference room, Bond opens a folder that contains, among other things, a picture of "Françoise Derval & sister, Dominique Derval" — or so it's written on the back of the picture, as well as "Classi-

fied" and "Hunt Photo, Nassau, blah blah blah." When Bond shows what is assumed to be the same picture to M and to Moneypenny, the back of it is white: no writing, no stamp ... nothing. (00:41, 00:42, 00:43)

10. During an underwater adventure, Bond sets Domino free and swims with her to the surface wearing black flippers. While paddling around Domino's boat, she says, "I'm not with you," to which Bond replies, "You soon will be." At this point, Bond has no more flippers. But when he swims to Paula, he shows his black flippers again. (00:44, 00:45)

11. Because his motor is "conked out," Bond asks Domino to drive him ashore. Domino has a large comb in her left hand, then she doesn't, then she does again. (00:46)

12. Once on the beach, Bond and Domino walk side by side: 007 has a red shirt he's holding with his left hand. He casually tosses it on his left shoulder—but in the following shot, he's still carrying it in his hand. (00:47)

13. Q is about to show Bond "a miniature Very pistol." Bond has a special camera in his right hand but, in the following cut, it's in his left. (01:00)

14. While displaying all of the new props, Q hands Bond a special device that can replace oxygen tanks when underwater, but for a short period of time. "About four minutes," Q specifies. Yet, when he escapes Largo's men and jumps on the *Disco Volante,* Bond uses the device for about seven whole minutes (from 01:58 to 02:05). (01:00, 01:58)

15. While showing all the new devices to Bond, Q says, "Now pay attention" without moving his lips. (01:01)

16. 007 swims to the S.P.E.C.T.R.E. frogmen's rendezvous point. He gets out of the water, throws his flippers away, and appears barefoot. Right after that, he's wearing white shoes. (01:06)

17. While flying in a chopper with Felix, Bond passes over Largo's villa and points his binoculars at the shark pool. 007's wristwatch jumps from his left arm to his right, and his hair is parted on the wrong side. (01:10)

18. Bond steps out of Largo's Palmyra basement, and drops a very large white hatch—which doesn't make any noise. (01:18)

19. During the Junkanoo parade, a drunk black man shoves his bottle in the car where Bond is kept under surveillance: the man holds the bottle by its neck in the wide shots, by the body in the details. (01:26)

20. During the same parade, Bond is shot: at first in his right leg, which then becomes the left (in the second

detail), comes back to the right (in the following shot), and once again becomes the left (when he jumps on the float and then bandages it in the Kiss Kiss Club toilet). (01:26, 01:27, 01:29)

21. 007 finds the NATO bomber
 👀 and his chopper lands on the water: Felix, who's piloting the helicopter, had been wearing shorts up until that moment; yet as Bond dives (and when he emerges), Felix has long blue pants. They come back as shorts in between and after. (01:32, 01:34, 01:36)

> Editor Peter Hunt said about the continuity problems in *Thunderball* that sometimes you just can't fix them, and "It's better to maintain the pace of the film than to worry about continuity."

22. While on the chopper, Bond spots a manta ray in the water. The comment is, "Manta ray! Unusual to see them as far out as this." This line is said by Pinder, 007's assistant in the Bahamas— who is not on the helicopter at the moment (**NOTE:** fixed on the new Special Edition DVD). (01:33)

23. As the chopper lands on the water, Bond needs a way to dive safely among the sharks, so Felix shoots one. While the two talk, it's possible to see the shadow of the

props still rotating, though when Felix fires the gun (and when Bond dives as well) the props are motionless. (01:34)

24. Bond dives to verify that the lost plane is actually on the bottom of the sea. He has no wristwatch—except at the moment when he removes the name tag from Angelo's jacket, who's still trapped in the cockpit. (01:34, 01:35, 01:36)

25. After diving together, Bond and Domino walk to the beach, but she places her right foot on some poisonous sea egg spines. Bond, however, pulls the spines out of her left foot. (01:37, 01:38)

26. Largo's underwater stunt double's hair is blondish— but definitely different from the grayish hair of the "real" Largo. (01:54)

27. 007's blue mask is ripped off underwater by Largo. Bond swims to one of the S.P.E.C.T.R.E. dead men and takes his black mask. But after a quick turn, Bond has his blue mask back on. (02:02)

28. During the fight on the *Disco Volante*, 007 hits the captain for the second time: the captain's hat flies away but it's back in place as the man lies unconscious against the wall in the background. (02:05)

29. 007, Domino, and one professor jump in the water before the *Disco Volante* blows up. Bond and Domino are rescued; the professor must still

be somewhere between New York and Lisbon. (02:07, 02:08)

Questions

1. To stall his pursuers, 007 sprays them with water, using a device from his Aston Martin. Yet, to emit such a volume of water, the car would have to have a tank larger than the car itself. Where was it? (00:04)

2. To take revenge for a massage that turned into torture, Bond enters a room through a door that says "Massage." After getting even with Count Lippe, bond exits the same room through a door that says "Sitz Bath & Heat Treatment." All right, but . . . ? (00:17, 00:18)

3. While swimming with the sharks in Largo's pool, one shot seems to reveal the glass between the fish and the actors: Bond's right hand seems to be "glued" to the glass as a shark swims by. Are we seeing things? (01:21)

Fun Fact

When a Sidney parade passes by, you can see a dog "relieving itself" in the middle of the crowd. (01:27)

TITANIC (21)

1997, color, 194 min.

Director: James Cameron

Cast: Leonardo DiCaprio (Jack Dawson), Kate Winslet (Rose DeWitt Bukater), Gloria Stuart (Old Rose), Bill Paxton (Brock Lovett), Billy Zane (Caledon "Cal" Hockley), Kathy Bates (Molly Brown), Victor Garber (Thomas Andrews), Danny Nucci (Fabrizio DeRossi), Frances Fisher (Ruth DeWitt Bukater), Lewis Abernathy (Lewis Bodine), David Warner (Spicer Lovejoy), James Lancaster (Father Byles), Ioan Gruffudd (Fifth Officer Lowe).

Fox and Paramount pay over $200 million for a ship, then it sinks.

Bloopers

1. Old Rose has blue eyes. Young Rose has green eyes. (00:11, 00:21)

2. There is no proof that there was precious jewelry on the *Titanic*. The most expensive jewel was a double-string of pearls that was around the neck of a woman who saved herself. (00:15)

3. Old Rose says about the Heart of the Ocean diamond: "I only wore it this once," while checking the drawing they found in the *Titanic* safe. But during her tale, Cal places it around her neck way before the drawing session. That would qualify for a second wearing. (00:16, 00:46, 01:25)

4. While the computer simulation of the boat's sinking plays on a screen and Mr. Bodine explains to Old Rose what happened, the lights on the CGI *Titanic* go out—and

do the same thing again, in a long shot. (00:18)

5. No proof exists that there were any priceless paintings on the *Titanic*. Picasso's *Les Damoiselles d'Avignon* is currently on exhibition at the Museum of Modern Art in New York and Degas's *Ballerina* rests inside the Louvre Museum in Paris—not on the bottom of the Atlantic Ocean. (00:28, 02:31)

6. During the cruise, heavy smoke is coming out of all four chimneys. On the real *Titanic*, only three of the chimneys were coming from the engines; the fourth one was dedicated to the kitchen. The producers said that during the cruise the kitchen was fully operative—true, but what in the hell could they be cooking, in order to produce that much smoke? (00:31, 00:56, 01:29)

7. Jack and Fabrizio run to the edge of the handrail to see dolphins jumping in and out of the water. The *Titanic* sank in the North Atlantic. Those are Pacific dolphins. (00:31)

8. While trying to save Rose from a fatal jump, Jack talks about his memories of fishing in Lake Wissota in Wisconsin. The man-made lake was created in 1917, five years after the sinking of the *Titanic*. (00:40)

9. Jack talks to a suicidal Rose and tries to convince her to come back on the ship. He rests on his right arm while saying, "I'm telling you. Water that cold, like right down there . . ." But in the following wide shot, as he says "Which is why I'm not looking forward to jumping in there after you," he's resting on his left arm. (00:40)

10. While talking to Rose, Jack mentions going to the Santa Monica Pier in Los Angeles and says that he and Rose could ride the rollercoaster. The pier was originally open to the public in 1909; however, construction of the "pleasure pier," including the Blue Streak Racer rollercoaster, didn't even start until 1916. (00:53)

11. Jack teaches Kate how to spit, but when the two are caught, they quickly turn to greet the newcomers. The drop of saliva on Jack's chin changes shape, size, and location. (00:55)

12. As Jack goes to the rich folks' dinner, a waiter opens a beautiful door—a door that reflects the image of a steadicam operator. (00:56)

13. When Jack reaches the dining room, he is approached by Molly ("Care to escort a lady to dinner?"). Jack grabs both Rose and Molly and follows Cal to the table. Jack takes a couple of steps, but in Cal's shot ("Sweet Pea?") it's possible to see Jack in the background, standing motionless next to Rose. Molly

is approaching him—again. (01:00)

14. Jack climbs up to the first-class deck and passes by a kid who's playing with a string-wound top. The kid spins the top—and in the following shot, he spins it again, even if he hasn't had time to get it back, pull the string around... (01:16)

15. Jack sneaks onto the first class bridge and "kidnaps" Rose, as she's alone. He opens the door of a rec room, and the two leave a deserted deck—but as they enter the room, an old couple is seen passing by the door—they probably were doing laps around the deck, because they weren't there before! (01:17)

16. Rose "flies" on the bow of the ship. A beautiful sunset frames the whole whimsical atmosphere... but the *Titanic* is sailing in the wrong direction. Since it's sailing from Great Britain to New York, the sun should have been on the opposite side of the ship. The direction from which the sun shines means that the *Titanic* was sailing North and not West. (01:20)

17. Rose gives the finger to Spicer Lovejoy as she gets down with Jack to the E deck via elevator. That gesture was already around at the beginning of the century, but it's hard to believe that a high society woman would

be aware of its use, much less use it. (01:31)

18. Looking for some help to set Jack free, Rose bumps into an ax and decides to use it. She smashes the glass using a hose, and—with the sole exception of one sliver—the glass is gone... until the next shot, in which it's almost entirely back in the frame. Broken, but back. (02:04)

19. You can see only about half of the passengers' breaths in the cold Atlantic night air (for instance, Jack and Rose breathe steam while Father Byles, who's praying at the same time in the same spot, doesn't). (02:37, 02:38)

20. The crew of the lifeboat is coming back looking for survivors, and Officer Lowe yells "Is there anyone alive out there? Can anybody hear me?..." After every yell there's an echo. How? There's nothing around to create an echo. (02:52)

21. In order to attract the attention of the rescuers, Rose swims in the cold water, grabs a metal whistle, and blows it. But in the freezing water, the metal would have stuck to her lips. (02:57)

Non-Blooper

Jack hands a secret message to Rose while leaving the dinner table. The note looks to be written on a yellow piece of paper, but when Rose opens it, it's a white

JUST WHAT THEY "KNEED"

... but didn't intend for us to see.

LL Cool J in *Deep Blue Sea*   Blooper No. 5
A guard in *The Matrix*   Blooper No. 22
A woman in *The Towering Inferno*   Blooper No. 5

piece of paper. Actually it's only yellow because of the light cast by a nearby lamp. (01:04)

TOWERING INFERNO, THE (6)
1974, color, 165 min.

Directors: John Guillermin and Irwin Allen

Cast: Steve McQueen (Fire Chief O'Halloran), Paul Newman (Doug Roberts), William Holden (James Duncan), Faye Dunaway (Susan Franklin), Fred Astaire (Harlee Claiborne), Susan Blakely (Patty Simmons), Richard Chamberlain (Roger Simmons), Jennifer Jones (Lisolette Mueller), O. J. Simpson (Jernigan), Norman Burton (Will Giddings), Mike Lookinland (Phillip Allbright), Carlena Gowen (Angela Allbright).

Very big, very tall, very in-flammable building is a disaster waiting to happen.

Bloopers
1. Will Giddings runs to push one of the guards away from a door with a fire behind it. Flames erupt from the door and Giddings is set ablaze. But when Doug yells, "get those drapes," Giddings is clearly wearing flame-retardant protective gloves as he's crawling on the floor. (00:38)
2. An elevator filled with party guests accidentally opens on the 81st floor, where the fire is, and catches everyone unprepared: the firemen, the security guards, the guests in the car—who jump in fear. They are so scared they do it twice, making the same exact gestures (it's the same shot from two slightly different angles). (00:56)
3. On the 87th floor, Mrs. Mueller runs to the door of an apartment where she suspects two kids and their deaf mother may be trapped. She's spotted on one of the surveillance monitors. It seems that the surveillance camera uses film (?) and is somehow only a few inches from Mrs. Mueller's face ... ? (01:00)
4. As Doug is about to use a shovel to open an air vent, he

crouches down to talk to little Phillip. In the detail, the shovel has rotated 90° in Doug's hands. It'll be back in its original position when he stands up again. (01:26)

5. The first and only attempt to help the trapped guests with a chopper goes so badly that the helicopter explodes on the roof of the Glass Tower. Two women who were trying to reach the vehicle fall flat on the floor. As Doug helps the second woman stand up, her dress hikes up a little too much—and she's wearing knee-pads. (01:51)

6. After everyone is ordered to tie him or herself up, there's a shot of the Glass Tower: a large explosion sends a huge cloud of white smoke out of a window ... but the cloud vanishes in an instant—even though the flames keep erupting from other windows. (02:20)

TOY STORY (13)
1995, color, 81 min.

Director: John Lasseter

Cast: Tom Hanks (Woody), Tim Allen (Buzz Lightyear), Don Rickles (Mr. Potato Head), Jim Varney (Slinky Dog), Wallace Shawn (Rex), John Ratzenberger (Hamm), Annie Potts (Bo Peep), John Morris (Andy), Erik Von Dotten (Sid), Laurie Metcalf (Mrs. Davis), R. Lee Ermey (Sergeant), Sarah Freeman (Hannah).

Toys have feelings, too, as well as the ability to reap tremendous box office receipts.

Bloopers

1. Little Molly grabs Mr. Potato Head and bites him, causing his right arm to fly to the ground. Later, when "the coast is clear," and Mr. Potato Head is lying on the floor, his arms are both in place—but he wouldn't have had time yet to fix himself. (00:01, 00:03)

2. When the soldiers go to spy on the birthday gifts Andy is about to receive, they use a Playschool baby monitor. But they screw up, because they take the receiver section, while the transmitter (the one that you have to leave in the baby room if you want to hear him) stays with Woody and the others. And they commit the same mistake twice. (00:09, 01:15)

Director John Lasseter said that no one realized that they had the wrong end, but "For those parents there, they probably know."

3. When RC, the radio-controlled car, hits the corkboard, Buzz finds himself under a waterfall of pins that stick into the desk. But as the globe rolls along the same desk, all the pins have departed. (00:26)

4. At the Dinoco gas station, Buzz and Woody are almost run over by a large truck. The double license plates of the vehicle are EL 4994 and DF 3443. Also, there's a red square with 1203 written in the middle. Later on, the Eggman Movers truck used for moving Andy's family has, as license plates, EL 4994 and DF 3443, but no square with 1203. So, (a) what are the odds? and (b) with all the money made in merchandising, Disney could at least rent two different trucks. (00:31, 01:07)

5. Buzz talks while staring at the moon from underneath a truck. The moon is a thin crescent curving to the right. When the moon's reflected in Buzz's helmet, it also curves to the right, but the reflection should curve to the left. (00:32)

6. Woody tries to rescue Buzz while hiding in a string of lights and calling Sid's sister. When the two puppets get out of the room, the string of lights has disappeared. It'll reappear a few shots later. (00:49, 00:50)

7. In order to talk to his friends, Woody opens Sid's window. When Sid enters the room, he straps a rocket to Buzz, then walks to a closed window and looks disappointed because of the rain. As he slams Buzz on the table, the window that Woody opened is now closed—and nobody touched it. (00:50, 00:55)

8. Woody tosses a string of Christmas lights to the other toys, from Sid's room to Andy's. But when he plays with Buzz's arm (and Rex says, "Hey, look! It's Buzz!"), there's one shot from behind the toys in which there's no string of lights at all. (00:51, 00:52)

9. Trapped in a milk crate, Woody hides underneath a booklet ("The Improvised Interrogation Manual TM 31-210"). The manual is still there when he tries to convince Buzz to help him, but it's gone as the two push the crate along the desk. (00:55, 00:56, 00:59)

10. Sid's alarm goes off at 7:00 A.M. As he leaves the room—immediately, since he wants to blow up Buzz—Woody asks for help from the other toys: a clock on the wall says that now it's 3:10 (even if there's less than one minute between the shots of the two clocks). After very little time, the same clock on the wall says it's 10:00 (but it's still daytime). (01:01, 01:02)

11. Sid grabs Woody from the barbecue, but in the shot immediately following, Woody is in a totally different position. (01:05)

12. Buzz and Woody are chasing the movers' truck. When Buzz climbs onto the platform, and also when Woody

does, we catch a glimpse of the lever to lower the ramp: it's black. When Flash operates it, the lever has turned bright red. (01:08, 01:11)

13. The toys lower the ramp of the movers' truck. However, when Buzz, Woody, and RC are flying toward the truck, before they drop the car, the ramp disappears. As Woody and Buzz jet up into the sky, the ramp is back. (01:13)

Question
Buzz Lightyear demonstrates that he can fly and proceeds to zoom around an orange car track. Wouldn't his wings have become trapped in the loop? (00:18)

Fun Fact
The toolbox that traps Woody in the milk crate is a Binford—the fictional brand of tools that sponsored *Tool Time*, the TV show within Tim Allen's sitcom *Home Improvement*. (00:55)

TWISTER (12)
1996, color, 117 min.

Director: Jan de Bont

Cast: Helen Hunt (Jo Harding), Bill Paxton (Bill Harding), Cary Elwes (Dr. Jonas Miller), Jami Gertz (Melissa), Lois Smith (Aunt Meg), Alan Ruck (Rabbit), Philip Hoffman (Dusty), Richard Lineback (Father), Rusty Schwimmer (Mother), Alexa Vega (Jo—5 Years Old).

Storm chasers face a bunch of CGI tornadoes.

Bloopers
1. The third shot (after the shot of an oil rig and the shot of a bridge) shows a fence. Right in the middle of the screen a piece of grass is blowing in the wind. But this shot has been looped to "stretch" its length, so the piece of grass bends and then is standing up straight, motionless. Then it bends, then it's standing straight again, and so forth. (00:01)

TRUCK TRICKS

Some of these trucks don't stay on the track.

A truck in *Forrest Gump*	Blooper No. 3
The "Today in Fashion" van in *Mars Attacks!*	Blooper No. 6
A truck in *Raiders of the Lost Ark*	Blooper No. 7
The moving truck in *Toy Story*	Blooper No. 13
A windshield in *Twister*	Blooper No. 11

2. As the camera approaches Bill's truck, it's possible to see the reflection of the helicopter on the side of the vehicle. (00:06)

3. Bill asks Jo to sign the divorce papers. He shows her the whole stack—holding it with two hands from the front angle, but only with one from the rear angle. (00:11)

4. When Bill leafs through the same papers, he stops at a page with a red flag on it. He shows it to Jo (and he covers the flag with his left hand—but it's still there). However, when Jo checks the page, there are now two flags. (00:11)

5. The twister drops Jo's truck in front of Melissa's van, which seems to have the driver's window rolled up. Melissa screams, swerves, and as she passes by the totaled truck, her window is rolled all the way down. But when Dusty opens the door to see if she's OK, the window is rolled up again. (00:33)

6. Chasing a tornado, Bill steps on the gas. The odometer of his truck reads 000902. A few minutes later, when Bill hits the brakes, the odometer reads 000239. (00:36, 00:38)

7. Bill hits the brakes of his truck, and Dr. Miller's five-car caravan passes him. Bill has all the time to explain to Jo what his plan is, and when he backs up the truck . . . the

caravan passes him by one more time. (00:38)

8. Bill's truck is on a muddy road, headed toward a lake where they'll find a "sister" twister. Right after the flying cow, through the back window of Bill's van it's possible to see a red vehicle driving in the opposite direction on another lane of a highway—not a muddy road. (00:41, 00:42)

9. After the loss of Dorothy I, Melissa gets close to Dusty with a large umbrella. Her hair alternates between dry and wet during the whole sequence—and finally remains dry when Jo's coworkers say that the situation "is stable." (01:00, 01:02)

10. One of the twisters causes a pole to fall on Bill's truck: the pole smashes Dorothy I and the truck's back gate comes off of its right hinges and swings to the left of the vehicle. When the tornado dissolves, the gate is nowhere to be seen, but when the truck backs up (while Jo protests), the gate is back in place without anyone fixing it. (01:01, 01:02, 01:03)

11. Bill and Jo race in the tornado; they zigzag among flying trucks and a lot of debris. The windshield of their vehicle is smashed by a pole, then is fixed again (and again and again and again) all throughout the sequence. (01:35)

12. Bill and Jo tie themselves to a pipe in order not to be

sucked up by the final, humongous tornado. Bill grabs a strip of leather, twists it around the pipe, and tells Jo to "wear" it. And so she does. Twice. (01:41)

Questions

1. It's presumably night, since little Jo is in bed and the sky is totally dark. A twister is about to hit the house. The father, the mother, and little Jo run for the storm cellar, scattering a bunch of chickens that are outside. What the heck are the chickens doing out at night . . . having a hoedown? (00:01, 00:02)

2. They run to the shelter as the huge tornado is approaching. Still, the trees behind them (one of which is hit by a bolt of lightning) seem quite indifferent to the extremely powerful wind. Were they "out of the loop" about the storm? (00:02)

3. After the first meeting with a twister and the loss of her truck, Jo's hair looks filthy and muddy. A few minutes later she's in Bill's truck chasing another storm, but now her hair looks pretty darned clean. Did they make a stop at Supercuts for a quick wash? (00:33, 00:36)

U

UNDER SIEGE (7)
1992, color, 102 min.

Director: Andrew Davis

Cast: Steven Seagal (Casey Ryback), Tommy Lee Jones (William Stranix), Damian Chapa (Tackman), Troy Evans (Granger), David McKnight (Flicker), Lee Hinton (Cue Ball), Patrick O'Neal (Captain Adams), Gary Busey (Commander Krill), Glenn Morshower (Ensign Taylor), Leo Alexander (Lieutenant Smart), John Rottger (Commander Green), Brad Rea (Marine Guard).

The USS Missouri *is hijacked by a gang of terrorists who have a foolproof plan. But they didn't count on the cook being a hero.*

Bloopers

1. Captain Adams talks to Commander Krill about an unauthorized helicopter landing on the USS *Missouri*. The pencils in his cup change from being all together to being spread out. (00:09)

2. Stranix has a T-shirt with a large, pale, purple spot in the middle. When he gets out of the chopper and steps onto the ship, the size of the spot changes—now it's smaller, and the color is more intense. Its size will change again during the singing welcome, and again in the captain's cabin . . . and so on. (00:14, 00:16, 00:24)

3. When Stranix introduces "The Fabulous Bail Jumpers," the microphone he's holding jumps from his right hand to his left. (00:16)

4. Walking in one of the main rooms of the ship, Casey kicks a party cake away. The cake rolls on the floor, thanks to a cable that's pulling it (lower left corner of the screen). (00:43)

5. Casey prepares an explosive device using one of the bombs he finds on the ship. He unscrews the upper part and his wristwatch says 10:20. He removes the top at 10:30. He places the cylinder flat at 10:20.

He unrolls a condom at 10:35. And then he wraps it with black tape at 10:30. (01:15, 01:16)

6. After talking about Saturday-morning cartoons, Stranix says "Splendid work!" He grabs his jacket, and puts his right arm in the right sleeve. But in the following cut, he hasn't put any arm in any sleeve. (01:27)

7. Stranix is about to send two tomahawk missiles and says, "This little piggy . . ." and stops when his index finger is on the switch. In the next shot, he has his thumb on it instead. (01:28)

Questions

1. Casey tosses one of his knives at a dartboard, hitting the lower part of it. When he retrieves it while moving in the darkness, he finds it in another place on the dartboard. Did he throw it more than once? (00:08, 00:32)

2. On the radio with the submarine, Stranix identifies the sub as "Tweety Bird," the Navy as "Wile E. Coyote," and himself as "Road Runner." Later on when he talks to the sub he says, "Coyote, this is Road Runner." Did he reassign the names? (00:46, 01:13)

UNDER SIEGE 2: DARK TERRITORY (5)

1995, color, 99 min.

Director: Geoff Murphy

Cast: Steven Seagal (Casey Ryback), Eric Bogosian (Travis Dane), Everett McGill (Penn), Katherine Heigl (Sarah Ryback), Morris Chestnut (Bobby Zachs), Peter Greene (Merc No. 1), Patrick Kilpatrick (Merc No. 2), Scott Sowers (Merc No. 3), Afifi (Female Merc), Andy Romano (Admiral Bates), Royce D. Applegate (Ryback's Cook).

Same as before, only this time on a train.

Bloopers

1. Casey uses his Apple Newton to send a fax to the Mile High Cafe. Since the line is busy, Casey hits a button and he's promptly informed, "Redial in 30 secs." He then fights with a thug, a plane is blown up, a decoy is destroyed, and when he grabs the Newton again, 1 minute and 34 seconds later, the display reads, "Redial 21 secs" and counting. (00:42, 00:43)

2. During a fight between train cars, Casey throws one man off the train, into a shack. The man destroys the shack and lands on some rocks . . . which bounce. (00:52)

3. When Casey's fax eventually goes through, it arrives on top of another curly sheet in the Mile High Cafe's machine. Yet when one of the cooks gets it, he removes only the faxed page, and there's nothing else on the tray. (00:55, 00:58)

4. The man who's tossed the "you're f***ed" bomb quickly explodes in a ball of fire . . .

and even more quickly finds a safety mask over his face. (01:02)

5. The countdown to the destruction of the Pentagon reaches 1 minute remaining, then goes 00:59, 00:58 . . . Fifty seconds later, it hits 00:48, 00:47 . . . (01:32)

UNTOUCHABLES, THE (7)
1987, color, 119 min.

Director: Brian De Palma

Cast: Kevin Costner (Eliot Ness), Sean Connery (Jim Malone), Charles Martin Smith (Oscar Wallace), Andy Garcia (Giuseppe Petri, alias George Stone), Robert De Niro (Al Capone), Richard Bradford (Mike, Police Chief), Jack Kehoe (Payne), Brad Sullivan (George), Billy Drago (Frank Nitti), Patricia Clarkson (Ness's Wife), Vito D'Ambrosio (Bowtie Driver), Steven Goldstein (Scoop).

Al Capone gets harrassed by a goody-two-shoes Treasury agent.

Bloopers

1. Eliot visits Jim to ask him to join in the fight against Al Capone. Jim puts a tea tray away, then declines the invitation. During the whole dialogue, Jim's shirt collar buttons and unbuttons by itself, in one shot after another. (00:24)

2. Eliot shoots a mobster in a shack. The man falls back dead. Jim reaches the scene after a few minutes, and the man's body has turned 180°. (00:57, 00:58)

3. After Wallace has been "touched" in the elevator, Eliot walks away. In the background, Jim grabs Wallace and lowers him to the floor. When Jim is seen again, he grabs Wallace and lowers him to the floor—again. (01:07)

4. Giuseppe passes the ledger book to Eliot, then mumbles: "We gotta bust these guys," and walks away. Eliot holds the book under his arm—but in the wide shot, he holds it in his hand by his side. (01:11)

5. When the killer armed with the knife looks inside of Jim's apartment, it's possible to see the steadicam reflection on the windows, especially when the window is about to be opened. (01:19)

6. On the roof of the courthouse, Nitti fires at Eliot, who falls off the building. When Nitti approaches the ledge to check on his victim, the sky is cloudy. When Eliot fires his gun at Nitti's hat from some scaffolding, the sky is perfectly blue. (01:42)

7. During the closing credits, the romanza "Vesti la Guibba" by Leoncavallo is listed. The correct spelling is "Vesti la GIUbba." Sorry, one of us is Italian. (01:58)

Question

During the first failed attempt to intercept illegal whiskey, Eliot specifies that "the liquor cases are marked with a red maple leaf." If that refers to Canadian whiskey, the symbol is a little ahead of its time: the movie takes place during the 1930s. The maple leaf was adopted by Canada in 1965. So, is this an anachronism, or just a coincidence? (00:10, 00:14)

DVD Blooper

When Jim tells the others that his medal is Saint Jude, the protector of lost causes and policemen, Giuseppe says, "Santo Giuda." The captioning, however, says "Santo Judaea." (00:36)

USUAL SUSPECTS, THE (11)

1995, color, 106 min.

Director: Bryan Singer

Cast: Stephen Baldwin (Michael McManus), Gabriel Byrne (Dean Keaton), Benicio Del Toro (Fred Fenster), Kevin Pollak (Todd Hockney), Kevin Spacey (Verbal Kint), Chazz Palminteri (Dave Kujan), Pete Postlethwaite (Kobayashi), Suzy Amis (Edie Finneran), Giancarlo Esposito (Jack Baer), Dan Hedaya (Jeff Rabin), Paul Bartel (Smuggler), Carl Bressler (Saul Berg).

WHO IN THE HECK IS KEYSER SOZE?

Bloopers

1. All right, all right, it's a fake flashback! Nonetheless, Keyser Soze shoots Keaton bare-handed, yet he drops a match with a gloved hand. (00:03, 00:04)

2. During the lineup, Keaton has his jacket folded on his left arm and he's holding his right hand in front of his face. When Fenster says his line, Keaton's jacket jumps onto his right arm and his left hand is now in front of his face. (00:08, 00:09)

3. Keaton enters the cell wearing his jacket. After he walks in front of McManus, the jacket is only draped over his shoulders. (00:12)

4. At the beginning of the interrogation, Verbal is given an almost empty cup of coffee. He takes a sip, complains about it, and the cup is now almost full. (00:25)

5. After the lineup, Keaton gets out of prison and lights a cigarette. But in the following shot the cigarette seems unlit. Oddly enough, Keaton's cigarette vanishes from his mouth, and he only seems to blow smoke out of his mouth, but never inhales it. (00:26)

6. The smuggler's plane that lands at the airport has four engines in the approaching shot but only two in the reverse shot as it's about to land. (00:31)

7. To escape from the flaming

car, the two cops and the smuggler open their doors and jump out. However, the smuggler was in the backseat, but the back doors of all police cars are locked from the inside. (00:34)

8. After Redfoot leaves, Hockney sits on the steps of an Asian temple, while Mc-Manus walks to him—but in the long shot Hockney is standing. (00:45)

9. When McManus kills Kobayashi's associates in the elevator, the blood that splatters in the car changes shape and size when Kobayashi reaches the 20th floor. (01:08, 01:09)

10. According to Verbal, Keaton asked him to stay hidden, adding "Just do what I say." But when Kujan convinces Verbal that Keaton had a master plan, Verbal relives the moment. Only this time Keaton says, "Just do what I tell you." (01:16, 01:33)

11. Hockney gets shot in front of a crate filled with money. The plastic bag containing the "blood" explodes out of his clothes. (01:21)

Questions

1. During the police car attack, McManus tosses his lit Zippo onto the gas-soaked car. A shot from above reveals three separate fires on the car: on the hood, the roof, and the trunk. How did one flame start all these? (00:34)

2. McManus enters a porthole, but, before going down, takes off his sweater. After a brief shot of Keaton, McManus enters the hole . . . but there's a body lying in front of him. Where in the heck did it come from? (01:22)

V

VARSITY BLUES (8)
1999, color, 104 min.

Director: Brian Robbins

Cast: James Van Der Beek (Jonathon "Mox" Moxon), Amy Smart (Jules Harbor), Jon Voight (Coach Bud Kilmer), Paul Walker (Lance Harbor), Ron Lester (Billy Bob), Scott Caan (Charlie Tweeder), Richard Lineback (Joe Harbor), Ali Larter (Darcy Steers), Tiffany C. Love (Collette Harbor), Eliel Swinton (Wendell Brown), Thomas F. Duffy (Sam Moxon), Jill Parker-Jones (Mo Moxon).

Mutiny on the gridiron.

Bloopers

1. Mox jumps on Billy Bob's truck and sits by Bacon the pig, who turns 180° in an instant: first it faces the back, then the front. (00:04)
2. Coach Kilmer takes Mox's binder and finds the Vonnegut book in it. Kilmer holds the binder in his right hand, then in his left. (00:13)
3. When Kilmer grabs Mox's helmet because the kid has a "bad attitude," his grip switches from underhand on the bottom of the face mask to overhand on top of it, and back. (00:20)
4. Lance is hit and his knee takes a licking. While he's yelling on the ground, his left shoulder pad switches from underneath his jersey, to over it, then to underneath it again. (00:29)
5. Mox kisses Darcy, who's wearing a whipped cream bikini, and some of the whipped cream winds up on the left side of Mox's T-shirt. When he pulls back, his shirt is spotless. (00:53)
6. Billy Bob grabs his "Most Improved Player at Liman Camp" trophy, which is in the shape of an athlete, and tosses it to use as a target. But when the trophy lands on the field, it has become a football-shaped trophy. (01:10)
7. Billy Bob fires twice at his trophy, then cocks his shotgun but doesn't fire it. Later, he

passes the weapon to Mox who, before shooting a Kilmer poster . . . cocks the shotgun again. (01:11, 01:13)

8. During the final game, the scoreboard shows that Gilroy leads 17 to 7. After Lance takes Kilmer's place as coach, they pass the ball to Mox (No. 4). The scoreboard in the background says 7 to 14. (01:31, 01:32)

Questions

1. The police car Tweeder "borrows" is very clearly marked "sheriff" on the side. Later on, in a bar, it's said that he stole a "state trooper" car. Are state troopers and sheriffs the same in Texas? (00:39, 00:42)

2. Tweeder drives a police car that appears to be empty. As he stops in front of Mox, three naked girls are sitting in the car with Tweeder. Where'd they come from? (00:40)

VERTICAL LIMIT (7)

2000, color, 124 min.

Director: Martin Campbell

Cast: Chris O'Donnell (Peter Garrett), Robin Tunney (Annie Garrett), Scott Glenn (Montgomery Wick), Izabella Scorupco (Monique Aubertine), Bill Paxton (Elliot Vaughn), Nicholas Lea (Tom McLaren), Alexander Siddig (Kareem Nazir), Robert Taylor (Skip Taylor), Temuera Morrison (Major Rasul), Stuart Wilson (Boyce Garrett), Augie Davis (Aziz), Steve Le Marquand (Cyril Bench).

The hills are alive with the sound of avalanches.

Bloopers

1. While flying to base camp, Major Rasul and Peter talk about Peter's sister. Rasul's earphones keep moving over and away from his right ear. (00:12)

2. Peter enters a tent looking for Skip, but meets Monique. Peter has a longer, more unshaven beard (and he's slightly chubbier) than he was in the following scene, where he finds Skip at the command tent. (00:18, 00:19)

3. It's possible to see the crew reflected in Annie's sunglasses— as well as in Tom's—at the end of the first radio transmission. (00:32, 00:34)

4. When the chopper lands to get Wick, it lands over two marks in the snow that look suspiciously like . . . chopper marks. Can anyone say, "take two?" (00:57)

5. During the prayer to Allah, the sun moves pretty quickly in the sky: check Kareem's shadow on the mat. It's behind him, then to his left, then almost in front of him, then to his left side again. (01:07)

6. In front of Wick's dead wife's body, Peter shows Wick a metal box. The position of Peter's hand changes between

the front and back angles. (01:34)

7. Once again, radios are used like telephones, where everyone can interrupt one another. Impossible with radios, folks. (01:37)

Question

Peter checks the inside of his tent, then zips it closed. But when the chopper flies over it, everything in the tent flies away. Isn't it vaguely defective then, since its primary use is as a shield from the wind? (00:08)

Fun Fact

The toeless foot that appears in the movie belongs not to Montgomery Wick, but to mountaineer Mark Wetu, who lost his toes during a 1994 attempt to climb Everest. (00:15)

VERY BRADY SEQUEL, A (6)

1996, color, 90 min.

Director: Arlene Sanford

Cast: Shelley Long (Carol Brady), Gary Cole (Mike Brady), Christine Taylor (Marcia Brady), Christopher Daniel Barnes (Greg Brady), Jennifer Elise Cox (Jan Brady), Paul Sutera (Peter Brady), Olivia Hack (Cindy Brady), Jesse Lee (Bobby Brady), Henriette Mantel (Alice Nelson), Tim Matheson (Roy Martin / Trevor Thomas), Whip Hubley (Explorer / Dead Husband), Whitney Rydbeck (Auctioneer).

Here's a sequel / of a lovely lady . . .

Bloopers

1. Caught by Bobby and Cindy (who were looking for Kitty Carryall), Roy says, "Boy, you kids scared the living sh—" and he closes the closet door twice. (00:31)

2. Alice enters Mr. Brady's den to make Roy's bed. When she comments about the mushrooms, the bed is in more disarray than before—and she hasn't touched it yet. (00:35)

3. When Alice drops Roy's bag, a few items scatter on the floor: the bag with the mushrooms and the shaving brush shift position before she picks them up. (00:35)

4. Jan takes a card for a male service: 555-HUNK. The last three digits she dials, however, are 1, 2, 1 ("HUNK" on a phone is 4-8-6-5). (00:47)

5. Bobby finds a picture of Roy with the words "My Assistant Trevor" written on the top right corner. The words are there when Bobby shows the picture to Marsha and Greg, but are gone when he hands the photo to his mom. (01:01, 01:03, 01:04)

6. To make Roy get in the car to go shopping with the Bradys, Marsha tilts her seat forward twice. (01:32)

Forgettable Vacation?

While flying to Hawaii in *A Very Brady Sequel*, Mr. Brady explains to his kids the origin of the islands, as if they didn't know or have never been there (01:07). But in *The Brady Bunch Movie*, Mrs. Brady said, "We used our savings to go to the Grand Canyon and Hawaii." (00:10) Hmmm . . . amnesia?

VIRUS (4)
1999, color, 99 min.

Director: John Bruno

Cast: Jamie Lee Curtis (Kit Foster), William Baldwin (Steve Baxer), Donald Sutherland (Captain Robert Everton), Joanna Pacula (Nadja Vinegradova), Marshall Bell (J. W. Woods Jr.), Sherman Augustus (Richie), Cliff Curtis (Miko), Julio Oscar Mechoso (Squeaky), Yuri Chervotkin (Colonel Kominski).

Deadly space entity invades Russian ship's computers and starts to control-alt-delete humanity.

Bloopers

1. The space entity invades the *Mir* space station and Nadja realizes that "something is very wrong." She takes off her glasses and stares at the monitor in front of her. Her image appears on a monitor on board the *Mir* station: Nadja is still wearing glasses. (00:03)
2. As the tug first approaches the *Volkov*, there is a red lifeboat hanging off the *Volkov*'s port side. The inside of the lifeboat faces out from the boat. As the tug gets closer, the lifeboat faces toward the bow of the boat. The tug gets closer, and the lifeboat is now facing as it was before. (00:15)
3. Squeaky notices a cable being pulled into a hole. He moves closer to investigate and places his radio on a table, on

---

SOUNDING OFF

Listen to these low-fidelity bloopers:

Taping Danny DeVito in *Batman Returns*	Blooper No. 4
The letter-reading in *Robin Hood: Prince of Thieves*	Blooper No. 3
An answering machine in *The Terminator*	Blooper No. 4
John Wood's typing in *Wargames*	Blooper No. 10
Meg Ryan's e-mail in *You've Got Mail*	Blooper No. 2

top of a map. He then grabs a flashlight from the same table—the same flashlight that in the wide shot was far away from the map, but which is now on top of it in the detail shot. (00:30)

4. Steve examines a door that has been welded shut: he uses a flashlight, which he holds in his left hand, his thumb on the bottom, his four fingers on top of it. But in the matching shot, he's holding it with his four fingers on the bottom and his thumb on top. (00:46)

W

WARGAMES (10)
1983, color, 112 min.

Director: John Badham

Cast: Matthew Broderick (David L. Lightman), Dabney Coleman (John McKittrick), John Wood (Stephen W. Falken), Ally Sheedy (Jennifer K. Mack), Barry Corbin (General Beringer), Juanin Clay (Pat Healy), Kent Williams (Cabot), Dennis Lipscomb (Watson), Joe Dorsey (Conley), Irving Metzman (Richter), Michael Ensign (Beringer's Ride), William Bogert (Mr. Lightman), Susan Davis (Mrs. Lightman).

Computer whiz kid breaks into a state-of-the-art defense system and almost causes World War III . . . just for fun.

Bloopers
1. To call all the numbers in Sunnyvale, California, David places the phone in the modem: the wire is toward us. When he gets home with Jennifer, and the computer is still dialing, the phone has turned 180° in the modem. (00:25, 00:27)
2. David gets distracted by Jennifer and his Galaga spacecraft blows up. The screen says "Game Over," but there are still two extra lives indicated in the bottom corner. Crappy videogame. (00:26)
3. Just for fun, David books a reservation for two tickets to Paris. Later on, when he's questioned by McKittrick, David is asked, "Who are you going to Paris with?" because he has reservations for two. Well, not exactly: the name David made the reservations under was Jennifer Mack. (00:29, 00:58)
4. Playing Global Thermonuclear War, David decides to list his targets: Las Vegas, Seattle, and so forth. The phone in the modem has the wire pointing toward the monitor. When Jennifer says, "Oh, attack!" (before David is

called by his Dad to take out the garbage), the phone has turned 180°. (00:41, 00:44)

5. Before going to a meeting, McKittrick gives his gum to Pat; he places it in her right hand, she eats it from her left. (00:54)

6. General Beringer gives the order to "Scramble two F-16s." But the footage shows two F-15s. (01:20)

7. The "1 minute and 30 seconds to impact" lasts 2 minutes 29 seconds. (01:35)

8. The first time the missile launch code appears, it's JPE 1704 TKS. After the failed attempt to play chess with Joshua, the launch code has become CPE 1704 TKS. (01:40, 01:43)

9. Joshua launches virtual attacks and then lists them on a side monitor. The first attack is "U.S. First Strike," the second is "USSR First Strike," and so on. In the side list, the attacks are listed as the USSR being the first strike, the U.S. the second . . . and so on. (01:46)

10. Professor Falken is finally greeted by Joshua. He approaches the keyboard and types (with loud keystrokes), "Hello, Joshua." The screen only says "Hello." (01:48)

WATCHER, THE (6)
2000, color, 97 min.

Directors: Joe Charbanic and Jeff Jensen

Cast: James Spader (Joel Campbell), Keanu Reeves (David Allen Griffin), Marisa Tomei (Polly Beicman, Ph.D.), Ernie Hudson (Ibby), Chris Ellis (Hollis), Robert Cicchini (Mitch), Yvonne Niami (Lisa), Jenny McShane (Diana), Gina Alexander (Sharon), Rebekah Louise Smith (Ellie Buckner), Joseph Sikora (Skater), Jill Peterson (Jessica), Quinn Yancy (Campbell's Secretary).

Serial killer loves both his work and the detective who's investigating him.

Bloopers

1. Campbell opens the first FedEx envelope and places it flat on the table with the "FedEx" logo side visible. The detail shows him still holding the envelope, but this time the back side of it is visible. (00:16)

2. To stop a kid who has hijacked a Honda, Hellis jumps and tosses his phone, which lands in the middle of a wooden pier. When he retrieves it, the phone is much much closer to the edge of the pier than it was earlier. (00:18)

3. Campbell gets the picture of "Jane Doe 1" (Ellie), and everyone is frantically looking for her. Oddly enough, after talking about a possible reward, Campbell's secretary has a picture of Jessie on her computer's monitor, the woman who hasn't yet stepped into the picture and who will be known as "Jane Doe 2." (00:28, 00:31)

4. Outside a Chinese restaurant, Campbell looks for Griffin's car. When Griffin backs up to exit the parking and rear-ends another car, it's clear that his Ford doesn't have a rear license plate. When Campbell runs after him, a license plate suddenly appears. (00:46)
5. To get to the cemetery, Campbell takes a cab from the hospital. Or does he? Maybe he took two: the taxi that drives among the gravestones, taxi No. 43, has yellow rearview mirrors. The taxi Campbell gets out of, taxi No. 8789, has black rearview mirrors. (01:14)
6. When Griffin shows Campbell a business card of his next victim, the blood stain on it changes from the detail to the wide shot (particularly the spot on the top right corner). (01:16)

Fun Fact
Griffin breaks into Polly's file cabinet. As he produces Campbell's file, it's possible to see her filing system: Cantors is followed by Candra and then by Carry. So much for alphabetical order. (01:10)

WAYNE'S WORLD (11)
1992, color, 94 min.

Director: Penelope Spheeris

Cast: Mike Myers (Wayne Campbell), Dana Carvey (Garth Algar), Rob Lowe (Benjamin Oliver), Tia Carrere

(Cassandra), Brian Doyle-Murray (Noah Vanderhoff), Lara Flynn Boyle (Stacy), Michael DeLuise (Alan), Dan Bell (Neil), Lee Tergesen (Terry), Donna Dixon (Dreamwoman), Charles Nolan (Ron Paxton), Robert Patrick (Bad Cop), Frank DiLeo (Frankie Sharp / "Mr. Big").

It's party time! Excellent!

Bloopers
1. Mr. Paxton is on the first *Wayne's World* episode with his invention, the Suck Kut. As he sits on the couch, the black tube of his device is in front of Garth. In the following shot, it has moved behind him. (00:01)
2. Garth tests the Suck Kut. Wayne tells him, "OK, OK, Garth, just sit there, and he's gonna put that thing on your melon, OK?" But later on, when Benjamin shows a tape of the same episode, Wayne says, "OK, Garth, just sit there, all right; he's gonna put that thing on your—on your melon." (00:02, 00:17)
3. Garth spots his Dreamwoman as she's placing a few slices of pie on different trays of a rack. She places one slice in the middle tray, one on the top tray—but then the one in the middle has vanished, and then comes back again. (00:10)
4. Wayne and Garth enter Gasworks while Cassandra is performing "Fire." After Garth says, "And they got a pool

table, too," there's a shot of the band playing. The drummer is way out of sync with the sound. (00:13)

5. When Garth wears the belt with his electric weapon, it's over his shirt. When he reenters Gasworks, the belt has moved under his shirt. (00:13, 00:14)

6. Garth is about to use his device: a woman wearing a red top is standing and watching him just to his left. As Garth juggles the weapon, the woman disappears. When he puts it back in the holster, she's back. (00:14)

7. In a garage, Garth fumbles with some tools and scratches a car door: the scratch starts above the handle, the detail shows the scratch as being below the handle, and then it moves back above again. (00:21)

8. Garth and Wayne are playing hockey in the middle of the road. When a blue van drives by, it reflects the boom operator. (00:42)

9. During the new and improved "Wayne's World," the first guest Wayne has is Mr. Vanderhoff. During the interview, Wayne flips through some cue cards, revealing some funny lines. One of these is "He blows goats. I have proof," followed by "This man has no penis." But as they cut to commercial and Wayne lowers the cue cards, the card he's holding is "He blows goats. I have proof." (01:07)

10. Wayne drives on a road with no cars. When he goes through an intersection and is chased by the Bad Cop, the road is filled with cars... which all vanish when we see Wayne in his car again. (01:17)

11. Frankie Sharp (Mr. Big) checks out Wayne's show from his limo. On the screen, Wayne holds the microphone with his left hand, pointing to the camera with his right. But as we cut to the studio, it's Wayne's left hand that is pointing to the camera. (01:24)

Question
Mr. Vanderhoff says that he does his own arcade commercials and that he doesn't "mention the games in the commercials, because technology moves so much faster than the advertising." (00:19) So then why did he have a commercial at the beginning of the movie where he mentioned "Zantar, Bay Wolf, Ninja Commando, Snake-Azon, Psycho Chopper . . ."? (00:00)

WEDDING SINGER, THE (6)
1998, color, 97 min.

Director: Frank Coraci

Cast: Adam Sandler (Robert J. "Robbie" Hart), Drew Barrymore (Julia Sullivan), Christine Taylor (Holly Sullivan), Allen Covert

(Sammy), Mathew Glave (Glenn Gulia), Ellen Albertini Dow (Rosie), Angela Featherstone (Linda), Alexis Arquette (George Stitzer), Christina Pickles (Angie), Jodi Tehlen (Kate), Frank Sivero (Andy), Steve Buscemi (David Veltri, The Best Man), Jon Lovitz (Jimmy Moore), Patrick McTavish (Tyler), Gemini Barnett (Petey).

As the 80s unravel with their tacky fads and fashions, a wedding singer and a waitress find true love.

Bloopers
1. During his embarrassing speech as a best man, David's azure bow tie keeps popping out and then hiding under the right collar of his shirt. (00:03)
2. When "Freddie Krueger" hands Robbie the picture of the wedding he retouched, his hands and the position of the picture switch in the matching shot. (00:18)
3. After performing "Love Stinks," Robbie lays in a dumpster. While talking to Julia, the garbage that's covering him (especially a piece of round plastic) keeps changing positions, back and forth. (00:29)
4. When everyone is tasting a sample of the wedding cake, Robbie winds up with a plate with two pieces. As he passes one to an ugly woman, they both vanish. One comes back

to the plate a few seconds later. (00:49)
5. Zig-zagging between the cones, Sammi's limo loses both hubcaps on the right side. Yet when the limo fishtails away after the bride and groom are inside, the right hubcaps are both back. (00:50)
6. When Holly is telling Julia she kissed Robbie, Julia's hands are both on the table—but in the following close-up, her left hand is up to her chin. (01:04)

Question
The story takes place in 1985, as is stated at the very beginning. Still, when Kate is yelling at Andy because they're late, he replies that he's watching *Dallas*: "I think J. R. might be dead or something. They shot him." That episode was aired as a cliffhanger for the '79–'80 season. Has Andy lived in a hole for five years? (00:30)

WILD THINGS (9)
1998, color, 108 min.

Director: John McNaughton

Cast: Kevin Bacon (Ray Duquette), Matt Dillon (Sam Lombardo), Neve Campbell (Suzie Toller), Theresa Russell (Sandra Van Ryan), Denise Richards (Kelly Van Ryan), Daphne Rubin-Vega (Gloria Perez), Robert Wagner (Tom Baxter), Bill Murray (Ken Bowden), Carrie Snodgress (Ruby), Jeff Perry (Bryce Hunter).

Steamy, sexy swamp thriller is all twisty and turny.

Bloopers

1. During the senior seminar, Sam writes "SEX" on the board. As he starts to write "CRIMES," we see that "SEX" is written differently. He underlines "CRIMES" once. In the next shot, "CRIMES" is double-underlined and the words are higher up on the board. In the next shot, the words are written differently yet again. (00:05, 00:06)

2. When the detectives tape Kelly's description of the rape, she's first seen through the viewfinder of a video camera: the microphone on the table is to her left. When the interview continues on a Sony TV screen, the microphone has moved to her right. And the interview doesn't seem to have been stopped or edited, for she completes the story. (00:21)

3. Sam leaves Smilin' Jack's Fish Camp in his jeep. There's no cover between the roll bars. Sam drives along the swamps, and there's still no cover. A car eventually rams the jeep and pushes it into the water—and there's now a cover between the roll bars. (00:30, 00:31)

4. The TV reporter lets us know that the second day of the trial is commencing, and the camera pans across the courtroom. After the camera pans across the Van Ryans and Baxters, look closely. An extra in a blue shirt sits with his arm around a woman on the aisle. As he gets into the shot, he gives a "thumbs up" sign for the camera. (00:42)

5. Kelly sneaks into Sam's motel room to celebrate, and as they're making out, right after Kelly says, "Yeah, I'm crazy. Ask my mom," she rubs the back of Sam's neck with her left hand, turning up his collar. In the next shot, the collar is back down. (00:54)

6. Detective Duquette finds a joint in Suzie's hands. He takes it and keeps it up in front of her eyes: the length of the joint varies between the front and back shots. (01:03)

7. When Duquette invites Hunter to question Sam, he opens a glass door that has "Authorized Personnel Only—Display your I.D. beyond this point" clearly marked on the other side. Neither Duquette, nor Hunter, nor even Perez have any I.D. displayed on their persons while they are in the "I.D." area. (01:07, 01:08, 01:10)

8. Kelly and Suzie pull up to the beach in the Range Rover, and the rearview mirror is visibly tilted. But in the two-shot it's straight. (01:11)

9. On the boat, Sam guesses right when he says, "Poison." His shirt is entirely open. Suzie throws him overboard, and in the glimpse of him floating out to sea, his shirt is partially buttoned. (01:38, 01:39)

HAIRDOS, AND DON'TS

Have you ever had a bad-hair movie?

A native in *King Kong* (1933)	Blooper No. 2
Keanu Reeves in *The Matrix*	Blooper No. 16
Sean Connery in *Thunderball*	Blooper No. 17
Jami Gertz in *Twister*	Blooper No. 9
Judy Garland in *The Wizard of Oz*	Blooper No. 4

WIZARD OF OZ, THE (21)

1939, black & white / color, 101 min.

Director: Victor Fleming

Cast: Judy Garland (Dorothy), Frank Morgan (Professor Marvel / Guardian of the Gates / "Wizard" of Oz), Ray Bolger (Hunk Andrews / Scarecrow), Bert Lahr (Zeke / Cowardly Lion), Jack Haley (Hickory Twicker / Tin Man), Billie Burke (Glinda, The Good Witch of the North), Margaret Hamilton (Miss Almira Gulch / The Wicked Witch of the West), Charley Grapewin (Uncle Henry), Pat Walshe (Nikko), Clara Blandick (Auntie Em).

"Follow the yellow brick road!"... to oodles of classic bloopers.

Bloopers

1. Dorothy's hair changes length during the movie. Medium-length at the beginning, longer when she meets the scarecrow, and even longer when the witch tries to steal her slippers. After the witch turns the hourglass a minute later, Dorothy's had a noticeable trim! (00:01, 00:33, 01:16, 01:17)
2. Running home to tell Auntie Em "what Miss Gulch did to Toto," Dorothy has two spots on her dress; but as she walks with Toto, the spots vanish. (00:02)
3. Auntie Em's counting the chicks she's taking out of the incubator: "sixty-seven, sixty-eight..." Then she takes out five more chicks (plus one from Dorothy) to place them in a cage. She then proclaims, "Seventy." Close. That makes seventy-four. (00:02)
4. Dorothy falls in the pigpen—but she gets up clean as a whistle. (00:04)
5. As the tornado bursts into the house, it lifts up everything—except for a small oil lamp that was on the table, but which vanishes just before the window is opened by the wind. (00:10, 00:16)

6. The basket that Dorothy constantly carries around is gone the moment before the tornado bursts one window open. (00:16)

7. With the twister in the background, Dorothy enters the house while everybody else goes for the underground hideout. But as she reaches the door of the hideout, the background is different from the one shown earlier. (00:16)

8. As the tornado bursts into the house, a few bottles look awfully attached to a table (which is shaking like everything else). (00:17)

9. As Dorothy steps out of the house and into Oz, she hugs Toto (from the front angle), but from behind her arms are wide open. (00:19)

10. Dorothy is given a bunch of flowers that vanishes when she's following the yellow brick road. (00:24, 00:33)

11. Dorothy is also given a lollipop that also vanishes after the entrance of the Wicked Witch. (00:28, 00:29)

12. When the Good Witch sends the snow over the gang, it's snowing only in the long shots: in Dorothy's close-up it has already stopped. In the following shot, it's still snowing. (00:56)

13. The Lion's crown, made out of a broken vase, bounces on the floor when it falls down. (01:07)

14. The Wicked Witch says, "I've sent a little insect..." to stop Dorothy and the others. But she didn't. (01:14)

15. As the flying monkeys storm over the four heroes, the Lion bends over to pick up Dorothy's basket. When they run away, the basket is on Dorothy's arm. (01:15)

16. When the Wicked Witch goes to grab the hourglass, Dorothy steps off screen to the left. Yet, as the Witch turns to talk to Dorothy, she looks to the right. (01:17)

17. The Tin Man smashes the Witch's door with an ax he wasn't carrying when he went upstairs in the castle dressed as one of the soldiers. (01:23)

18. The Wizard faces the Tin Man, the Scarecrow, Dorothy, and the Lion. In the following shot he faces the Tin Man, Dorothy, the Lion, and the Scarecrow—in that order. Nobody has moved. (01:29)

19. A proud Wizard hands the Scarecrow a degree of Th.D. The paper is rolled up, but on the over-the-shoulder shot it is open. (01:30)

20. In order to prove that he has a brain, the Scarecrow recites a theorem that doesn't make any sense at all. It is simply wrong (but the degree he was holding is now rolled up). (01:30)

21. The Lion shows his medal by holding it up with one paw— yet the detail has the medal on the Lion's chest and no paws are in sight. (01:32)

Non-Blooper

THE REAL TRUTH: The figure that moves in the background IS NOT SOME GUY WHO COMMITTED SUICIDE ON THE SET. It is just a large bird, such as a heron or something. (00:47)

Questions

1. If he doesn't have a brain, how come the Scarecrow outsmarts the apple trees and finds a solution to save the gang from the army of the Witch? (00:39, 01:24)

2. Why does the "Witch's Castle" appear as "Witches Castle" on the sign? Is there more than one witch in that castle? Sure doesn't seem like it. (01:13)

X

X-MEN (7)
2000, color, 104 min.

Director: Bryan Singer

Cast: Hugh Jackman (Logan / Wolverine), Patrick Stewart (Professor Charles Francis Xavier / Professor X), Ian McKellen (Erik Magnus Lehnsherr / Magneto), Famke Janssen (Dr. Jean Grey), James Marsden (Scott Summers / Cyclops), Halle Berry (Ororo Munroe / Storm), Anna Paquin (Marie / Rogue), Tyler Mane (Victor Creed / Sabretooth), Ray Park (Mortimer Toynbee / Toad), Rebecca Romijn-Stamos (Raven Darkholme / Mystique), Bruce Davison (Senator Robert Jefferson Kelly), Matthew Sharp (NSC Agent Henry Peter Guyrich), Brett Morris (Young Magneto), Kenneth McGregor (Magneto's Father).

"Yes, but are they a mutated band of superheroes?"

Bloopers

1. Magneto's father has a star of David on his coat, to the left. But when Magneto is separated from his father, the star jumps to the right. (00:01, 00:02)
2. During her speech, Jean answers Senator Kelly with, "Yes, but not to live." Then she keeps talking in a wide shot. Or at least this is what is heard, because it seems that Senator Kelly is the one who's really talking in this shot. (00:06)
3. In his truck, Wolverine smokes a cigar and the window is up. But when he stops after hearing a rattle, the window is rolled down, then half way up. (00:14)
4. When Wolverine stops to find Rogue in his trailer, the truck tires leave a clear line in the snow. But when he leaves, the truck's tracks are gone. (00:14, 00:15)
5. Senator Kelly is on a chopper talking on his cell phone: he's in full sunlight, but when the shot goes to Henry Guyrich,

Kelly is completely in the shade. (00:30)

6. Mystique has "replaced" the boat captain, who's lying on the floor. But when she pulls in by the Statue of Liberty, the captain's head is visible, as if he were leaning against one of the walls of the cabin. He'll be lying flat again when Rogue looks at him. (01:06, 01:07)

7. In the Statue of Liberty, Cyclops reaches up to his visor with his left hand and blows away a door that is trapping him. Yet from behind he's lifting up his right hand. (01:14)

Questions

1. Wolverine runs away from the school lab, chasing a voice. Doesn't the noise he makes sound a lot like shoes . . . even if he's barefoot? (00:22, 00:24, 00:25)

2. Logan ridicules the X-Men and their enemies because they have funny nicknames, like "Sabretooth," "Storm," "Wheel" (he makes that one up). But isn't it true that when he was fighting in a cage he was introduced as "The Wolverine?" (00:26)

3. When Guyrich pockets Kelly's cell phone, he turns into Mystique. So where did she put the phone, exactly? (00:30, 00:31)

X-Men Cameo

When the mutated Senator Kelly walks onto the beach, he approaches a hot dog stand: the owner is Stan Lee, executive producer of the movie and creator of the *X-Men* comics. (00:43)

Y

YOU ONLY LIVE TWICE (14)
1967, color, 117 min.

Director: Lewis Gilbert

Cast: Sean Connery (James Bond 007), Akiko Wakabayashi (Aki), Mie Hama (Kissy Suzuki), Tetsuro Tamba (Tiger Tanaka), Teru Shimada (Mr. Osato), Karin Dor (Helga Brandt), Donald Pleasence (Blofeld), Bernard Lee (M), Lois Maxwell (Miss Moneypenny), Desmond Llewelyn (Q), Charles Gray (Henderson), Tsai Chin (Chinese Girl—Hong Kong).

For his fifth adventure, Bond goes to China.

Bloopers

1. The "corpse" of 007 touches the ocean floor after his burial at sea. Bond's head lands close to a rock, but when two scubadivers retrieve the body, it's lying entirely on the sand. (00:09)

2. Bond and Aki leave a sumo wrestling arena, and Aki's car has the steering wheel on the right. As they reach Mr. Henderson's place, the wheel has moved to the left. It'll be back to the right later on, when Bond marches out of the Osato building. (00:19, 00:27)

> Charles Gray, who plays Henderson, one of Bond's contacts in *You Only Live Twice* (00:20), played Ernst Stavro Blofeld in *Diamonds Are Forever* (01:14). Ironically, Henderson is killed by one of Blofeld's men.

3. The rear propeller of a chopper that lands on Osato's building stops in a vertical position. Yet when Mr. Osato and his secretary get out of the chopper, the propeller is horizontal. (00:38)

4. During a chase, the villains' car is lifted by one helicopter with a large magnet underneath it. 007 follows the whole operation on a monitor, as if the scene were filmed by a second heli-

copter. But there is no other helicopter. (00:42, 00:43)

5. Miss Brandt traps Bond in a small plane, then jumps out of it. When she jumps, the landing gear is down, but when Bond frees himself and reaches the controls, the landing gear is up, and 007 has to belly-land the plane. (00:50)

6. Q and one technician remove the red safety braces from the propeller of Little Nellie (the small chopper), yet the front brace is back in place when 007 is putting on his helmet. (00:53)

7. Bond, riding Little Nellie, is chased by four helicopters that fly in formation. When the first pilot is seen, another helicopter in the background is flying away from him—and not in formation, as every other shot indicates. (00:55)

8. During the Russian missile launch sequence, palm trees are visible in the foreground. (00:58)

9. Bond wears black shoes when he jumps off the boat. When he swims toward land with Kissy, he's barefoot. But once on land, he's wearing the black shoes again. (01:25)

10. 007 is also wearing his salmon-colored shirt and a pair of pants when he dives in. But when he reaches the top of the fake volcano, he removes the shirt, revealing a Ninja outfit equipped with a set of suction cups. Nobody knows where this uniform came from. (01:25, 01:30)

11. 007 and Kissy have to swim underwater in a cave filled with poisonous (phosgene) gas. Yet later on, Bond and the army of Ninjas swim in the very same cave, heads above the water, and couldn't care less about the gas. (01:25, 01:52)

12. Bond asks for one last cigarette. Blofeld agrees, and a technician brings 007's cigarette holder, opening it twice. (01:43)

13. Bond struggles with the automatic destruction button: the timer in front of him goes, 00:13, 00:12, and in the following shot, 00:25. (01:51)

14. When Bond and Kissy's raft is rescued by a submarine, the shot is in reverse—check out the waves. (01:54)

Question

Why didn't 007 correct Henderson when he prepared his martini "Stirred, not shaken?" Bond only drinks his martinis "shaken, not stirred." But in this case he says that it's perfect. (00:21)

Fun Facts

1. Q complains about his journey to Japan. As he walks, four technicians are standing by with four large cases, apparently waiting for Q and his cue. As the camera is on them, they all begin to walk. (00:52)

2. Blofeld's base is attacked, and 007 sarcastically remarks, "Im-

pregnable?" Look at Blofeld's poor cat: it's freaking out! (01:46)

YOU'VE GOT MAIL (9)
1998, color, 119 min.

Director: Nora Ephron

Cast: Tom Hanks (Joe Fox), Meg Ryan (Kathleen Kelly), Parker Posey (Patricia Eden), Jean Stapleton (Birdie), David Chappelle (Kevin), Steve Zahn (George Pappas), Dabney Coleman (Nelson Fox), Greg Kinnear (Frank Navasky), Heather Burns (Christina), John Randolph (Schuyler Fox), Deborah Rush (Veronica Grant), Hallee Hirsh (Annabelle Fox, Joe's Aunt).

Can one catch a virus from cyber love?

Bloopers

1. When Joe is drinking orange juice in the morning and Patricia frantically walks back and forth, the bottle of OJ moves across the table and spins to show the label. (00:05)

2. Joe, as NY152, receives an e-mail from Shopgirl, and we hear her voice off screen reading it aloud. She says, "What will NY152 say today? I wonder . . . I wait impatiently as it connects." Yet in her e-mail she wrote "What will he say today? I wonder . . . I wait im-patiently as it boots up." Oh, well. (00:06, 00:07)

3. Frank places one sheet of paper in a typewriter and types in the upper part of the sheet. Yet, when he and Kathleen lean over onto the typewriter, the sheet has scrolled down by itself. And then it comes back to its original position. (00:19)

4. Trying to toss a ring around a bottle, little Annabelle is given a red ring but tosses a green one. (00:22)

5. At Café Lalo, Joe sits at Kathleen's table and removes his coat twice. (01:03)

6. When Joe "leaves" the table, he places down a rose, the flower toward Kathleen. But when he returns to the table, the flower has turned 180°. (01:04, 01:05)

7. Joe fixes a couple of drinks for his dad and himself. When they're talking about a certain Jillian, Joe puts an olive in one of the glasses. Twice. (01:33)

8. While eating at an outside café, Joe and Kathleen are passed by a woman pushing a red cart. She then leaves in the background, twice. (01:45)

9. Walking home with Joe before her appointment with NY152, during the "what if" speech, Kathleen is wearing a thin wristwatch. But when she walks up the steps to her door, the watch is gone. (01:49, 01:52)

Z

ZERO EFFECT (6)
1998, color, 116 min.

Director: Jake Kasdan

Cast: Bill Pullman (Daryl Zero), Ben Stiller (Steve Arlo), Ryan O'Neal (Gregory Stark), Kim Dickens (Gloria Sullivan), Angela Featherstone (Jess), Hugh Ross (Bill), Sarah DeVincentis (Daisy), Matt O'Toole (Kragan Vincent), Michele Mariana (Maid), Robert Katims (Gerald Auerbach), Tyrone Henry (Staffer No. 1), Aleta Barthell (Staffer No. 2).

Very peculiar detective unravels a case and probably his life.

Bloopers
1. Halfway through a tuna snack, Daryl slams the can on the counter. The can stops in an almost vertical position against an appliance, but a few seconds later it appears to be lying flat. (00:13, 00:14)
2. A few bystanders can be seen reflected in the windshield as Stark boards the 119 train to Portland. (00:31)
3. While rummaging through Gloria's apartment, Daryl opens a drawer in her nightstand: he opens it with his palm against the drawer, but the detail shows the back of his hand against it. (00:56)
4. Getting mad at Steve because he's about to retire, Daryl yells and screams in his motel room. A sign is on the doorknob behind Steve, but when he leaves for a beer, the sign is gone. (01:19, 01:23)
5. While screaming, Daryl pushes almost everything from the top of a chest of drawers, except for the lamp. But when he asks Steve, "So, what am I supposed to do?" there's a newspaper lying flat by the lamp. And after Steve leaves, the paper is gone. (01:19, 01:21, 01:23)
6. When Kragan Vincent discovers young Gloria in her mom's motel room, he moves the bed behind which she's kept. But in the following shot of Gloria, the bed looks to have not been moved at all. (01:44)

DO IT AGAIN! AND AGAIN AND AGAIN!

Just when you thought you'd had enough.

Catherine O'Hara in *Beetlejuice*	Blooper No. 4
John Belushi in *The Blues Brothers*	Blooper No. 10
Gary Cole in *The Brady Bunch Movie*	Blooper No. 2
Tom Cruise and Kevin Pollack in *A Few Good Men*	Blooper No. 6
Dana Kimmel in *Friday the 13th Part 3D*	Blooper No. 7
King Kong in *King Kong* (1976)	Blooper No. 5
George Kennedy in *Naked Gun 33⅓: The Final Insult*	Blooper No. 4
Dan Aykroyd in *1941*	Blooper No. 12
Martha Plimpton in *Parenthood*	Blooper No. 4
Christopher Reeve in *Superman III*	Blooper No. 5
Tom Hanks in *You've Got Mail*	Blooper No. 5

COMING ATTRACTIONS

JUST WHEN YOU THOUGHT IT WAS SAFE TO GO BACK TO THE
VIDEO STORE . . .

OOPS! They Did It Again!

Featuring

Aladdin
The Birds
Crouching Tiger, Hidden Dragon
The Empire Strikes Back
Frankenstein
The Lord of the Rings: The Fellowship of the Ring
Gone With the Wind
Live and Let Die
A Nightmare on Elm Street
Saving Private Ryan
What Lies Beneath

Special Appearances by

American Graffiti
Cast Away
Dr. Seuss' How the Grinch Stole Christmas

Guest Star

Friday the 13th Part VIII: Jason Takes Manhattan

. . . and many, many more!